SCHOLASTIC

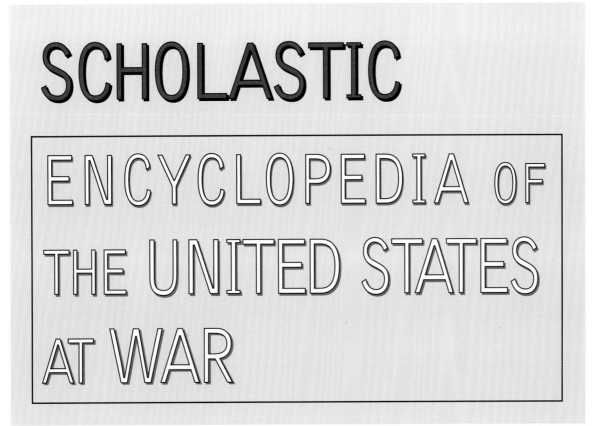

ENCYCLOPEDIA OF THE UNITED STATES AT WAR

SCHOLASTIC

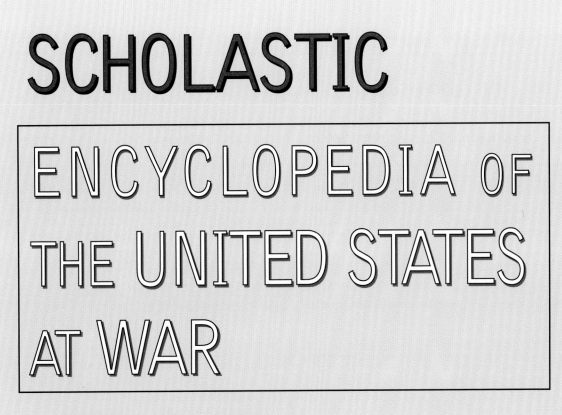

ENCYCLOPEDIA OF THE UNITED STATES AT WAR

JUNE A. ENGLISH

THOMAS D. JONES

This book is dedicated to
Sara and Gordon Myers.

Editor: Carolyn Jackson

Design: Todd Cooper/Bill Smith Studio

Advisor: LTC. (ret) Clair G. Myers, U.S.A.

Cover Design: David Saylor/Nancy Sabato

Consultants: Mary Habeck, Richard Steins

Film Consultant: Clifton Titus

Editorial Research: Jessica Chesler, Sara Myers, Julie Winterbottom, Amy Simon Hopwood

Photo Research: Ned Campbell (U.K.), Mary Kate Coudal,
Bobo Xavier Curtis (Germany), Justine Price

ACKNOWLEDGMENTS: For their assistance in the preparation of this manuscript, grateful acknowledgment to:
Kate Waters, Scholastic; Todd Ensign, Citizen Soldier; Randy Hackenberg, USAMHI; Kay Scott, The Chosin Few; Crossing
the Delaware Reenactment Staff: Mary Jean and Robert Goetz, Sarah and Matthew Goetz, Alicia and Bernard Kayes

Library of Congress Cataloging-in-Publication Data

English, June
    Scholastic encyclopedia of US at war / June English, Thomas Jones.
      p. cm.
Includes index.
Summary: Discusses all of the major wars in which the United States
has participated beginning with the American Revolution and concluding with
the Gulf War of 1991.
ISBN 0-590-59959-3
1. United States—History, Military—Encyclopedias, Juvenile. [1. United States—
History, Military—Encyclopedias.] I. Title.
E181.E64
973—dc21   97-46492
                                                                          CIP

10 9 8 7 6 5 4   0/0 01 02

Printed in the U.S.A. 23
First printing, September 1998

Copyright acknowledgements and permissions are on page 188.

CONTENTS

INTRODUCTION

The United States was born in war and, throughout its history, war has shaped this nation. It has framed its government and expanded its borders. It has united its citizens in fervor and divided them in dissent and grief. Perhaps most importantly it has called into question who, as a nation, we truly are.

The Declaration of Independence defined us as a nation based on justice and liberty. The **American Revolution (1775–1781)**, in which a tiny country waged war against Great Britain, then the greatest power on earth, forged a powerful and lasting symbol: human beings grabbing back their rights from tyrants. It was an image which would haunt not only the world, but, in time, ourselves.

The eighteenth century American struggle with the British continued with more practical overtones in the **War of 1812 (1812–1814)**. Here Americans sought, among other things, to secure the right to trade on the seas and expand into the West.

LAND WARS. By the middle of the nineteenth century, the nation's sense that it had a superior government and culture led it to push that expansion even further. At mid-century, epic U.S. land-lust led to the **War with Mexico (1846–1848)**; the U.S. victory in that war pushed its frontiers to the Pacific.

U.S. territorial expansion caused bloodshed not only on its border, but all across the continent. Throughout the nineteenth century, the country battled dozens of Indian nations contesting possession of land that other Americans—many of them immigrants—sought to settle or exploit. American Indians, treated as savages and not citizens, weren't provided the privilege of self-government that Americans had demanded for themselves.

A NATION DIVIDED. Nor were those rights given to black Americans, the tragic human commodity in the country's centuries-old slave trade. The **Civil War**

U.S. WAR CASUALTIES

Source: U.S. Dept. of Defense

- American Revolution: 4,435
- War of 1812: 2,260
- Mexican-American War: 13,283
- Civil War: 498,332
- Indian Wars: Not Available
- Spanish-American War: 2446
- World War I: 116,708
- World War II: 407,316
- Korean War: 33,651
- Vietnam War: 58,168
- Gulf War: 293

0   100,000   200,000   300,000   400,000   500,000

(1861–1865) begun as a battle over the rights of states to secede from the Union, ended in a victory against enslavement. That liberation, though, was bought at terrible price. In Abraham Lincoln's words: "every drop of blood drawn with the lash...[would be] paid by another drawn with the sword."

The Civil War was, by far, the worst conflict this country ever participated in, taking more American lives than any other war before or since. The extreme savagery and scope of those battles set precedents for what "modern war" would come to mean in the following century.

WAR IN EUROPE. By that time, Americans, who had proved themselves capable of waging war in the extreme, had had enough of it. With the exception of the short-lived **Spanish-American War (1898)**, the United States remained determinedly isolationist until **World War I (1914–1918)** began in Europe.

Most Americans wanted no part of that conflict either. But U.S. insistence on neutrality gave way when Germany tried to entice Mexico into joining its cause. American doughboys joined the ranks of other Allied (British, Canadian, and French) soldiers. Millions of them had already been machine-gunned and gassed in a war that, even today, remains outstanding in its sheer, mindless brutality. A last-ditch U.S. effort helped to finally defeat Germany, but the hard-fought victory took from the United States 100,000 of its children.

World War I was supposed to be the war to end all wars. Instead, in just twenty years, it was followed by an even more murderous conflict: **World War II (1939–1945)**. Again Americans resisted being drawn into the European bloodbath. Long-standing tensions, though, between the United States and Japan exploded at Pearl Harbor in 1941. With the pride of the U.S. fleet bombed and blazing, U.S. neutrality vanished. The nation, driven to its knees by years of depression, rose up to fight the war of wars. The titanic conflict would send millions of GIs across the seas, push women out of their kitchens into factories, and ignite both heartbreaking sacrifice and bigoted intolerance.

THE COLD WAR.

The United States and the Soviet Union—allies in World War II—emerged as the super-power victors at its end. But their opposing ideologies and their interest in influencing nations around the world guaranteed further conflict. Soon the Soviets and the United States each had a nuclear arsenal, and the Cold War began. Each country was now striving for superiority in a race that threatened the survival of humankind.

This Cold War fostered both the **Korean War (1950–1953)** and the **Vietnam War (1964–1973)**. The United States, seeking to preserve some semblance of democracy in Southeast Asia, was confronted with the pro-communist sympathies of former colonies. In neither Korea nor Vietnam were United States forces allowed to wage total war. And in neither case did they achieve total victory. In Korea, the U.S. managed to reestablish the status quo of two separate countries. In Vietnam, the United States withdrew its forces and South Vietnam eventually fell entirely to the communist regime of North Vietnam.

Faced with the continued threat of nuclear confrontation, the United States increasingly resorted to covert (secret) acts to influence the affairs of other governments during the 1980s. These efforts were often not very successful. Most often they produced not democracies but strong-man dictatorships. However, in the following decade the United States once again turned to conventional military tactics in its victory (with United Nation's forces) in the **Gulf War (1991)**.

COSTS OF WAR.

Perhaps the most important lesson armed conflict has taught the people of this country is that, while war may sometimes be the only solution, it is always a terrible solution. War has cost this nation hundreds of thousands of its children on battlefields at home and around the world. But the cumulative effects of war carry on long after the battlefield dead are mourned and buried. They are felt by children who have to live without their parents and parents who must bury the children whose lives they expected to share. They are felt by wounded and disabled veterans whose struggle is often forgotten when the war is over. Perhaps most strongly, they are felt by those whose brutal memories no longer allow them to sleep at night.

The consequences of warfare in this age, however, are more than just personal. They are universal. With the arrival of nuclear weapons, the lives of everyone on the planet hang in the balance of peace. However, if the course of history has taught one repeated lesson, it is that peace seldom lasts for long where there is no justice.

LEGACY OF A REVOLUTION.

The United States has created powerful armaments and participated in many wars. Still the most powerful weapon this nation ever produced was the notion that human beings have a value not determined by their governments. That very American idea has confronted tanks and toppled tyrants, and, to this day, makes the enemies of freedom sleep fitfully in their beds. Though tyranny and oppression still abound in the world, and injustice is not absent within our own borders, that idea of freedom still thrives.

Today the United States is the most powerful country on earth. But we still have an obligation not to betray the principle which gave the United States its life and still gives it its honor. "Those who deny freedom to others deserve it not for themselves," said Abraham Lincoln. We can best honor those who have fought for us by fulfilling our nation's pledge of justice, both in war and in peace.

"The government of the United States...gives to bigotry no sanction, to persecution no assistance," said George Washington two centuries ago. Though we have sometimes lost sight of it, our nation continues to carry the promise to defend and not oppress the freedom of others. If we abandon that promise, we abandon the foundation of our nation. Our great American Revolution—fought so desperately so long ago—can still be won or lost.

J.A. English
New York, New York

T.D. Jones
Houston, Texas

THE
AMERICAN REVOLUTION

The American Revolution began long before the War for Independence actually started. John Adams, one of the Revolution's leaders and later United States president, wrote: "The Revolution was in the hearts and minds of the people...long before a drop of blood was shed..."

Many have debated just what that Revolution was about. The signers of the Declaration of Independence insisted it was about liberty and democracy, the people's right to choose how they should be governed. Later, others insisted the Revolution was really about money and trade. The British were taking all the colonies' profits, and the Americans wanted them for themselves.

In fact, the Revolution was about both issues. The lofty sentiments of the Declaration of Independence and the bare-knuckled struggle for trade were linked together in the colonists' revolt. To live the way they wanted, the colonists needed a kind of freedom that gave Britain's King George nightmares. The result was a British-American war—and much more.

"We have the power to begin the world again," wrote Thomas Paine, urging his fellow Patriots to take arms against the British. True enough, the tiny American nation's revolt against the greatest military power on earth sparked wars and uprisings throughout Europe in the decades to follow. The Declaration of Independence would inspire the makers of governments for centuries to come.

American rifleman,
Revolutionary War

1770–1774	1775	1776	1777	
Boston Massacre *(March 5, 1770)*	American Revolution begins at Lexington and Concord, Mass. *(April 19).*	Declaration of Independence *(July 4)*	British take Fort Ticonderoga, N.Y. *(July 5).*	Washington's army suffers through a terrible winter at Valley Forge, Pa.
British defeat an American militia in Alamance, N.C. *(May 16, 1771).*		Washington's Army crosses the Delaware River, capturing 1,000 Hessians at Trenton, N.J. *(Dec. 25–26).*	Major American victory at Saratoga, N.Y. *(Oct. 17)*	
Boston Tea Party *(Dec. 16, 1773)*				

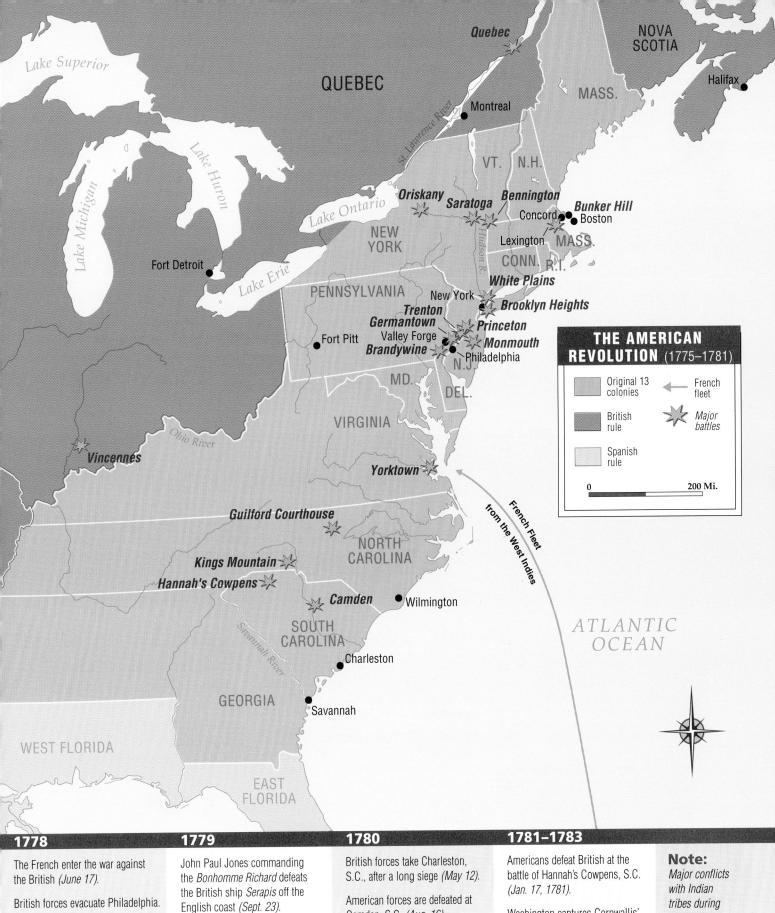

THE AMERICAN REVOLUTION (1775–1781)

- Original 13 colonies
- British rule
- Spanish rule
- French fleet
- Major battles

0 ————— 200 Mi.

Lake Superior

Lake Michigan

Lake Huron

Lake Ontario

Lake Erie

QUEBEC

Quebec

NOVA SCOTIA

Halifax

Montreal

St. Lawrence River

MASS.

VT. N.H.

Oriskany
Saratoga
Bennington
Bunker Hill
Concord
Boston
Lexington
MASS.
CONN. R.I.

NEW YORK

White Plains

Fort Detroit

PENNSYLVANIA

New York
Brooklyn Heights
Trenton
Germantown
Princeton
Valley Forge
Monmouth
Brandywine
Philadelphia
N.J.

Fort Pitt

MD.
DEL.

Hudson R.

VIRGINIA

Ohio River

Vincennes

Yorktown

French Fleet from the West Indies

Guilford Courthouse

NORTH CAROLINA

Kings Mountain

Hannah's Cowpens

Camden

Wilmington

SOUTH CAROLINA

Savannah River

Charleston

GEORGIA

Savannah

ATLANTIC OCEAN

WEST FLORIDA

EAST FLORIDA

1778

The French enter the war against the British *(June 17)*.

British forces evacuate Philadelphia.

Major battle at Monmouth, N.J., ends in a draw *(June 28)*.

British forces take Savannah *(Dec. 29)*.

1779

John Paul Jones commanding the *Bonhomme Richard* defeats the British ship *Serapis* off the English coast *(Sept. 23)*.

American forces spend a brutal winter at Morristown, N.J.

1780

British forces take Charleston, S.C., after a long siege *(May 12)*.

American forces are defeated at Camden, S.C. *(Aug. 16)*.

Americans blockade British in New York.

1781–1783

Americans defeat British at the battle of Hannah's Cowpens, S.C. *(Jan. 17, 1781)*.

Washington captures Cornwallis' British Army at Yorktown, Va. *(Oct. 19, 1781)*.

Europe's Treaty of Paris formally ends the American Revolution *(Sept. 3, 1783)*.

Note:

Major conflicts with Indian tribes during the American Revolution are covered in the Indian Wars chapter.

5

PRELUDE TO WAR

By 1763, the French and Indian War (fought by France against England and her American allies) was over. England was now the strongest power in North America. After years of bickering with France over land, the English had practically kicked the French off the continent.

However, the cost of winning the war was enormous, and the English found themselves in serious economic trouble. King George III and his minister George Grenville decided that the thirteen colonies—which had benefited from the British war effort—should help pay the war debt. The British Parliament began to levy taxes on the colonies as a way to raise revenue. The Sugar Act of 1764 imposed taxes on virtually all items imported to the colonies. Immediately the Americans were faced with an economic crisis of their own.

Along with the taxes came new restrictions on American trade. The British now told the colonies where they could and could not sell their goods. To make matters worse, Parliament soon dreamed up another money-making scheme, the Stamp Act.

This new tax required all papers—legal documents, newspapers, marriage licenses, ships' papers, etc.—to carry a large blue paper seal, as proof that a tax had been paid. The stamps were expensive, and the colonists didn't appreciate this latest version of England telling them what to do.

SONS OF LIBERTY. By 1765, the British Quartering Act required the colonists to provide housing and food for British soldiers. This new act, together with the Stamp Act, caused serious grumbling among the colonists. An underground organization, the Sons of Liberty, was formed by angry Americans looking for a way to put a stop to British interference.

Not all protest was going on underground. American displeasure could already be seen in the streets. Many colonists refused to buy the stamps; others harassed or occasionally attacked the Stamp Masters. Trade came to a standstill because nobody would buy the stamps, and ships were not allowed to leave the harbor without properly stamped papers.

The colonists formed a Stamp Act Congress and sent a Declaration of Rights and Grievances to London to protest the tax. The declaration outlined the reasons why Parliament should repeal the Stamp Act. It noted that taxing the colonists without representation was a violation of civil liberties.

The king finally backed down and repealed the Stamp Act. But he wasn't about to drop Parliament's leash on the colonies. He insisted on issuing a Declaratory Act, which stated that Parliament had the right to tax the colonies without their consent.

SETTING THE REVOLUTION'S FIRES

Thomas Paine, Samuel Adams, and Patrick Henry established their reputations as the Revolution's three firebrands.

A firebrand is someone who is always stirring

up trouble—Sam Adams definitely fits this description. He founded the Sons of Liberty and was known to the British as one of the worst troublemakers in New England. He used every opportunity to pit the colonists against the British Parliament. Adams organized resistance to the Stamp Act and was a major instigator of the Boston Tea Party. Sam Adams was in favor of making a clean break with England, and he wasn't alone.

Thomas Paine spoke out against the British monarchy in favor of independence. He wrote a pamphlet entitled "Common Sense," outlining the reasons why the colonies needed to be free from England. Paine used harsh language when talking about King George III, calling him a "royal brute." His pamphlet was an instant

best-seller in the colonies and in Europe.

The third firebrand was also a radical for his time and a powerful speaker. Patrick Henry was elected to the Virginia House of Burgesses as a young lawyer. He was adamantly opposed to Britain's policy of taxation and saw the Stamp Act as a threat to liberty.

In 1775, when the port of Boston was closed and British soldiers were all over the colonies, Henry gave his most famous speech. In a secret meeting of the House of Burgesses he raged, "Is life so dear, or peace so sweet, as to be purchased at the price of chains and slavery? Forbid it, Almighty God! I know not what course others may take, but as for me, GIVE ME LIBERTY, OR GIVE ME DEATH!"

Colonists tar and feather a British tax official in a political cartoon. Independent Americans resented being told what to do.

TOWNSHEND AND THE BOSTON MASSACRE.

A year later the British were up to their old taxing tricks again. In 1767, the Townshend Act restated Britain's right to raise revenue through taxation to pay for the defense of the colonies.

The colonists could not swallow this new measure. They began boycotting British goods. The king sent troops to the colonies to help enforce the new laws, but the colonists, in direct opposition to the Quartering Act, refused to house them.

A "massacre" in Massachusetts pushed the issue to its limit. On the evening of March 5, 1770, a gang of men in Boston began pelting some off-duty soldiers with snowballs and rocks. British troops were called to the scene. In the confusion, one soldier fell, and his musket likely misfired. The accidental shot gave way to a ragged volley—the soldiers ended up killing five Americans and wounding seven others. Among the dead was a black freedman, a laborer named Crispus Attucks. The Boston Patriots used this incident to unite the other colonies against England, calling it the Boston Massacre.

Militias in the South were also countering the British, though not with much success. In Alamance, North Carolina, 2,000 lightly armed men, calling themselves the Regulators, were bested by a thousand British soldiers. The British rounded up what prisoners they could, executing some of them. The rest of the militiamen escaped. Later some would rejoin Washington's forces in the Revolution.

> *"If this be treason, make the most of it!"*
>
> —Patrick Henry, March 1775

THE BOSTON TEA PARTY.

In 1773, Parliament gave the financially ailing East India Company a monopoly on the tea trade to the colonies. This was more than the colonists could bear. They objected to the idea of a monopoly being given to anyone, fearing that there was nothing to prevent England from putting all American importers out of business if they wanted.

Many Americans marched to the ports in each of the colonies and refused to let the tea land. In Massachusetts the governor, in alliance with England, refused to let the ships leave the harbor unless the tea was unloaded. The colonists appealed to him to let the ships return to England still loaded with tea. The governor refused.

LIBERTY TREE

On the night of December 16, 150 Bostonians, disguised as Mohawk Indians, boarded the ships and dumped 23,000 pounds of tea overboard. The next day everyone in Boston was singing "Rally, Mohawks! Bring out your axes and tell King George we'll pay no more taxes..."

FIRST SHOTS

King George III was furious at the outrage in Massachusetts. He closed the Boston port to all commerce until the dumped tea was paid for in full. The Coercive Acts, known to the Americans as the Intolerable Acts, went into effect, a punishment for the colonists' "tea party."

PREPARING TO FIGHT. The First Continental Congress met in Philadelphia in September 1774. The representatives from twelve colonies declared the Intolerable Acts null and void. They wrote a Declaration of American Rights, denying that Parliament had any authority over internal colonial affairs. The king was not moved. "The colonies," he said "must either submit or triumph."

As Britain continued to send troops and arms to America, Patriots began to amass cannonballs and gunpowder. The British soon found out about a supply of rebel weapons in Concord, just outside of Boston, and General Thomas Gage, the British commander, planned to march to Concord to destroy the munitions.

The Boston Patriots learned of the British plan. They sent riders out to warn the people in Concord. Paul Revere, a silversmith, and dozens of other "expresses," rode through the night, thumping houses along the roads outside Boston. Trained to respond instantly, minutemen scrambled out of bed. Families went to work melting their pewter dishes into musket balls. Others continued to spread the alarm.

LEXINGTON AND CONCORD. British soldiers and local militiamen confronted one another on the village green in Lexington on the morning of April 19, 1775. The British commander screamed at the colonists: "You Rebels disperse, damn you, disperse!" Shots rang out. When the smoke cleared, eight Americans were mortally wounded. A Lexington townsman who lived opposite the green dragged himself bleeding to his doorway. He died on his doorstep as his young wife watched in horror.

Hours later more minutemen met the British at the North Bridge in Concord. The men from Concord were now joined by colonists from other towns. The redcoats were bloodied badly. Colonists sniped at them from the woods all along the way back to Boston.

BUNKER HILL. With no formal military training and little equipment, the American army was unprepared to fight the highly trained British. But the British were slow to respond to the colonial forces. This gave the Americans time to plan. In Boston, the minutemen fortified Bunker (actually Breed's) Hill overlooking the city in the middle of the night. Early the next morning the British spotted the Americans on the hill.

General Gage was worried about what kind of fight the Americans might put up. As he stared through a spyglass at the hill, he saw a tall man striding along the barricades. Gage's aide identified the man as his own brother-in-law, William Prescott. "Will he fight?" asked Gage.

"I cannot answer for his men," replied Gage's aide, "but Prescott will fight you to the gates of hell."

WOMEN REBELS

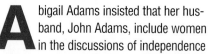

Abigail Adams insisted that her husband, John Adams, include women in the discussions of independence

and freedom. She wrote, "…I desire you remember the ladies…if particular care and attention are not paid to the ladies we are determined to foment a rebellion and will not hold ourselves bound to obey laws in which we have no voice or representation."

Outspoken women like Abigail Adams helped shape and defend the Revolution's ideals. Mercy Otis Warren, for instance, used her skills to write a play that mocked the British and championed the Revolution. She used her wit to turn Loyalists into Patriots.

Many women worked on the home front forging cannon and concocting gunpowder. Others became "Molly Pitchers," carrying supplies and water to men on the battlefield.

Some women actually joined the fighting. Mary Ludwig Hayes saw her husband fall from his gun at the battle of Monmouth. Though she was seven months pregnant, she rushed to replace him. A cannonball crashed between her legs, carrying away her petticoats.

Others actually enlisted. Deborah Sampson disguised herself as a man and joined the Continentals. Anna Marie Lane enlisted along with her husband, keeping her identity a secret from all except him. She was the only woman to receive a Revolutionary War soldier's pension. The exact number of women who served in the war is unknown because most fought in disguise.

BOSTON

CHARLES TOWN

The battle of Bunker Hill seen from Charlestown Harbor. The British took the hill but paid dearly for the victory.

As the 1,500 redcoats charged headlong again and again at the American entrenchments, they took staggering casualties—more than 1,000 men soon lay fallen on the slopes of the hill. Eventually, the Americans ran out of gunpowder and had to abandon their positions. The British owned the hill, but the victory was costly. "We could scarcely afford such another," wrote Gage.

> *"If they mean to have a war, let it begin here."*
> —Captain John Parker,
> Massachusetts Militia
> commander at Lexington

WASHINGTON APPOINTED. In the aftermath of Lexington and Concord, 20,000 Americans had joined the colonial militia. They were now eager to fight but needed someone to lead them. Congress named George Washington to be general of the Continental Army. Washington immediately went to Boston to take control of the soldiers gathered there. Meanwhile, the Continental Congress tried once again to make peace with England. They sent the Olive Branch Petition to King George III, asking him to consider their grievances. The king refused to even read it.

CANADA INVADED. During the next month, the Americans occupied Fort Ticonderoga and Crown Point, both on Lake Champlain. In a gutsy move, the Patriots now began planning a military expedition into British-held Canada. They hoped they could convince the French-speaking Canadians to join their fight. They also wanted to lay their hands on badly needed guns and powder stored by the British in Quebec.

In the summer of 1775, two colonial forces headed north into Canada. One was led by Irish-born General Richard Montgomery and the other by the American Colonel Benedict Arnold. Montgomery led his troops to Montreal, while Arnold led his troops through terrible flooding and snow, on toward Quebec. The two armies met up outside Quebec after Montreal surrendered to Montgomery.

The Canadians, however, refused to help the ailing American troops. To make matters worse, the enlistments of the majority of Arnold's troops had expired, and the men refused to stick around for the siege of Quebec.

Montgomery and Arnold decided to risk everything with a brave, desperate move. In the middle of a New Year's Eve blizzard, they stormed the city walls. Unfortunately their bravery did not pay off. Montgomery was killed, and Arnold was wounded in the leg. The British took 424 men prisoner. The rest of the Americans were forced back to their forts on Lake Champlain.

The Patriot defeat in Quebec was softened somewhat by an American victory in Boston. The Continentals sledded cannons captured at Fort Ticonderoga to Boston, and Washington managed to run the British out. As 1776 began, there was no trace of the British army left in the thirteen colonies.

INDEPENDENCE

In April 1776, the Continental Congress announced that American ports were open to ships of all nations except Great Britain. The colonists, with fewer than a dozen ships, had no real naval power to enforce the act, but the announcement served as a grand snub to Britain. The colonists were becoming bolder and gradually moving toward a complete separation from their British keepers.

WE HOLD THESE TRUTHS. In May, Richard Henry Lee, a delegate from Virginia, insisted: "...these United Colonies are, and of right ought to be, free and independent States..." The Congress set up a committee of five men, including Thomas Jefferson, John Adams, and Benjamin Franklin, to draft a longer document.

The Declaration of Independence put forth a rationale—or reason—for the Revolution and a new philosophy of government. Thomas Jefferson drafted the document by himself, basing it on the principles of the English philosopher John Locke.

Congress was not completely pleased with Jefferson's work, making a total of eighty-four changes. Jefferson himself considered the edits of his work "deplorable," but

the Declaration was formally adopted on July 4. With this open statement, the Congress was justifying the Revolution to the world.

As the American Revolution began to blaze, most of Europe was enjoying a time of peace. Unemployed European soldiers offered their services to both the English and the Americans. Benjamin Franklin went to France to drum up financial support and ended up enlisting many men to fight.

The most famous Frenchman to join the American cause was the young Marquis de Lafayette. He arrived in Philadelphia with his own ship full of soldiers and volunteered to serve. He soon became a general on Washington's staff. Britain also employed foreign troops, mainly Hessian mercenaries (paid soldiers) from Germany.

NEW YORK INVADED. Even before the Declaration of Independence was signed, the British sensed that the final break with the colonies was coming. They decided not to let the rebels get the upper hand. Under General William Howe's command, the British assembled a force of 30,000 soldiers and a huge fleet and headed to New York.

General Howe opened his assault on New York City by landing on Long Island. The English outnumbered the Americans by more than two to one. Before the Americans knew what had happened, they were flanked by the British and nearly cut off. The Americans had to fall back to their fortifications in Brooklyn at the end of August.

Thinking he had the Americans trapped, General Howe halted his redcoats in front of the American trenches. Washington, however, was not about to surren-

JEFFERSON AND HIS WORDS

Just over a year before independence was declared, Thomas Jefferson wrote a letter to his friend John Randolph in England. Jefferson was still hoping for a solution to the colonial crisis.

But on one point he was adamant: "...rather than submit to the...British parliament," he insisted, "[I] would lend my hand to sink the whole Island into the ocean."

Though Jefferson's hand did not have the power to drown Britain, it did have the skill to shake that island mightily. In June 1776, the thirty-two-year-old Jefferson was appointed to write out the document declaring the American colonies free and independent.

Little in the American Declaration of Independence was completely new. Jefferson borrowed heavily from other authors of political philosophy. Much of what the Declaration contained had been outlined in the pamphlet *The Rights of the British Colonies Asserted and Proved,* written by the original American firebrand, James Otis, in 1764.

What made the Declaration a powerful statement had to do with the ideas it contained—but those ideas were made radiant

by the writing skills of Jefferson himself. The Virginia delegate defined the notions of equality and self-government with precision and elegance. The Declaration gave the profound idea of human worth an equally profound voice.

Though Jefferson fought to keep passages he wrote against the slave trade in the Declaration, he was outvoted, and the lines were stricken. And though he disapproved of slavery in principle, Jefferson continued to hold slaves throughout his life, freeing only two upon his death. Nevertheless, the Declaration asserting the equality of all men remained one of Jefferson's proudest accomplishments, "an expression," he said, "of the American mind."

Thomas Jefferson's corrections on his draft of the Declaration of Independence. His words would shake the world.

der his force. With no American navy to come to his aid, the Virginia general nevertheless rounded up every small boat he could find. In the midst of a raging thunderstorm, 9,500 men rowed across the East River to the safety of the Manhattan shore. While the brilliant escape saved half of the American army, Washington lost the biggest American seaport to the British.

WASHINGTON CROSSES THE DELAWARE. On September 15, the British attacked across the East River, driving Washington and his men into retreat. By the middle of December, Washington, with no more than 6,000 men, had fled to the Pennsylvania side of the Delaware River near Trenton, New Jersey.

> *"We hold these truths to be self-evident: that all men are created equal..."*
> —*The Declaration of Independence*

The British now occupied New York City, all of northern New Jersey, and Newport, Rhode Island. General Howe left a small force in New Jersey to keep an eye on Washington's weary troops and settled in at Newport for the winter.

Washington had not achieved one clear victory since he had taken command. He once counted an army of 20,000; now he had barely 3,000 men under his command. Their enlistments would expire in a matter of days. Time was running out for Washington and the Revolution. "If every nerve is not strained to recruit the new army, I think the game is pretty near up," wrote the desperate commander.

But fate was about to smile on George Washington. In late December he received intelligence that the town of Trenton was being held by fewer than 1,500 Hessian troops. On the bitter cold Christmas night in 1776, the American army crossed the Delaware River back into New Jersey. Chunks of ice choked the frigid waters. None of the Americans were prepared for the bitter weather; few if any had winter uniforms. Arriving onshore, the troops were frozen and exhausted. But the journey was far from over. Covering nine miles in the early morning hours, the American army marched through the snow with their feet tied in rags, leaving a trail of bloody footprints.

Though they arrived too late to attack at dawn, Washington's army managed to surprise the Hessian troops in Trenton, who were still asleep after a festive Christmas celebration. The fighting was over in just an hour, and almost a thousand Hessian soldiers were taken prisoner.

The very next day, Washington's forces pulled off yet another surprise victory at Princeton.

STRUGGLE FOR THE HUDSON

American morale got a boost after Washington's victories in New Jersey. But in June 1777, word came that a large British army of 10,000 men and 138 cannons was headed south from Canada. Many thought the American Revolution would soon be over.

SARATOGA. General John Burgoyne had bet a year's wages that after one decisive blow against the Americans, he would return to England victorious. Burgoyne believed that by striking down the Hudson River he would cut off New England and New York from the rest of the colonies and end the rebellion.

After recapturing Fort Ticonderoga, Burgoyne headed toward Fort Edward. But when the Patriots saw him coming they abandoned the fort and took to the woods. Crack riflemen, positioned behind—and sometimes in—the trees, bloodied the advancing British soldiers. In a series of skirmishes, the British lost close to 1,000 men.

The attacks slowed the British down, and by the time they reached Saratoga, the Americans were ready for them. General Horatio Gates, commander of the American forces, placed his men on a high bluff called Bemus Heights, overlooking the road to Albany. American cannons were trained on the approaching British. Burgoyne had only two choices: march down the dangerous narrow road to Albany or fight the Americans.

American farmers, led by Benedict Arnold, soon joined the furious assault upon Gates' troops. After losing another 600 soldiers, Burgoyne, who swore he would never surrender, did just that. The Americans marched the British army to Boston and put them on ships returning to England.

The victory at Saratoga finally convinced the French to join the war on the American side.

VALLEY FORGE. Saratoga had turned the tide of the war, but George Washington was going through some tough times. Trying to protect Philadelphia, he had lost two battles in Pennsylvania at Brandywine and Germantown. On September 26, General Howe finally captured Philadelphia. A despairing Washington brought his exhausted army to Valley Forge, Pennsylvania.

It was a good spot for a winter camp. The land was high enough so the American troops could keep an eye on Philadelphia. Yet it was far enough away that they didn't have to worry about surprise attacks.

Unfortunately, the winter of 1777–1778 was terrible. There wasn't enough clothing to go around, and there was never enough to eat. Nearly 2,000 soldiers died, and another 2,000 deserted. The survivors, though, emerged in the spring as a new, thoroughly trained army.

MONMOUTH. In June 1778, hearing that the French fleet was on the way, British General Henry Clinton pulled his troops out of Philadelphia and pushed them northward toward New York. Washington's army caught up with him near Monmouth, New Jersey.

On June 28, Washington ordered his second in command, Charles Lee, to lead the attack on Clinton's force. Lee, however, didn't like Washington's plan and issued

WAR RESISTERS

Some Americans refused to take arms against the British for reasons of conscience. Members of religious groups like the Quakers, Shakers, and Amish were often exempted from fighting. Those exempted, though, often had to pay for a replacement. Quakers were particularly outspoken against the war and refused even to pay the imposed fines.

"We cannot take up arms…or [help in] the destruction of our fellow creatures," said a meeting of Virginia Quakers. A few were put in prison. Yet Quaker Societies continued to disown members who joined the war or hired a substitute to replace themselves in military service.

Although most conscientious objectors were left alone, occasionally some took abuse. In September 1779, fourteen Virginia Quakers were arrested and forced to march to Washington's army encamped near Philadelphia. General Washington sent them home.

Some of those who refused to fight were sons of famous Patriots. Patrick Henry was probably the most outspoken advocate for war with the British. But it was his son, John Henry, who ended up in the decisive battle against the British near Saratoga. John Henry witnessed the terrific struggle at Bemus Heights, where Burgoyne's army was slaughtered as they tried to retreat. Though the Americans won the day, their ranks, too, were shattered in the close fighting.

After the battle, young John Henry trudged through the blood-soaked fields, searching for faces of friends lost in the fight. The sight of the broken bodies proved more than the revolutionary's son could take. He threw down his sword and cried in anguish among his dead friends. Two months later he went home to Virginia, refusing to fight any longer.

Molly Pitcher loads the guns at Monmouth. American women fought for liberty—for their country and themselves.

orders that confused the troops. In places where they might have easily advanced, he ordered them to fall back. When the retreat was reported to Washington, the commander was so amazed he had the messenger arrested for spreading false reports. Washington's disbelief soon turned to fury, though, when he caught his second in command riding away from the battle. The general reportedly swore at Lee "until the leaves shook on the trees."

"I have beat them. I have beat all the Americans."

—George III, just before the Battle of Saratoga

Washington then halted the retreat and spurred his troops once again to turn and attack the enemy. The general was aching for a victory, but daylight was fading. During the night Clinton's army slipped away.

A French force arrived in New York harbor too late to stop the British escape. The French briefly blockaded New York, but their fleet was damaged in a storm. On August 10, however, they joined forces with the Americans for an attack on Newport, Rhode Island.

The British and Hessians had made much fun of the American militia, calling them a "flock of ducks." But an all-black regiment, the 1st Rhode Island, forced them to choke on their words. In a series of furious assaults, the Rhode Islanders inflicted four times as many casualties on the Hessians as they took themselves.

WAR IN THE WEST. Long before the war began, Britain had forbidden American colonists to move west over the Appalachians. For years, though, settlers had been pushing back this frontier. Now Britain had recruited local Indian tribes as their allies and used them to attack American settlements.

A Virginian, George Rogers Clark, was determined to end the raids and made plans to seize British forts along the frontier. With about 150 hard-traveling men, he braved the white water of the Ohio River to the mouth of the Tennessee. Slipping overland through the forest he arrived before spring in Illinois territory. By February, Clark's men had violently taken Vincennes in Indiana.

THE DARKEST DAYS

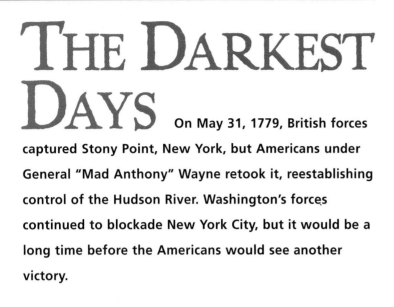

On May 31, 1779, British forces captured Stony Point, New York, but Americans under General "Mad Anthony" Wayne retook it, reestablishing control of the Hudson River. Washington's forces continued to blockade New York City, but it would be a long time before the Americans would see another victory.

STALEMATE AND STARVATION.

In the northern colonies during 1779 and 1780, the Revolution had reached a stalemate. Many believed it was worse than that; they thought that the war was all but lost.

The fighting with Britain had gone on now for four years. The American economy was shattered—the Continental dollar worth almost nothing. Fields and barns across the country had been picked clean to feed the army. The country's resources were evaporating, and the spirit of the Revolution was disappearing with them. At the same time, war profiteers who took advantage of shortages were rampant.

Bitter soldiers, away from home, worried about the survival of their wives and children. One woman wrote to her husband: "I am without bread and cannot get any. My children will starve or, if they do not, they must freeze."

Anguished by such pleas and without food themselves, many men deserted. From winter 1779 through 1781, Washington found himself putting down mutiny after mutiny.

The weather didn't help. As the Continental Army wintered at Morristown, New Jersey, in 1779, it found itself in the midst of the worst winter in memory. Drifts as high as eight feet surrounded the huts of shivering and desperate men, who could not even count on food to eat. "We were absolutely, literally starved," wrote one young soldier.

SIEGE OF CHARLESTON.

The Revolution still burned, though the real fighting had now switched to the South. By 1779, all of Georgia had fallen to the British. The next year a combined French and American effort failed to dislodge them. The British now had their eye on the important city of Charleston, South Carolina.

General Henry Clinton was encouraged by the English success in Georgia. In 1780, he and Lord Charles Cornwallis sailed south with an 8,500-man army. They landed in Charleston in February and spent the next few months adding to their army until it was 10,000 strong.

The British army in Charleston was now twice the size of the Continental army there, and the Patriots were quickly wiped out. After the surrender of Charleston, the British seized as much of the South as possible, raiding and burning towns along the way.

DISGRACE AND DEFEAT.

In August 1780, at Camden, South Carolina, Cornwallis dealt the Americans another crushing defeat. Most of the Patriot soldiers were

THE *BONHOMME RICHARD*

One of the worst problems the Americans had was their lack of a navy. Without one, they were at the mercy of the powerful British Navy, and the French were as yet unwilling to use their ships in the Patriot cause. The American navy remained more illusion than reality, although it did claim one intrepid captain.

Scottish-born John Paul Jones had fled to America from England to avoid prosecution for killing a mutinous sailor. Commissioned by Washington, Jones conducted several raids on British shipping during 1778.

In September of 1779, the Scotsman immortalized himself when his *Bonhomme Richard* met the British ship *Serapis* off the English coast.

Moments after the battle began, one of the *Bonhomme's* cannons exploded, maiming many of her crew. The British called on the American captain to surrender. But Jones was undaunted. He lashed his crippled ship to the *Serapis* and continued fighting at close range until the *Serapis*, too, was about to collapse.

The British crew, astonished at Jones' crazed struggle, were too frightened even to try to haul down the British flag in surrender. *Serapis'* own captain was forced to pull down her colors. The *Bonhomme Richard* sank three days later, and Jones sailed off victorious on the captured British vessel.

"Don't Tread on Me" was one of the first American flags. Its message was clear: Interfere with our liberty at your peril.

sick and half-starved when they met the well-fed British forces in the middle of the night. When the redcoats charged with bayonets, four fifths of the American army fled from the field. Worse, their commander, Horatio Gates, ran with them, spurring his horse from the scene and riding all the way out of the state.

Gates' disgraceful behavior was paid for in blood by an astonishingly brave group of Maryland and Delaware soldiers. Led by a Bavarian volunteer, Johann DeKalb, these 600 men stood their ground until Cornwallis threw his entire force, more than 6,000 men, against them. DeKalb himself, leading from the front, was wounded three times and finally bayoneted to death. The broken remnants of his command fled the field to avoid capture.

SOUTHERN PARTISANS. The Americans had lost two armies, but the dismal defeats at Charleston and Camden did not end the fighting in the South. Instead a strong guerrilla army rose up to harass the British.

"These are the times that try men's souls."
—Thomas Paine

As the British moved farther inland, these private American armies repeatedly attacked British supply lines to the coast. Small bands would strike the British suddenly and then ride off before they could be captured. While bleeding the king's forces, they also battled the many Loyalists and former Patriots who had joined the British cause.

One guerrilla force under Francis Marion was an especially sharp thorn in the British side. Lord Cornwallis was so incensed by this Swamp Fox's constant attacks that he sent out his crack officer, Banastre Tarleton, to catch Marion. Tarleton, who had a reputation for being unstoppable, dogged Marion but could not chase him down. "The devil himself could not catch him," he complained.

CIVIL WAR. After the Declaration of Independence, it became an act of treason to take a pro-British stance. As many as 80,000 citizens left the colonies, half of them going to Canada. In the South, though, many Loyalists stood their ground. When the war came to these colonies, the fighting between Loyalists and Patriots created scenes of "devastation, bloodshed, and deliberate murder." Houses and fields were burned and their owners' throats cut.

Retaliations had reached a fevered pitch by early October 1780. The climax came when an American force of 1,400 frontiersmen, mountainmen, and guerrillas encircled 1,100 British Loyalists at Kings Mountain in South Carolina. This battle—pitting Americans against Americans—revealed clearly that the Revolution had become a civil war as much as a struggle for independence. After the violent confrontation on Kings Mountain, American Loyalists lay in heaps. More than 150 were killed outright and 600 were captured. The gruesome battle finally turned back the pro-British tide. The victory also brought new recruits into the American ranks and warned other Southerners against joining the Loyalist side.

COWPENS TO YORKTOWN

In December 1780, Nathaniel Greene took command of the Continental Army in the South. Greene, a Quaker, had left his pacifist beliefs behind to fight in the Revolution. Now George Washington was counting on him to save that Revolution from being extinguished.

GREENE TAKES COMMAND. Though he had fought alongside Washington in many battles, Greene was not anxious for command. Now, into his hands fell an army that was, in his own words, "wretched beyond description." The ragged Southern troops numbered only 3,000 and had scant food or supplies. The British General Lord Cornwallis, on the other hand, had 4,000 experienced and disciplined troops ready and eager to grind the Americans into the ground.

Against all rules of warfare, Greene promptly divided his small force. He knew that Cornwallis could not chase one half without risking being attacked from the other. Greene dispatched 600 of his men west under the direction of the hard-fighting, rum-swilling Daniel Morgan. Morgan's crack riflemen had been key to the American victory at Saratoga.

Cornwallis, in turn, divided his own force, sending half of it in pursuit of Morgan. Commanding these troops was Banastre Tarleton, whose name was infamous throughout the South. It was Tarleton who refused to allow Americans to surrender after Charleston, personally cutting down a soldier who raised the white flag and overseeing the slaughter of men who had laid down their arms. When Nathaniel Greene received word that Tarleton was on Morgan's trail, he sent him a message. "Colonel Tarleton is said to be on his way to pay you a visit. I doubt not but he will have a decent reception."

HANNAH'S COWPENS. Morgan had a reception in mind, all right. He and his men had gathered near the border between the Carolinas at a place called Hannah's Cowpens. With their backs to the river and no place to go, Morgan knew his men would fight hard. Still, he was aware that many of them were inexperienced militia. These men weren't part of the Continental Army. They were defending their homesteads. Most couldn't be expected to stand and shoot for long.

Morgan knew how to get the best from the motley group he commanded. As the British approached, he assembled his troops in three lines. Up front he put a row of his own sharpshooters, men who could pick off British officers at a distance. Behind them he put a line of the green militiamen, assuring them that they only

---

"TURNING ARNOLD"

In 1780, toward the end of the Revolution, a British fleet with 1,200 troops sailed up Virginia's James River and took Richmond with little resistance. The most shocking detail about the British raid was its commander—the American, Benedict Arnold.

Arnold was one of the Revolution's most passionate Patriots and a superb general. Early in the war he had led an epic march of nearly 400 miles through the Maine wilderness into Canada. His daring but failed attack on Quebec during a blizzard nearly cost the general his left leg. The wounded Arnold had to drag himself bleeding more than a mile back to his lines. He did not retire but went on to be a key figure in the American victory at Saratoga.

Had the Revolution ended earlier, or had Arnold died at Quebec, he would be standing proudly by Washington's side in U.S. history books. Instead Arnold's name is pure mud.

Arnold's real problem was not lack of belief in the revolutionary cause. It was greed. Like many other Patriots, Arnold had used his own money to finance his expeditions. Members of Congress—not generally fond of Arnold—refused to reimburse his expenses or to raise his salary, even when George Washington himself pleaded Arnold's case.

Arnold's lifestyle was lavish. As he slipped increasingly into debt he began war profiteer-ing—dealing in goods that were in short supply. The trade was illegal, and Congress censured him. Arnold reacted furiously to the criticism, having, as he said, "made every sacrifice of fortune and blood, and become a cripple in the service of my country."

But Arnold did more than complain; he began to conspire. He agreed to turn over the plans of his new command, West Point, in return for a generalship in the British Army. Though Arnold's treachery was soon discovered, he managed to escape to a British vessel.

Months later, when Arnold captured Richmond, the unrecognized general asked Virginians what they would do if they ever caught up to the infamous Benedict. One local replied that he would cut off Arnold's left leg (wounded in Quebec) and bury it with full military honors. The rest of him he would hang.

Washington and Lafayette at Yorktown. The French-American alliance had trapped Cornwallis' British army.

needed to fire two shots before running for cover. At a distance behind the militia, Morgan lined up a third row of disciplined Continental soldiers.

At dawn on the morning of January 17, Tarleton sent in cavalry scouts to see what the Americans were up to. Morgan's sharpshooters promptly dumped them from their saddles. Tarleton then sent in the first lines of his troops. As soon as the militia saw the redcoats, they fired their two rounds and broke for the American flanks. The British mistook the militia's move for a retreat and pounded headlong toward the American lines. Before Tarleton's troops knew what was happening, they ran smack into the ferocious Continentals.

> ## "Oh, God! It is all over!"
> —British Prime Minister Lord North

Tarleton, now a bit desperate, sent in his Highlanders, crack British troops. The Americans—hit hard—now fell back, and the British charged them once again. But as the redcoats approached the American lines, the Continentals turned suddenly around, firing a "sheet of flame" into their enemies' faces.

The British broke ranks and ran. Within thirty minutes, over 900 men, 90 percent of Tarleton's force, were killed or captured. Morgan and his soldiers sped over the Carolina border to rejoin their commander. Nathaniel Greene would much appreciate the reception Daniel Morgan had given Banastre Tarleton.

YORKTOWN. In mid-September, Cornwallis brought his troops up to Yorktown—a river port on the Chesapeake Bay—to await supplies from New York. Washington sent General Lafayette and 1,200 troops south to confront the British commander.

When Washington heard that a French fleet was en route to America, he planned a combined French and American attack on Yorktown. On September 28, 1781, more than 8,000 Americans and 7,800 French soldiers arrived in Yorktown to fight Cornwallis' weary army of 7,000. The allies dug trenches, moved up their cannons, and before long had the British trapped against the York River. The French and American army then started shelling the outnumbered and despairing British.

Cornwallis had no options. On October 17, 1781, a British officer braved the bombardment and waved a white flag over his lines. Cornwallis' stunned army was ready to surrender if necessary.

Nobody realized that Yorktown was the end of the war. King George was prepared to continue the fight, but an annoyed and bankrupt Parliament put an end to it. A treaty was signed in Paris on September 3, 1783, formally ending the Revolutionary War.

AFTERMATH

In the years following the Revolution until the War of 1812, the American colonies organized themselves into a nation. And they multiplied: In two decades, the infant nation grew from thirteen to seventeen states. U.S. territories stretched west to the Rocky Mountains and south to the Gulf of Mexico.

THE U.S. CONSTITUTION. A nation, however, is more than just territory. The colonists had defeated the British, but that victory was won by separate states, not by a real country. After the Treaty of Paris was signed, Congress began the process of forming a nation.

The Articles of Confederation had been in effect since 1777. With it, the colonies had been able to fight the British in unison. But now that the British were defeated, the colonists needed a stronger bond. They needed a constitution.

On May 25, 1787, a Federal Convention convened in Philadelphia to form a new government. The old Congress was expanded into two houses: the Senate and House of Representatives. This legislative body would be balanced by a strong executive, the president. In addition a Supreme Court would decide issues of federal law. No single person or body would have total power; the government of the people would be shared.

The Constitution was ratified by all the states. The newly formed government began in earnest on September 13, 1788. Presidential electors chose George Washington as the nation's first leader.

The new government stood upon shaky legs. It had no money and many debts. It was surrounded by old enemies: the British were still in control of Canada. Tribes of hostile Indians did not recognize the sovereign nation; many had traditionally sided with the French or British. Now Britain was encouraging them to form a state of their own.

Washington had sent the American army home after the war. Now all that remained were fewer than 700 officers and soldiers and no American navy to patrol the seas.

BARBARY PIRATES. The lack of a navy was a particular problem. Soon after the war, pirate ships in the

---

FOUNDING FATHER

For nearly 200 years schoolchildren learned the following about George Washington: 1) he never told a lie; 2) he chopped down his father's cherry tree, but admitted doing it; and 3) he had wooden teeth. All of these things became part of Washington's revered history. In fact, historians only know for sure that our first president did have wooden false teeth.

Washington came from a wealthy family, but he never went to college. He was much more interested in the outdoors and the military. When he tried to join the navy as a teenager, his mother refused to let him go. He did, however, finally join the Virginia militia as an officer. During the French

and Indian War, Washington gained fame leading campaigns against Indians along the American frontier.

Though he retired from the military at twenty-six, the experience stuck with him. Washington was a strong advocate of using force to gain independence from England. Once he became American commander, Washington much preferred European military training. He hoped to shape the Continental Army into a fighting force that would rival that of the British.

That shaping required discipline, and Washington did not shy away from the power of command. During the winter at Valley Forge, courts-martial were held every day, and soldiers were punished, even executed, for dis-

obeying even very basic orders.

Despite his austere authority, Washington was admired by his troops. During 1781, a group of soldiers in the Continental Army were considering mutiny. They were furious that they had fought for so long and Congress was neglecting to pay them. Washington coaxed the mutineers out of their revolt. He had sacrificed as much for his country as anyone. He had earned the right to ask sacrifice of others.

Unlike countless other successful military leaders, Washington never tried to seize control of the country and form his own government. Given his success in the Revolution, he might well have succeeded had he tried.

Instead, after the war, Washington dismantled his army and went home. It was the newly formed United States that came calling for Washington. He served as its president for eight difficult years when the United States was groping for its place in the world.

This army recruiting notice appeared in 1799 as war with France threatened. George Washington was compelled to dust off his uniform.

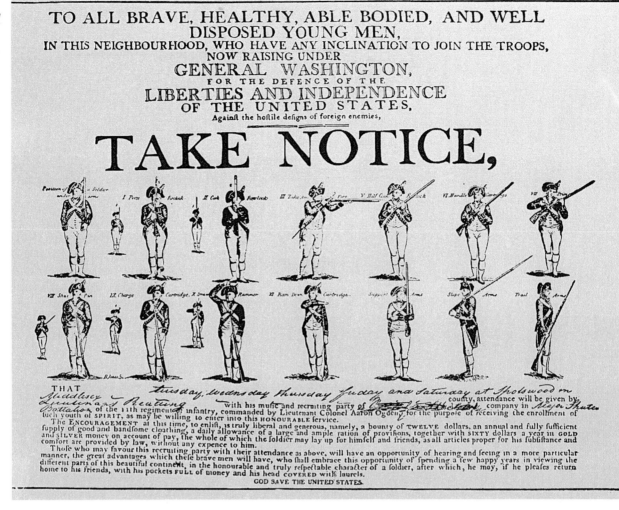

TO ALL BRAVE, HEALTHY, ABLE BODIED, AND WELL DISPOSED YOUNG MEN, IN THIS NEIGHBOURHOOD, WHO HAVE ANY INCLINATION TO JOIN THE TROOPS, NOW RAISING UNDER GENERAL WASHINGTON, FOR THE DEFENCE OF THE LIBERTIES AND INDEPENDENCE OF THE UNITED STATES, Against the hostile designs of foreign enemies,

TAKE NOTICE,

GOD SAVE THE UNITED STATES.

Mediterranean began attacking American vessels. Without a navy to protect them, these merchant ships were easy prey. Crewmen from the ships were locked up in dungeons or forced to do hard labor until ransom was paid.

Finally, the Congress responded by building new warships. American sailors and marines defeated the Barbary pirates of North Africa. But it took ten years—and $2 million in ransom money—before U.S. vessels were able to sail the Mediterranean in peace.

Spurred on by American independence, the French Revolution erupted in 1789. In its wake, much of Europe was thrown into a state of war. The French and English would exchange blows from 1793 to 1815.

The United States took a neutral stance in the European free-for-all. However, distinct political parties had now formed in the U.S. government. Both Republicans and Federalists had their own views as to what "neutral" meant.

The Federalists took a pro-British stance, sealing it with Jay's Treaty in 1794. This treaty was meant to secure English and American interests by regulating commerce. It would also establish the country's neutral rights during wartime.

FRENCH NAVAL WAR.

European trade, though, remained a problem. In the aftermath of the French Revolution, Napoleon Bonaparte came to power in France. His armies gained victories across Europe. The French, feeling betrayed by Jay's Treaty, began attacking American merchant ships with a vengeance.

President John Adams sent a mediator to Paris to resolve the situation. But Napoleon's government refused to negotiate unless the United States first paid a $250,000 "tribute" plus a $10 million loan.

The United States refused to pay the bribe; instead it began to arm its merchant vessels. The American navy and marine corps were refitted and rebuilt. Impressive, tall, and fast sailing ships like the *Constellation* and *Constitution* advertised American power on the sea. U.S. vessels were ordered to capture any French armed vessels that crossed them.

In the north, fearful of a French invasion from Canada, the U.S. Army readied its guns. Even George Washington was obliged to dig his uniform out of storage to lead a force of 3,000.

Fortunately the French threat was short-lived. By 1799, France was, once again, acting reasonably.

THE WAR OF 1812

Unlike the Revolution, no grand issues of fundamental rights would be wrangled over in the War of 1812. Instead the United States, now a constituted nation, would battle its old enemy for the right to be left alone. Americans wanted to trade on the seas and be left alone to grow west to the Mississippi and beyond.

The British had other ideas. Having lost the Revolution to the upstart colonists, they were as yet unwilling to lose the entire American continent. The conflict that began in 1812 would set the limits of British power in North America once and for all.

PRELUDE TO WAR When the new president, Thomas Jefferson, and his fellow old-style Republicans took over, they began a new foreign policy. It was governed by three main principles: 1) protect U.S. interests on the seas; 2) clear America's western territories of foreign troops and influence; and 3) break free from all dependence on Europe. The rallying cry of the Republicans was "no entangling alliances."

IMPRESSMENT. Still, Americans continued to be entangled. When the war in Europe (Napoleonic Wars) started up in 1803, the French and English again began preying on neutral American ships.

The British policy of impressment infuriated Americans. The British claimed that deserters from their navy were working on American ships—and many were. The British navy would actually stop ships and force seamen—some American, some British—to join their crews. About 6,000 Americans were "impressed" by the British from 1803 to 1812. The British also interfered with American trade, seizing and searching U.S. ships in American waters.

The United States responded by passing the Non-Importation Act in 1806. This act prohibited the importing of English goods that could be bought somewhere else or made at home. The English, for their part, established a full naval blockade of the European coast.

SHOTS FIRED. In 1807, the English warship *Leopard* stopped the American ship *Chesapeake*. The British demanded the surrender of four crew members who they claimed were British deserters. When the Americans refused to give up the men, the *Leopard* opened fire on the *Chesapeake*, killing three and wounding eighteen. The *Chesapeake* finally surrendered, and the British carried the alleged deserters off the ship. The incident enraged Americans, and many now demanded a war with England.

The British worsened the situation by passing a series of new laws that required all neutral trade with Europe to pass through England first. They claimed the measure was a necessary response to Napoleon's decree forbidding trade with England.

Nevertheless, Americans felt the English were using the war in Europe as an excuse to destroy their commerce. They had hard evidence to back their claim. Between 1807 and 1812, England and France had seized about 900 American ships and some 4,000 naturalized American citizens.

CONGRESS DEBATES. The 12th Congress met on November 4, 1811. The possibility of war with England was on everyone's mind. The War Hawks, a new faction in Congress, were wholeheartedly in favor of doing battle once more with Britain.

President James Madison, in office since 1809, did his part to push the Hawk cause along. He sent a message to Congress that accused England of declaring war on American commerce. In response, Congress ordered war preparations to begin.

The British, meanwhile, were trying to avoid war and move toward a more peaceful relationship with the United States. The *Chesapeake* affair was settled in 1811. By the spring of 1812, the British were treating American ships with a new respect. In fact, as war grew more certain, the British offered to give the United States an equal share of trade in Europe.

Just two days before war was declared, Britain gave up the naval blockade of Europe. Unfortunately, communication across the Atlantic was slow. It would be weeks before the United States heard of the British concessions. By then it was too late.

WAR OF 1812 (1812–1814)

United States	Disputed area
British Territory	British Blockade
Spanish Territory	Major battle

0   200 Mi.

BRITISH NORTH AMERICA (CANADA)

Newark
Fort George — Fort Niagara
Lewiston
Niagara Falls — Fort Schlosser
Fort Chippewa — Niagara River
Fort Erie — Buffalo
Lake Erie

Montreal

Chrysler's Farm
Sacket's Harbor
Lake Champlain
Chateaugay
York (Toronto)
Battle of the Thames River
Lake Ontario

MASS.
VT. N.H.
MASS.

MICHIGAN TERR.
Lake Erie
Ft. Detroit
Ft. Niagara
Buffalo
NEW YORK
CONN.
R.I.
N.J.

Ft. Dearborn

ILLINOIS TERR.
INDIANA TERR.
OHIO
PENNSYLVANIA
DEL.
MD.

River
Baltimore
Washington
Ft. McHenry
Chesapeake Bay

VIRGINIA

Ohio River
KENTUCKY
—OURI —TORY

TENNESSEE
NORTH CAROLINA

Mississippi River

SOUTH CAROLINA

MISSISSIPPI TERRITORY
GEORGIA

—SIANA
Pensacola
New —leans

FLORIDA (Spanish)

ATLANTIC OCEAN

Gulf of Mexico

U.S. Naval officer, War of 1812

Congress had already decided that if the USS *Hornet*, expected from Europe, did not bring word of concessions, then war with Britain would begin. When the *Hornet* arrived without any good news, the Hawks pushed President Madison toward a declaration of war.

Madison resisted making a direct call for war. He said, "We behold...on the side of Great Britain a state of war against the United States; and on the side of the United States a state of peace towards Britain." But Madison's careful words forged no compromise.

1812

America declares war against the British *(June 18)*.

British forces take Fort Mackinac *(July 17)*, Dearborn *(Aug. 15)*, and Detroit *(Aug. 16)*.

A U.S. invasion of Canada is thrown back at Queenston *(Oct. 13)*. British blockade U.S. coastline.

1813

American forces raid York (Toronto) *(April)*.

Battle of Lake Erie. Oliver Perry captures British flotilla *(Sept. 10)* and takes Detroit *(Sept. 29)*.

Battle of the Thames. British and Indian forces defeated by Americans at London, Ontario *(Oct. 5)*.

British and Indian forces take Fort Niagara *(Dec. 18)*, then capture and burn Buffalo *(Dec. 29–30)*.

1814

American forces invade Canada *(July)*.

British forces take Washington, D.C., burning the White House, Capitol, and other buildings *(August)*.

British forces attack Baltimore, but meet defeat at Fort McHenry *(Sept. 13–14)*.

The Treaty of Ghent ends the War of 1812 *(Dec. 24)*.

1815

Americans shatter British forces laying siege to New Orleans *(Jan.)*.

Note:

Major conflicts with Indian tribes during the War of 1812 are covered in the Indian Wars chapter.

1812

War between the United States and Britain began officially on June 18, 1812. The Republicans were happier to be at war than the Federalists. The Republicans were anxious to win "free trade and sailors' rights." They also wanted to put an end to Britain's influence over American Indians in the western territories. Britain had been encouraging certain tribes to attack American settlements. The British had even talked of setting up an Indian nation to limit American expansion.

WAR AIMS. The Republicans also believed the war would serve as a sort of second war for independence. The war would allow the United States to prove to the rest of the world that it was a true nation now and couldn't be bullied.

In fact, though, the United States wasn't really prepared to fight anyone. The army's enlisted men had little experience and even less discipline. Furthermore, no one had planned exactly how to fight a war with the British, if it should come.

The Republicans felt that British Canada might be a good target to attack because it was weakly defended. As Henry Clay claimed, Americans did not want to conque Canada. They only felt it was important to strike wher the enemy was weakest. Canada would be "the instru ment by which...redress was to be obtained."

The invasion of Canada, though, would prove mor difficult than anyone imagined.

A BATTLE PLAN. President Madison adopted a war pla that called for a three-pronged attack in the north. Th United States would move against Montreal, the Niagar River, and Detroit.

The Detroit operation was led by William Hull, th governor of the Michigan territory. Hull was an ol Revolutionary War hero. When the new war agains Britain was declared, he assembled an army of 2,000 me and headed to Fort Detroit. The fort was on the Detroi River, which connected Lake Erie to Lake Huron. By Jul Hull had crossed the river and led his troops into Britisl territory. Hull was forced to retreat back to the fort though, when he found out his fellow Americans hac been defeated on Mackinac Island.

THE INDIAN CARD. The British commander, Genera Isaac Brock, knew that Hull was terrified of Indians. H decided to use Hull's fear to advantage. He forged a doc ument stating that a large number of Indians were set tc attack Detroit. Brock arranged for the paper to fall intc Hull's hands. At the same time, Brock moved his troop: into position to attack Fort Detroit.

Hull panicked, as expected, surrendering the fort or August 16. One observer reported that "even the womer

---

THE NAVAL WAR

The land war in 1812 had proved nearly a complete disaster for the Americans. If there were bright lights in the war against the British, they were shining out at sea. Though the British had blockaded the American coast, U.S. naval and merchant marine forces were taking serious shots at the English fleet. Most of the really rough fighting was being done by American privateers. These hard sailors liked to call themselves the "militia of the sea." Their greatest thrill was wreaking havoc on English commerce.

The tiny United States Navy wasn't standing still, either. Against a "sea monster" of 600 ships, the United States put to sea just over a dozen large vessels and about 200 gunboats. Though seriously outgunned and outnumbered, the Americans did have a group of excellent frigates, used during the French Naval War. They were supremely fast and sturdy, able to outrun anything in the British fleet.

The *Constitution*, in particular, gained a reputation for getting the best of British ships. In August 1812, she was commanded by Isaac Hull, when the British *Guerrière's* sails were sighted. Hull closed in on the British ship to just fifty feet and let loose. Grapeshot ripped through *Guerrière's* rigging and shredded her sails. In just a quarter of an hour, the blood-spattered British ship was incapable of maneuvering. *Constitution's* guns then turned for the kill, raking the crippled ship, while sharpshooters picked off the rest of *Guerrière's* helpless crew.

In minutes the British ship was dead in the water. The U.S. Navy had achieved a stunning victory. "Never before in the history of the world," said the *Times* of London, "did an English frigate strike to (lower her flag to) an American."

The British warship Guerriére *falls to the U.S. frigate* Constitution. *The victory at sea kept American hopes alive.*

were indignant at so shameful a degradation of the American character."

Before the surrender Hull had ordered the evacuation of Fort Dearborn near present-day Chicago. During the Dearborn retreat, a group of Potawatomi Indians slaughtered the American soldiers. The British now held both Fort Detroit and Fort Dearborn. Hull was later court-martialed and convicted of cowardice and neglect of duty.

> *"Now, boys, hull her!"*
>
> —*Isaac Hull, ordering the raking of the British ship* Guerrière. *(In his excitement, Hull bent over and ripped the seam out of his trousers.)*

By the end of the summer, Mackinac, Dearborn, and Detroit were all in the hands of the British. The entire Northwest was open to a British attack (see main map). By autumn, the Americans had nothing to show for their land war except dead soldiers.

WAR IN THE EAST. The Eastern campaign, under Major General Stephen Van Rensselaer, didn't fare much better. Van Rensselaer planned to seize Queenston Heights on the British side of the Niagara River. By October, he had amassed a force of more than 6,000 troops. They faced 2,000 British and Indian soldiers across the river.

Though the British were outnumbered, General Brock, fresh from his victory in the west, had arrived to take care of British defenses. The Americans managed to crush Brock's force and kill him as well.

But mistakes plagued the Americans. During the fight with Brock's forces, some American troops made their way across to the British-held side of the Niagara. But the Van Rensselaer forces refused to follow them (see sidebar on page 24). As a result, the gains made by almost a thousand brave American soldiers were overturned. The British captured or killed nearly all the men who had crossed over to the other side.

INTO MONTREAL. Another Revolutionary War veteran was chosen to lead the third and most important part of the campaign. Henry Dearborn, who, at age sixty-one, had come to be known as "Granny," led an army nearly 8,000 strong to Lake Champlain in November. Some of the troops crossed into Canada to fight. Once again, though, the rest of the army refused to leave U.S. soil. Dearborn was forced to give up his attempt to reach Montreal and retreated.

At the end of the year, the United States had altogether failed in its attempts to conquer Canada. In the words of one newspaper, the campaign was filled with "disaster, defeat, disgrace, and ruin and death."

1813

Americans had some reasons to cheer up in 1813. The United States had approximately 30,000 troops by the spring, twice as many as when the war began. U.S. strategy seemed solidly grounded. Canada was still the main focus of the U.S. attack. Now, though, the army realized the key to the campaign was controlling the Great Lakes. By the end of 1812, the United States had enough ships to try to force the British to give up their stranglehold on the region.

TERROR IN YORK. In April 1813, Navy Captain Isaac Chauncey led 1,700 men to York (present-day Toronto). York was defended by 700 British and Indian troops. The Americans took York and 290 British soldiers as well. U.S. soldiers, however, then took it upon themselves to loot and destroy the city. They torched everything, including government buildings.

In May, the British responded by attacking Sackets Harbor, New York. While the British took their revenge in the West, the United States was assembling a force of 4,500 men in the east, across from Fort George. The fort was located on the Canadian side of the Niagara River and was held by at least 1,100 British soldiers ready to fight.

On May 24, American troops opened fire from a small town across from Fort George. A few days later, Captain Chauncey directed a landing of U.S. troops right next to the fort. He was helped in his cause by Oliver Perry, who had directed the campaign in Lake Erie. The U.S. soldiers attacked the fort from the rear.

The British had been waiting for an assault, but they were outnumbered. When they saw the odds against them, they turned and ran as fast as they could. U.S. soldiers nevertheless managed to inflict more than 300 casualties. More important, they had wedged open the door to the Niagara frontier.

BATTLE OF LAKE ERIE. In September, the Great Lakes became the "battleground" for warring ships. Under Oliver Perry's command, nine U.S. gunboats confronted a smaller British fleet in Lake Erie. The two squadrons eyed each other at a distance. The British knew that if they moved in any closer, they would be defeated.

Still, they decided to open fire, hoping to hit the Americans with their long guns without really risking themselves. Perry ordered his ships to close in. The fighting was fierce. In Perry's crew alone, eight of every ten men were killed or injured. Perry desperately ordered even the wounded to keep on fighting.

His hard line paid off. After another hour of fighting, the U.S. fleet had crippled all the British ships, forcing their crews to surrender. Perry's fight had secured Lake Erie for the Americans and tipped the balance of power in the west. By the end of 1813, the United States had recovered all the territory it had lost the previous year.

BATTLE OF CHATEAUGAY. The Americans now pulled almost all of their men off the Niagara frontier to prepare for an attack on Montreal. The campaign got underway in October. Seven thousand men marched to Montreal, following the Chateaugay River.

Again, however, many U.S. troops refused to cross the border. To make matters worse, the British had

AMERICANS INVADE CANADA: "WE WON'T GO!"

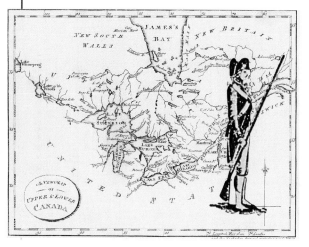

During 1812 and 1813, American troops prepared several times to invade Canadian soil. But more often than not, many soldiers refused to cross the northern border.

For the officers commanding these northern militias, the refusal verged on mutiny. But for many of the soldiers, saying no was just an assertion of their constitutional rights.

State militiamen were not constitutionally required to leave national territory. Their services could only be used to suppress insurrections or repel invasions.

It wasn't only individual soldiers who refused to follow orders. State governors did, too. When President Madison asked to use the Massachusetts militia in the action against Montreal, Massachusetts Governor Caleb Strong flatly refused.

Actually, Northerners may have had other motives for refusing to fight in Canada. Many thought that this was a war for Western and Southern interests and that Westerners and Southerners should be fighting it.

A cartoon depicts the controversy over the battle between the Chesapeake *and the* Shannon. *The British still held the seas.*

assembled a force of 1,400 French-Canadian soldiers to repel the attack. The two sides met on October 26 at the Battle of Chateaugay. The Americans were unable to break through the British defense and fell back. Stalled, the United States gave up its plan to invade Montreal altogether.

> *"Don't give up the ship.*
> *Fight her 'til she sinks."*
>
> —*Captain James Lawrence,*
> *as he died aboard the* Chesapeake

BURNING TOWNS. Now the British were busy with another plan. They decided to take advantage of the weak enemy positions along the Niagara frontier. By December, there were only about 250 men guarding the entire frontier. The Americans, fearing an attack, abandoned Fort George on December 10. But as they fled, they decided to burn the town of Newark, so that the British wouldn't be able to shelter there.

The British were incensed by the torching. They got their revenge eight days later. Together with their Indian allies, they surprised U.S. forces at Fort Niagara. Almost all the Americans were killed or taken prisoner.

Other British and Indian troops went on to Buffalo. They killed civilians—men and women alike—and burned the entire city to the ground. By the end of the year, nearly the entire frontier, from Lake Ontario to Lake Erie, was wrecked and in British hands.

BLOCKADE WAR. Meanwhile the British had bolstered their fleet in American waters. By the end of 1812, they enforced a blockade from Florida all the way up to the coast of Delaware. By November 1813, with the blockade covering most of the New England coast as well, it was coming close to destroying the American economy.

Not only was foreign trade cut off, the British blockade was disrupting trade even within the states. Because there were few good roads, Americans were unable to transport their goods fast enough over land. As a result, there were food and supply shortages throughout the country.

The Americans didn't have the power to break the British hold on the seas. In May, the USS *Chesapeake* ran into the HMS *Shannon* off the port of Boston. The U.S. ship was outmatched by the *Shannon*. The British took only fifteen minutes to destroy the *Chesapeake*. *Chesapeake*'s captain, James Lawrence, dying of his wounds, pleaded with his men not to surrender, but the crew had little choice.

The battle restored British confidence on the seas. The American naval victories of the year before faded like a dream. And there were nightmares yet to come.

1814

By 1814, the war had slid lopsided into British hands. Their fight with Napoleon practically over, the British were now able to send more men and supplies to America. By the fall of 1814, the British army in North America was 30,000 strong. Luckily for the United States, its army was rapidly improving with experience. With 40,000 soldiers, the United States thought it might still have a chance.

INTO CANADA ONCE MORE.

The fiercest fighting in the campaign of 1814 took place once again along the Niagara River frontier. The United States was still determined to overrun Canada. U.S. troops went on the offensive in July. A force of 3,500 men crossed the border into Canada. They attacked Fort Erie and quickly overpowered the main British force.

They found British and Indian troops at the Chippewa River on July 5. With much needed reinforcements, they managed to pull out a victory. After Chippewa, U.S. troops ran into British soldiers at Lundy's Lane. The bloody battle ended in a stalemate. Both sides suffered shocking casualties during the five-hour slaughter.

After the Battle of Lundy's Lane, the broken and exhausted Americans needed a rest. They retreated to Fort Erie. A month passed, then the British decided to retake the fort, beginning an attack that lasted two days. The fort held, but the British were determined. They brought in big guns to blast the defenders out.

The Americans held, but with heavy losses—more than 500 U.S. soldiers lost their lives. Still, the British kept up the pressure. By November 5, the Americans were forced to destroy the fort and evacuate the frontier.

ATTACK ON WASHINGTON.

The British found further success along the Atlantic Coast. Using their fleet to support landing troops, they easily captured Maine. They would hold the state until the end of the war.

The British then set their sights on Washington and Baltimore. Americans had done little to prepare the capital for an enemy attack. By August, the British had sailed up the Chesapeake Bay with twenty ships and plenty of troops. The invading English landed at Benedict, Maryland, and marched toward the Potomac River.

The British were nearly upon Washington before American officials realized they were in big trouble. Quickly, they got together 7,000 men to meet the invaders. But it was hardly enough. The British easily overpowered the militia and scattered them.

At this point almost everyone in Washington had fled the city in terror. The president's wife, Dolley Madison, refused to leave without packing first. She coolly determined to rescue the items she thought valuable. She managed to pack up all the Cabinet records and White House treasures, even though she had to leave behind her personal belongings.

THE CAPITAL BURNS.

When the British arrived in Washington, they put a torch to nearly everything. The Capitol building, the Library of Congress, the Treasury and War and State Departments all went up in smoke. Before setting the president's house on fire, British officers sat down and feasted on the meal that had been prepared for Madison's dinner that evening.

The British had scored a major and humiliating victory in Washington. Americans were thoroughly shamed by the burning of their capital. Now Britain determined to pile insult on injury. They would aim a decisive blow at the city of Baltimore.

★ ★ STAR-SPANGLED STANZAS ★ ★

It was the Maryland militia that finally stopped the British troops that had burned the nation's capital. And it was off the shores of Maryland, in the waters of the Chesapeake, where the new nation's anthem was born, penned by a lawyer named Francis Scott Key.

Key, who had been negotiating for a friend's release from the British, was under temporary confinement as the English fleet bombarded Baltimore's Fort McHenry. Through the night, Key anxiously watched as the 200-pound shells exploded over the harbor. Some 1,500 of them were fired in an attack that lasted twenty-four hours. The fort never surrendered, and Key continued to watch the shredded banner fluttering against the bomb-lit sky.

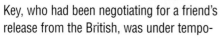

The vision set him to writing a single stanza on the back of an envelope: "Oh, say can you see by the dawn's early light/ What so proudly we hailed at the twilight's last gleaming?/ Whose broad stripes and bright stars, thru the perilous fight,/O'er the ramparts we watched were so gallantly streaming?"

The next day, at Indian Queen Inn in Baltimore, he finished the poem. The final stanzas set to music were designated the national anthem by an act of Congress in 1931.

British forces burn Washington. The nation, not yet forty years old, was on the brink of extinction.

Baltimore was ready, though. Residents of the city had been preparing for just such an attack since 1813.

On September 12, 4,500 British soldiers marched toward the city. Halfway there, they were met by American militia. There was a skirmish, but the British were able to resume their march. They stopped just

> "We should have to fight hereafter, not for 'free trade and sailors' rights,' not for the conquest of the Canadas, but for our national existence."
>
> —*A Republican senator*

before reaching Baltimore to coordinate with the Royal Navy's attack from the Chesapeake. The British plan was to have the navy bombard Fort McHenry, which guarded Baltimore harbor. Once the fort was destroyed, the British hoped to move in and attack the city itself.

Through the night of September 13–14, the British attacked Fort McHenry with everything they had. After twenty-four hours of bombardment, though, the fort was still standing (see sidebar). The failure to seriously damage Fort McHenry canceled their campaign against the city. By dawn on September 14, the attack was called off.

LAKE CHAMPLAIN. As the fighting flared along the Atlantic Coast, the British were also launching a major offensive in northern New York. They were planning to march down Lake Champlain and attack the city of Plattsburgh. Mustering an army of 10,000, the British crossed into the United States on August 31. The Americans were totally unprepared for the attack. A meager army of 3,400 men had been left behind to defend the area.

The British stopped at Lake Champlain and waited for their navy to back them up. The Americans, meanwhile, moved their ships into position to counter a British attack. Remarkably, the Americans were able to push back the British fleet. After the U.S. victory on the lake, British land forces picked up and skedaddled without firing a shot.

Throughout the remainder of 1814, the United States was able to fend off all British offensives. Still, neither side, after three years of fighting, could really claim the advantage. The war had settled nothing. As the year drew to a close, both sides were looking for peace.

AFTERMATH

By August 1814, both the United States and Britain had sent negotiators to Belgium to hammer out an agreement acceptable to both parties. While the finishing touches were being added to the treaty ending the war, the British decided to invade the Gulf Coast.

THE BATTLE OF NEW ORLEANS.

The British sent a sea and land force against New Orleans. The city, with a population of 25,000, was the largest in the West.

The Americans, under Andrew Jackson ("Old Hickory"), were prepared for the attack. Upon arriving in the city on December 1, Jackson immediately cut off the water approaches to the Gulf. The Battle of New Orleans took place on January 8, 1815, after a series of smaller engagements. The battle was a decisive victory for the Americans. Jackson's troops killed or wounded nearly 2,000 British soldiers under the command of General Edward Pakenham. The motley American force suffered only seventy casualties of their own. The once proud enemy was chased down to the sea (see sidebar).

TREATY OF GHENT.

Official news of peace didn't reach Jackson until March 13, long after the treaty had been concluded. On Christmas Eve, December 24, the two sides had come to an agreement. They had restored things to the way they were before the war began. Neither side came out of the war with more territory than it had when the conflict began.

The treaty was ratified by Congress and proclaimed by the president on February 17, 1815. The War of 1812 was formally ended.

The United States claimed victory when the Treaty of Ghent was signed. In fact, the United States hadn't achieved its prewar goals. Still, many cheered the conflict as America's "second war of independence." As one newspaper put it, "The administration has succeeded... against the encroachments of human ambition and tyranny."

SONG FOR ONE CLEAR-CUT VICTORY

The War of 1812 provided few opportunities for the United States to gloat. Defeated badly and often, on land and on sea—its capital burned—the nation was lucky to have gotten out alive.

The war produced little literature or other memorable effects—save "The Star-Spangled Banner"—but there was one high note. The Battle of New Orleans, though it was fought after the official end of the war, was a cause for celebration. The British, at long last, were defeated and sent packing.

In the late 1950s, songwriter Jimmy Driftwood captured the exhilaration of chasing the British Army off American territory for the last time.

Well, in 18 and 14, we took a little trip
Along with Colonel Jackson down the mighty Mississip'
We took a little bacon and we took a little beans
And we met the bloody British in the town of New Orleans...

Well, I seed Marse Jackson come a-walkin' down the street
And a-talkin' to a pirate by the name of Jean Lafitte;
He gave Jean a drink that he brung from Tennessee,
And the pirate said he'd help us drive the British to the sea...

Old Hickory said we could take 'em by surprise
If we didn't fire a musket till we looked 'em in the eyes
We held our fire till we sed their face well

Then we opened up our squirrel guns and really gave 'em well...

Well, they ran through the briars and they ran through the brambles
And they ran through the bushes where a rabbit couldn't go
They ran so fast the hounds couldn't catch 'em
Down the Mississippi to the Gulf of Mexico

They lost their pants and their pretty shiny coats
And their tails was all a-showin' like a bunch of billy goats.
They ran down the river with their tongues a-hanging out
And they said they got a lickin', which there wasn't any doubt.

Well, the guide who brung the British from the sea
Come a-limping into camp just as sick as he could be,
He said the dying words of Colonel Packenham
Was, "You better quit your foolin' with your cousin Uncle Sam."

The Battle of New Orleans was fought after the war's official end. Creoles and pirates helped send the British packing.

The nation, though, had paid a heavy price. Americans lost 2,260 soldiers in battle during the three years of the war. An additional 4,500 were wounded. The financial cost of the war was even more of a burden. The conflict cost the United States $158 million and came close to destroying the nation's economy.

A CHANGED COUNTRY. The war altered the American landscape and political scene. By destroying the power of the Indians in the West (see Indian Wars), the United States was able to expand with little opposition. Westward expansion, however, would renew arguments over the issue of slavery, leading eventually to the Civil War.

By the end of the War of 1812, the United States had learned the price of being unprepared. President Madison now called upon Congress to increase peacetime defense spending. He believed that "…preparation for war is not only indispensable to avert disasters in the onset, but affords also the best security for the continuance of peace."

As a result, a standing army three times the size of the prewar army was authorized. A program to fortify American coastal waters also went into effect. In addition, Congress appropriated $8 million (to be spent over eight years) to construct nine gunboats and twelve frigates.

The war enhanced the reputation of the United States in Europe. European powers, now at peace, no longer sought to regulate American trade and commerce. The British stopped impressing sailors. Now the United States was free to grow without any European influence.

In 1823, in fact, President James Monroe would assert the U.S. right to combat European influence within neighboring countries as well. In his seventh annual message to Congress, the president outlined the Monroe Doctrine, declaring that the Americas "are henceforth not to be considered as subjects for the future colonization by any European powers…[and] that we should consider any attempt on their part to extend their system to any portion of this hemisphere as dangerous to our peace and safety."

Though the United States did not yet possess the naval forces to enforce the doctrine, the idea stuck. Decades later, the principles of the Monroe Doctrine would be used to justify the American occupation of Haiti, the Dominican Republic, and Nicaragua in order to protect them from foreign influence.

THE MEXICAN-AMERICAN WAR

The Mexican-American War was the first offensive war fought by the United States. Though it wasn't the first American conflict fought over land rights, it was one of the most successful. By the time the war ended, the American government had control over much of what would become the continental United States.

PRELUDE TO WAR

In 1821, Mexico won its independence from Spain. As a result, Mexico inherited Spanish lands, including Texas, California, and New Mexico.

U.S. SETTLEMENT.

Mexican independence coincided with United States expansionism. Throughout the 1820s and 1830s, U.S. pioneers headed west, frequently settling in Texas. In fact, Mexico even encouraged settlement in its territory on the condition that U.S. settlers become Mexican citizens. Many agreed in return for cheap land. By 1836, there were more than 30,000 U.S. settlers living in Texas.

The Mexican government, run by the dictator General Antonio López de Santa Anna, began to worry about the increasing number of U.S. settlers. Likewise, settlers were angry at Santa Anna's rules. In 1830, Mexico banned the importation of more slaves into Texas. It also prohibited further U.S. immigration into Texas.

BATTLE AT THE ALAMO.

Texas declared its independence from Mexico on March 2, 1836. It set up a new government, naming Sam Houston commander in chief. Houston had fought with Andrew Jackson against the Indians in the War of 1812.

Santa Anna, with a force of 3,000 men, marched to San Antonio to crush the insurrection. He surrounded 200 Texans at the Alamo, an old, abandoned mission. The Texans, though, refused to surrender and held their ground against their attackers for ten days. But the Mexicans captured the Alamo and killed its defenders.

"Remember the Alamo!" became the rallying cry of the Texans' quest for independence. The next month, while Santa Anna's men took their afternoon nap at their camp near the San Jacinto River, Houston's troops attacked. The Battle of San Jacinto was over in twenty minutes. At its end, Santa Anna was captured. In exchange for his life, he promised to retreat from Texas and grant the Lone Star Republic (so named because the Texan flag had a single star) its independence.

> *"Young America demands the immediate annexation of Texas at any and every hazard."*
>
> —United States Journal, *1845*

MANIFEST DESTINY.

Mexico never officially recognized Texas as an independent republic. Sam Houston, however, governed it as though it was. He immediately asked the United States to annex the republic. In the United States, meanwhile, a new fever eventually known as Manifest Destiny was taking hold across the country. Manifest Destiny justified America's expansion. It did so by explaining that it was the country's God-given right to spread its superior institutions and moral culture across the entire continent. This idea was used to justify taking over Indian lands. Now with expansionist fever, Americans anticipated establishing control west across the continent and north to the border of Alaska.

When Texas asked to be annexed, many felt that this was further proof of Manifest Destiny and looked to expanding the U.S. border southward. The North and the South, however, were split on the issue. In 1836, the United States was made up of thirteen slave states and thirteen free states. Upon gaining its independence, Texas had established slavery as a legal institution. The North felt that by admitting Texas to the Union, the balance of power would tip the scales in favor of the South and slavery.

As a result, the Lone Star Republic was officially ignored until 1844, when President John Tyler reopened the issue. During his last days in office, Tyler succeeded in pushing a joint resolution through Congress allowing Texas to join the Union.

U.S. soldier,
Mexican-American War

MEXICAN WAR (1846–1848)

- United States
- Mexico
- Disputed area
- Major battle

0   400 Mi.

1836

Texas declares its independence from Mexico (March 2).

Alamo besieged (Feb. 23– March 6). A force of 200 Texans is killed when they refuse to surrender to the Mexican Army.

1845–1846

United States annexes Texas (1845).

War between U.S. and Mexico begins. Mexican Army defeated at Palo Alto (May 8), Resaca de la Palma (May 9), and Monterrey (Sept. 20–24).

American settlers revolt in California (June). American forces take California. California annexed by U.S.

1847

Mexico suffers major defeat at Buena Vista (Feb. 22–23).

Seaborne forces capture Vera Cruz (March 29) and defeat Santa Anna at Cerro Gordo (April 18).

U.S. forces attack Mexico City (Aug.) and force its surrender (Sept.14).

1848

War is ended under the Treaty of Guadalupe Hidalgo (Feb. 2). California and Southwest Territories ceded to U.S. Mexico recognizes American annexation of Texas.

LAND WAR

When the United States admitted Texas to the Union, Mexico cut all diplomatic ties with the United States. To make matters worse, the United States then insisted that the Rio Grande was the southern border of Texas.

The Mexicans were outraged. They claimed that the Texas border ended 150 miles to the north, at the Nueces River. They pointed out that even when Texas was part of Mexico, Texans never settled below the Nueces.

DECLARATION OF WAR

The new president, James K. Polk, offered to buy California and New Mexico in exchange for the Rio Grande border. The Mexicans refused to even consider the offer. Rumors of a Mexican invasion spread in Washington. Polk sent General Zachary Taylor and 3,500 troops to the Rio Grande in preparation.

U.S. troops were now stationed on land claimed and traditionally held by Mexico. On April 14, 1846, after declaring a defensive war, Mexico attacked. Mexican troops crossed the Rio Grande to kill sixteen of Taylor's men. President Polk finally had an excuse to ask Congress for a declaration of war. He said, "…Mexico has passed the boundary of the United States, has invaded our territory and shed American blood upon American soil." On May 13, 1846, Polk officially signed a declaration of war.

The Mexican war was a dirty one—literally. After the Battle of Monterrey, American troops were described "as dirty as they could be without becoming real-estate."

U.S. infantry, marching across dry ground, became covered with white dust that resembled the Mexican adobes. Soon the Mexicans were calling them "dobies," or doughboys. Unlike the dust, the name would stick for a hundred years.

VICTORY AT MONTERREY.

Without much opposition, the United States quickly captured California. Meanwhile, in May, U.S. forces defeated the Mexicans at Palo Alto and Resaca de la Palma. General Zachary Taylor then led a 6,000-man army 170 miles to the key Mexican fortress at Monterrey. The battle began on September 20, 1846, and three days later the Mexicans surrendered. Nearly 500 U.S. troops were killed or wounded in the struggle.

After winning a series of smaller victories, Taylor came face-to-face with Santa Anna. On February 22, 1847 at Buena Vista, Taylor's 5,000 troops defeated the Mexican force of 20,000 men. Santa Anna was forced to retreat.

The Mexican conflict divided the American people. Many questioned the legitimacy of a war on disputed territory. One senator spoke out against an "aggressive unprovoked war." He went on to say, "If I were a Mexican I would greet you with bloody hands and welcome you to [your] graves." Many felt the war was provoked out of greed for territorial expansion.

MEXICO CITY CAPTURED.

Polk decided that the United States had to capture Mexico City to ensure total victory. He appointed Winfield Scott to take charge of the troops that would storm the beaches at Vera Cruz and march inland toward the Mexican capital.

Upon reaching Mexico City, Scott's forces conquered the Chapultepec fortress. On September 13, 1847, Scott's 8,300 men faced 20,000 Mexican soldiers, and, by the next day, they had captured all of Mexico City.

The Treaty of Guadalupe Hidalgo was signed February 2, 1848, formally ending the war. The treaty called for Mexico to accept the Rio Grande as its boundary with Texas and stated that New Mexico, Texas, and California belonged to the United States. In exchange, the United States paid Mexico $15 million and assumed $3 million in unpaid claims by U.S. citizens against Mexico.

ANESTHESIA FOR THE WOUNDED

One of the greatest advances in battlefield medicine came during the Mexican-American conflict. Surgeons began treating their patients with a chemical compound called ether. This light, flammable liquid worked as an anesthesia, or sleep inducer. A little was poured on a handkerchief and put over the patient's face while the surgeon worked.

Patients in previous wars were given few options during amputations or other surgeries. Sometimes the injured were given opium. More often they were held down while they screamed. Ether was accepted quickly as a preferred anesthetic.

The compound did have serious side effects, though. It was hard to judge the amount needed to keep a patient asleep. After the surgery, the ether gave many people severe headaches and nausea. Eventually, it gave way to better and more controllable anesthetics. But for its time, ether was a medical miracle.

U.S. troops storm Independence Hill in Mexico. Some Americans wondered what they were doing there.

AFTERMATH

The Mexican War has been called the "most unjust war ever waged by a stronger against a weaker nation." Although this accusation is overstated, the war was probably unnecessary. The border issues could probably have been solved without bloodshed.

BUYING THE CONTINENT.

Zachary Taylor emerged from the war a hero and was elected president in 1848. The war also succeeded in reopening the issue of slavery. While the status of slavery in the newly acquired lands was temporarily settled by the Compromise of 1850, the issue divided Americans.

The United States bought even more territory from Mexico in the Gadsden Purchase of 1853. By 1853, the United States was one third larger than it was before the war. The acquisition of the new land created many problems for the United States, and also for the Mexican-Americans who had lived—some for generations—in these territories. They now lived as second-class citizens in a land that had once belonged exclusively to them. Many lost their lands and livelihood. It would take more than a hundred years before Mexican-Americans regained their rights under the law.

Relations with Mexico itself would also continue to be difficult. During the American Civil War, France attempted to take over Mexico while the United States was distracted with its own conflict. At the close of its Civil War the United States insisted that the French withdraw from Mexico and placed troops along the U.S.-Mexican border. The Mexican Republic was soon restored.

Revolution again struck Mexico in 1910 when an opponent of the Mexican dictator Porfirio Díaz escaped to the United States and began organizing an armed insurrection. About one million Mexicans died in the series of civil wars that followed. The revolutionaries were eventually successful, and their leader Francisco Madero became president, only to be assassinated in 1913.

Supported by Germany, another rebel leader, Victoriano Huerta, took power and began ruling as a dictator. The United States fought Germany's support of Huerta, even sending in troops to occupy Veracruz and blocking German gun shipments in 1914. Though Huerta was ousted, civil war continued, with the forces of Emiliano Zapata and Pancho Villa opposing the new government. In 1916, Villa's forces made a cross-border raid on Columbus, New Mexico. The United States sent in approximately 10,000 men to pursue Villa, but they were unsuccessful.

Remarkably, it was Germany's influence in Mexican-American affairs that led to the United States entering World War I (see pages 100–101).

THE CIVIL WAR

Confederate soldier, top
Union soldier, bottom

The principles of the Declaration of Independence and the U.S. Constitution were more radical and far-reaching than the nation ever realized. Thomas Jefferson's phrase "all men are created equal" referred only to white male landholders in the eighteenth century. By the mid-nineteenth century, that assumption was shattering. People of conscience had begun to protest the enslavement of blacks in a country that advertised itself as a free nation.

At the same time, Southerners demanded the right to run their states the way they wished. They protested the interference of the federal government, whose antislavery measures threatened to bankrupt them.

Both slavery and states' rights became fighting causes in the 1850s. Americans in conflict over basic human freedoms and economics waged their deadliest war ever. The conflict would take the lives of more of the nation's sons than any other war before or since.

UNORGANIZED TERRITORY

NEBRASKA TERRITORY

Arkansas

NEW MEXICO TERRITORY

Rio Grande

MEXICO

1854
Kansas-Nebraska Act starts fierce feuding over slavery in "Bleeding Kansas."

1856
Proslavery protesters sack Lawrence, Kansas *(May 21)*.

1859
Abolitionist John Brown attempts to start a slave revolt at Harpers Ferry, West Virginia *(Oct. 16)*.

1860
Abraham Lincoln is elected president.

1861
The Confederate States of America is formed.

Fort Sumter in South Carolina is bombarded by Confederates *(April 12)*.

Manassas/Bull Run, Virginia, is the first major battle of the war *(July 21)*.

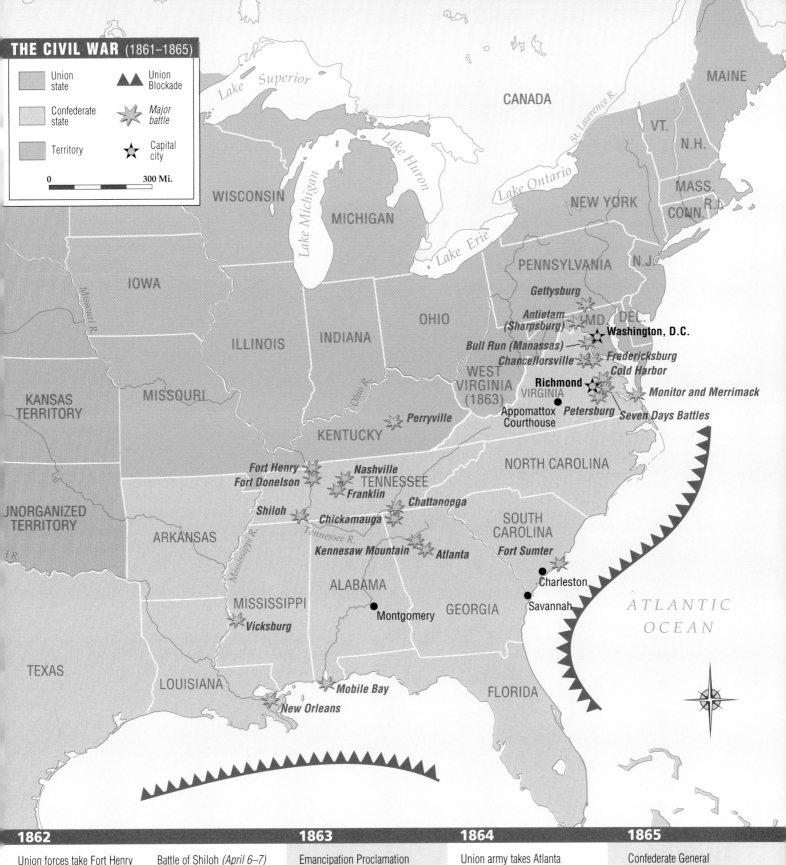

THE CIVIL WAR (1861–1865)

Union state		Union Blockade	
Confederate state		Major battle	
Territory		Capital city	

0 _____ 300 Mi.

CANADA

MAINE

VT.

N.H.

MASS.

R.I.

CONN.

NEW YORK

N.J.

Lake Superior

Lake Michigan

Lake Huron

Lake Ontario

Lake Erie

St. Lawrence R.

WISCONSIN

MICHIGAN

IOWA

ILLINOIS

INDIANA

OHIO

PENNSYLVANIA

MD.

DEL.

Washington, D.C.

WEST VIRGINIA (1863)

VIRGINIA

Richmond

Missouri R.

Ohio R.

Gettysburg

Antietam (Sharpsburg)

Bull Run (Manassas)

Chancellorsville

Fredericksburg

Cold Harbor

Monitor and Merrimack

Appomattox Courthouse

Petersburg

Seven Days Battles

KANSAS TERRITORY

MISSOURI

KENTUCKY

NORTH CAROLINA

Perryville

UNORGANIZED TERRITORY

ARKANSAS

TENNESSEE

Fort Henry

Fort Donelson

Nashville

Franklin

Shiloh

Chickamauga

Chattanooga

SOUTH CAROLINA

Kennesaw Mountain

Atlanta

Fort Sumter

Mississippi R.

Tennessee R.

_R.

ALABAMA

MISSISSIPPI

GEORGIA

Charleston

Savannah

Vicksburg

Montgomery

TEXAS

LOUISIANA

Mobile Bay

New Orleans

FLORIDA

ATLANTIC OCEAN

1862

Union forces take Fort Henry and Fort Donelson on the Cumberland River *(February)*.

First ironclad ships, *Merrimack* and *Monitor*, battle off Virginia coast.

Battle of Shiloh *(April 6–7)*.

Battle at Antietam/ Sharpsburg, Maryland, bloodiest day of the Civil War *(Sept. 17)*

1863

Emancipation Proclamation *(Jan. 1)*

Battle at Gettysburg, Pennsylvania *(July 1–3)*

Confederate Army of 30,000 surrenders at Vicksburg, Mississippi *(July 4)*.

1864

Union army takes Atlanta *(Sept. 2)*.

Union army under William Tecumseh Sherman marches through Georgia to Savannah.

1865

Confederate General Robert E. Lee surrenders at Appomattox Courthouse, Virginia *(April 9)*.

Abraham Lincoln is shot by an assassin *(April 14)*.

PRELUDE TO WAR

On the surface, at least, the United States was riding a wave of prosperity in the 1850s. The nation's harvests of food and raw materials were big and getting bigger. Manufactured goods were carried across the land on finished railroads, nearly 30,000 miles of them.

A DIVIDED ECONOMY. Still the country had a crack in it, and that crack was widening. Though economic times were good at mid-century, some parts of the nation were doing better than others. The industrial North grew more rapidly than the South during the 1850s. The South relied on agriculture and was growing at a slower pace.

Southerners were forced to buy all their manufactured goods from the North and had no choice but to accept low Northern prices for their plantation crops. Many Southerners resented this unequal partnership.

SLAVERY. The issues over trade were nothing compared to the disagreement over slavery. Slavery had been thriving since the seventeenth century. Though the North no longer relied upon slaves for labor, the South still did.

While only a minority of Southerners were plantation and slave owners, most white Southerners felt it was their natural right to hold slaves. Attacks on slavery struck at their pride in Southern traditions and institutions, at their way of life. They deeply resented Northerners having a say in how they should live and conduct their businesses.

While the North idealized John Brown and his antislavery beliefs, the South saw him as a murderer and terrorist.

Numerous Southerners also feared their slaves, many of whom had been treated mercilessly. There were 4 million slaves held in the South—nearly half the number of the total white population. In 1831, a slave in Virginia, Nat Turner, had led a local slave rebellion. Fifty-seven white people, as well as hundreds of blacks, had been killed. Southern whites were not only resistant to the idea of abolition, they were terrified by it.

Most Northerners felt that enslaving other human beings was morally wrong and evil. Abolitionists like Frederick Douglass, Wendell Phillips, and Harriet Tubman were active and persuasive. Clergy and people of conscience spoke out on the terrible treatment of blacks. Abolitionist William Lloyd Garrison put it simply: "Slavery," he said, "is sin."

STATES' RIGHTS VS. FEDERAL RIGHTS. At the core of the debate on slavery was another, even broader issue. Do the states themselves have the last say on the laws that they live under or does the federal government? The nation faced this issue head-on when the country debated whether new territories in the West should be open to the slave trade. In 1820, the Missouri Compromise allowed slavery in that state. But it prohibited slavery west of the Mississippi above Missouri's southern border. This law, after much conflict, was repealed in 1854.

In 1854, the new Kansas-Nebraska Act permitted the voters in each territory to choose whether they would enter the Union as a free or slave state. Armed men from both sides flooded into Kansas territory to influence the vote. One of those arriving was John Brown, a self-ordained preacher with a feverish hatred of slavery.

BLEEDING KANSAS. The vote, meant to settle the slavery issue for Kansas, settled nothing. The election was rigged, and the two sides formed rival state governments. Fighting erupted. In one particularly ugly raid in May 1856, a Southern mob sacked and burned the town of Lawrence, Kansas.

This was too much for John Brown. With a small band of followers, he murdered five proslavery settlers along Kansas' Pottawatomie Creek. In retaliation, Brown's son was killed by proslavery men. "Bleeding Kansas" was the first thin tap in the river of blood to come.

DRED SCOTT DECISION. In 1857, the Supreme Court ruled against Dred Scott, a slave who had petitioned the Court for his freedom. Scott argued that when his master had taken him to the free territory of Wisconsin, he (Scott) had become a free man.

The Court found instead that Scott, as a black slave, was not a citizen and could not sue. It also maintained that because Scott was his owner's property, he could not be freed by a move to a free territory.

Most important, the Supreme Court ruled that Congress had no right to ban slavery anywhere. The

Northerners considered secession treason, an illegal move that would destroy the Union.

Court declared that banning slavery would result in the taking of property without due process of law.

The South felt that its arguments for slavery had been proven right by the Court. But the case just widened the gulf between the states. Militia companies began to spring up in cities both North and South. War was in the air.

RAID ON HARPERS FERRY.
John Brown had waged a fiery war against the slaves' chains in Kansas. Now he brought his crusade to Harpers Ferry, (now West) Virginia. Brown hoped to seize the rifles in the town's federal armory. With them he would rouse the slaves in Virginia and begin a general uprising.

"...above your national, tumultuous joy, I hear the mournful wail of millions."

—*Frederick Douglass*

On the night of October 16, 1859, Brown grabbed the federal armory and arsenal and the local firehouse, too. His planned uprising, though, was a disaster. Only two slaves braved their masters' rage to join Brown. U.S. Marines killed or captured more than half of Brown's force of twenty-one men. The rest fled for their lives.

Brown was quickly tried for treason and sentenced to hang. During the trial, his courage and outspoken condemnation of slavery won admiration in the North. Brown's raid, however, fed Southern fears of a general slave uprising. The North's sympathy for this abolitionist also worried Southerners. Many were convinced that it was just a matter of time before Northerners forced the issue over slavery.

SEARCH FOR A COMPROMISE.
Abraham Lincoln was elected president in 1860. He had lost every state below the Mason-Dixon line (the traditional line dividing South from North). With Lincoln's election, Southerners truly felt that their cause was lost.

However, Lincoln was determined to avoid a split between the states. When he entered office in 1861, he tried to assure the South that a middle ground could be found between abolitionist and proslavery forces.

The issue though, was too much even for Lincoln's political skills. In December 1860, South Carolina pulled out of the Union. More states would follow, forming the Confederate States of America.

Lincoln had wanted to resolve the conflict between the states slowly and without bloodshed. Slavery, though, was an institution that had to be destroyed, not just dismantled. After two centuries, it was deeply implanted in this country. Its uprooting would be violent and bloodfilled, rattling the body—and soul—of the now divided nation.

FIRST FIGHTS

As more Southern states left the Union in January 1861, they took over federal property within their borders. Forts and weapons were among the first things to be seized.

SUMTER SURROUNDED. Most federal posts across the South gave up quickly. Southern militia commanders allowed Union soldiers to return home unharmed. But Union commanders in a few key Southern ports refused to give up without orders. One of these was Major Robert Anderson. He and sixty soldiers held a heavy brick fort in Charleston Harbor called Fort Sumter.

As winter turned to spring, Anderson's men were getting worried. They knew they were surrounded and couldn't help noticing the new rows of cannons facing the fort from the harbor. The threat was clear: If Anderson didn't get going and fast, the South Carolina militia would force him out.

Anderson had other problems as well. He was running out of food and short of ammunition. Some well-placed Confederate cannon shots had already turned back a Union ship filled with supplies and 200 reinforcements.

Meanwhile, the South got its own president. Former U.S. Senator and Secretary of War Jefferson Davis was elected to lead the seceding states, which called themselves the Confederate States of America. On February 18, 1861, Davis took office while spectators sang "Dixie," the new Southern anthem.

LINCOLN TAKES OFFICE. In Washington, the new president was to take office on March 4. Death threats had been made against Lincoln, so the president-elect from Illinois sneaked into the capital on a train just before the inauguration.

The War Between the States had not yet begun. In his inaugural speech Lincoln still offered hope that bloodshed could be avoided: "Though passion may have strained, it must not break our bonds of affection."

SUMTER ATTACKED. Nevertheless, just after he took office, Lincoln sent reinforcements to Fort Sumter. When word came to the Confederates that relief for Fort Sumter was on the way, Davis decided to act. He ordered the commander in Charleston, Brigadier General Pierre Gustave Toutant Beauregard, to demand that the Federals leave Fort Sumter or else.

Anderson, in reply, hinted to the Confederates that he would have to leave Sumter by April 15 due to lack of supplies. On the other hand, if help came in time, he might just stay and fight.

This was too much for the Confederates; they sent a short reply: "...we have the honor to notify you that [the General] will open the fire of his batteries on Fort Sumter in one hour."

At 4:30 A.M. on April 12 the Confederates fired the first shot of the Civil War. Huge cannonballs and exploding shells blasted the fort and set it on fire. A day and a half later, Anderson hung out a white flag. For all the noise

CIVIL WAR SPIES

Though codes and ciphers were used during the Civil War, most spying was done by amateurs. Some of the most valuable spies were women. They were less likely than men to be suspected and, if caught, less likely to be hung. Among them was a Confederate widow, Rose Greenhow. Greenhow was Southern by birth, and when war broke out she made no secret of her Confederate sympathies.

Living in Washington, Greenhow extracted important information about troop movements from friendly Union officers. In the first months of the war, she helped tip off General Beauregard to the Federal march to Manassas. As a result, Southern reinforcements arrived in the nick of time.

Because of her social standing, Union authorities were reluctant to arrest her. Still, Greenhow's spying proved so relentless, they had to do something. She was put under house arrest, but amazingly, continued to send out messages. The widow simply stuffed the information into her daughter's shoes.

Finally exiled to the South, Greenhow eventually went to England and wrote a book about her experiences. It made her famous in Europe and increased sympathy for the Confederate cause.

She left England abruptly in August 1864, perhaps carrying a secret message for Jefferson Davis. Off the North Carolina coast, her blockade runner, the *Condor*, ran aground. With a Union picket boat closing in, Greenhow again faced the prospect of arrest and prison. Along with several others, she tried to escape in a small boat. The tiny craft capsized in heavy seas. Rose Greenhow, weighed down by her sodden clothes, drowned.

Union troops train at their camp near Washington, D.C. Bull Run swept away hopes for a short, bloodless war.

and firepower, little blood was shed. One man (Union) and one horse (Confederate) were the only casualties.

CONFRONTATION AT MANASSAS.
The war was on. Thousands of volunteers streamed into Washington, answering Lincoln's call for recruits. The Union had few experienced generals (most Southern officers had already resigned), but Lincoln found a likely commander in Irvin McDowell. McDowell knew his green troops were not nearly ready to fight. Luckily for the Union army, the spring saw no major battles.

> *"Your little army...has met the grand army of the enemy and routed it.... We have taught them a lesson in their invasion of the sacred soil of Virginia."*
>
> —*Jefferson Davis*

Ready or not, McDowell's army moved south from Washington in mid-July. The 35,000 Union soldiers formed the largest fighting force ever seen on the continent. Their aim was to cut the rail lines at Manassas, Virginia, and march on Richmond, the Confederate capital.

General Beauregard, the winner at Fort Sumter, moved up to block the Union army. He had gotten news of the invasion from a Confederate spy in Washington (see sidebar). Beauregard's troops, like McDowell's, were inexperienced. Still, the Southern soldiers were convinced that each could whip a dozen Yankees. Both sides thought the war would be over in no time.

BATTLE AT BULL RUN.
The Confederates formed their line along Bull Run Creek. On the morning of July 21, as picnicking spectators eagerly watched, McDowell sent his forces across the stream. The confident Yankees sang as they marched to attack: "We'll hang Jeff Davis from a sour apple tree." They smashed into the Confederate positions on the left, driving the Rebels back.

The center of the Southern line, however, had not panicked. A Virginia brigade led by Thomas J. Jackson had been sent up to help hold the Rebel position. And they were holding it—the Union could not move them. One besieged officer shouted to his troops to look at Jackson's fresh Virginians, standing "like a stone wall!" The name stuck; Jackson became "Stonewall" forever.

In the late afternoon, Confederate General Beauregard counterattacked, ordering his men to charge, yelling like furies. Confederate reinforcements bolstered the attack, and the terrified Union army fell to pieces. Terrified spectators and panicked soldiers ran from the bloody field, "skedaddling back to Washington."

BATTLE FOR THE RIVERS

"Whatever nation gets...control of the Ohio, Mississippi, and Missouri Rivers," wrote Union General William Tecumseh Sherman, "will control the continent." Through the winter and spring of 1862, ironclad gunboats and mud-caked troops fought for control of these Western rivers that ran deep into Confederate territory.

FORT HENRY. In February 1862, a squat and ugly fleet of Union gunboats led by Commodore Andrew Foote steamed up the Tennessee River, heading for Rebel-occupied Fort Henry. The plan was to capture the Tennessee fort in a combined attack from land and water, and then take Fort Donelson, twelve miles east on the Cumberland River.

At Fort Henry, Union troops led by Ulysses S. Grant went ashore and marched toward the fort's earthen ramparts. But the soldiers bogged down in the muddy road already flooded from spring runoff. Waiting on the river, Foote grew impatient at the army's slow crawl. He decided to pound the fort from the water.

Foote's fleet steamed upstream to nearly point-blank range of the fort and opened fire. Huge, solid shot plowed gaping holes in Fort Henry's walls, wrecking the Rebel guns. With the rising river flooding in and only four guns firing, the fort's commander ran up the white flag. Union army troops never even made it into the battle.

To DONELSON. Most of the Confederates from Fort Henry escaped overland to Fort Donelson, reinforcing the troops already there. Grant's army followed, and the Union gunboats chugged up the Cumberland River intending to attack again from the water. Grant's troops quickly sealed the Rebels inside the fort and waited for the gunboats to begin shelling them out.

Foote's ships moved within close range of Fort Donelson. But unlike Fort Henry, Donelson was built high on a bluff. When the gunboats fired, their cannon-balls failed to hit their mark. Meanwhile, Confederate guns hammered away, cracking gunboat timbers and wrecking Yankee cannons. With two vessels crippled and the rest damaged, the fleet retreated downriver. Grant's army was left to take Donelson alone.

The Confederate garrison was in a tight spot. Though equal in number to the Union forces, the Rebels were trapped against the river. At dawn, under Confederate General Gideon Pillow, they tried for a breakout. In a battle that bloodied the snow all morning, the troops cut an escape route through the Union lines to Nashville. But just before noon, Pillow lost his nerve and pulled back most of his men.

Pillow's hesitation was Grant's opportunity. Union troops counterattacked and broke the Confederate lines, trapping the Rebels for good. General Buckner, left in

DAVID G. FARRAGUT

David G. Farragut joined the navy in 1810 at the age of nine; in the War of 1812 he was put in command of a captured British ship when only a twelve-year-old midshipman.

Before the Civil War he had lived in Virginia with his Southern wife, but when war broke out he had no doubt about which side he was on. "Mind what I tell you," he said to his rebellious neighbors. "You fellows will catch the devil before you get through with this business."

Capturing New Orleans in 1862 made Farragut a naval hero. Still, though he was already sixty, the triumph over the Southern port wasn't his last stroke of genius. In 1864, Farragut went after Mobile, Alabama, one of the last Confederate ports still open to blockade runners. In his flagship, the *Hartford*, Farragut led his fleet into the mouth of the bay at dawn on August 5, 1864.

Frail and desperately seasick, the Union commander had himself tied to the rigging of his ship as the fleet sailed single file past the blazing guns of Fort Morgan. Soon after the attack began, disaster struck. Farragut's lead ironclad, the *Tecumseh*, strayed out of the channel, struck a Rebel torpedo (mine), and plunged to the bottom. The *Brooklyn*, next in line, halted to avoid the torpedoes. This slowed all the Union ships right in front of Fort Morgan, whose guns blasted the *Hartford*'s deck, covering it with blood and slaughter. Farragut hesitated a moment, then shouted, "Damn the torpedoes! Full speed ahead!"

The *Brooklyn* scraped through the minefield and led the fleet into Mobile Bay. Later that morning, Farragut's ships pounded the Rebel ironclad *Tennessee* into surrender, ending the battle. Farragut, like Grant, believed that he could minimize battle losses by mounting an aggressive attack. His decisiveness made him the most successful naval officer of the war.

Ironclad gunboats helped force open the western rivers. Their invention rendered wooden ships obsolete.

charge when Pillow fled, had no choice but to surrender. A friend of Grant's before the war, Buckner expected generous surrender terms. He didn't get them. Grant demanded "unconditional and immediate surrender." His hard line earned him the nickname "Unconditional Surrender" Grant.

Tennessee's capital, Nashville, soon fell to the advancing Union forces. With that Southern jewel in their pocket and the control of the Western rivers, the Federal armies could now move south.

THE VITAL MISSISSIPPI.
In the spring of 1862, while the bloodiest battle in the West was raging at Shiloh in Tennessee, Union Admiral David G. Farragut (see sidebar) led a daring campaign to seize New Orleans, the South's largest city and busiest port. Farragut's gamble was part of the Union effort to take control of the Mississippi River and split the Confederacy in two.

To apply even more pressure, the Union Navy had been gradually blockading the Southern Gulf coast, cutting off trade and military supplies.

To reach the city, Farragut's ships had to get by two Confederate strongholds, Forts Jackson and St. Philip, seventy-five miles east of the city. The forts stood on either side of the Mississippi, and a heavy chain barrier stretched across the river between them. "Nothing afloat could pass the forts," a New Orleans resident remembered, and "Nothing that walked could get through our swamps."

Farragut thought he could first shell the forts, then push past the crippled defenses with his powerful fleet.

On April 18, mortar schooners opened fire on Fort Jackson, blasting the brick walls for the next five days. But little serious damage was done, and most of the Confederate guns still growled defiance. On April 23, Farragut decided to run past the forts, whatever the cost.

At 2 A.M. on April 24, Farragut's ships headed past the forts in the dark. Three nights before, two Federal gunboats had cut a gap in the chain barrier. The lead ship got through the gap before the Confederates spotted the fleet, but soon the night exploded with cannon shells. Burning rafts floated downriver, sent by Rebels to set the Federal ships ablaze.

Fighting the Mississippi current, Union warships steamed with agonizing slowness beneath the forts, firing as they went. But clouds of gun smoke spoiled the aim of the Rebel gunners. Only after the fleet made it through the barrier did a Union vessel go down. By dawn almost all of Farragut's ships had passed the forts.

A CITY SURRENDERS.
When Farragut arrived at New Orleans the next day, the city was at the mercy of his cannons. With Union troops arriving just behind Farragut, the city surrendered on May 1. The gate to the Mississippi, the Confederacy's largest trade route, was closed.

Union forces continued to press up and down the river, still trying to divide the Confederacy in two. Farragut headed north but couldn't crush the powerful Rebel guns at Vicksburg, Mississippi. He was forced to return to New Orleans. Union General Grant would soon grasp again for Vicksburg's valuable Mississippi port.

SHILOH, SHILOH

Union General Henry Halleck wanted to unite Ulysses S. Grant's army with General Don Carlos Buell's 35,000 troops out of Nashville. With the combined forces, Halleck hoped to move south and smash the Rebels at Corinth, Mississippi. Corinth was a key rail link between Memphis and the rest of the South.

CLOSING IN. Confederate commander Albert Sidney Johnston knew his 40,000 troops couldn't stand against Halleck's combined force of 75,000. He decided to act first and surprise Grant before Buell arrived from Nashville. On the evening of April 5, 1862, Johnston's Army of the Mississippi crept close to the Union camp at Pittsburg Landing, about two miles from the Tennessee River. Grant's men were scattered around the rural church named "Shiloh"—the Hebrew word for peace.

TAKEN BY SURPRISE. Yankee soldiers were boiling coffee and frying bacon for breakfast near a peach orchard when a wave of Confederate infantry rolled over their camps.

Screaming their high-pitched battle cry, the Confederates drove the stricken Yankees back toward the Tennessee River. Breaking one Yankee line after another, the Rebel attack seemed unstoppable.

The year before, at Manassas, such green troops had run away in terror when the battle had gone against them.

Some would run here—one officer was found curled up in a hollow log with two of his men. Some made for the river, swimming frantically to the other side. One private, caught in a fury of fire, shot his finger off so he could stand down.

Many, though, stayed and fought the Rebels. Thousands fell through the grim morning, raining blood on fallen peach petals.

THE HORNET'S NEST. By afternoon the Union soldiers had their backs to the river and could not retreat. Headlong Confederate charges continued to slam into their lines; the defenders were slashed with rifle fire from front and sides. If the bullets could not break the lines, screaming Rebels came charging with bayonets.

The Confederates fought bravely all morning, but now their courage was about to cost them. A stubborn Yankee division was using a sunken dirt road as a trench and could only be attacked across open ground. General Johnston urged his men on, thinking they could shove these stubborn Yankees out of the way, just as they had all morning. But the Union line would not budge. Grant had insisted that they hold the position "at all cost."

Finally the Confederates trained sixty-two cannons at point-blank range on the trench they called the Hornet's Nest. The position exploded, trees and men broken and thrown into the air in a "mighty hurricane."

Johnston, in the midst of a charge, was hit behind the knee by one of the thousands of bullets buzzing through the battle smoke. Helped from his horse by his staff, he bled to death before a surgeon could help him.

NIGHT TERROR. The Union division holding the Hornet's Nest was eventually surrounded. They finally surrendered

CHILD WARRIORS

Both sides needed males of fighting age to fill the ranks during a long war. The legal age of enlistment was eighteen, but many boys, excited by the idea of combat, enlisted as well.

Some young men got their parents' permission. Others ran off and lied about their age to the recruiters. A few preteens joined their home-state regiments as musicians, mostly drummer boys. The bands played on the march and in camp. After the battles, they carried the stretchers of the dead and wounded.

One drummer boy who became famous during the war was John Clem from Michigan. Reportedly, Clem was just ten years old when he was caught up in the terrible battle at Shiloh. A Rebel artillery shell smashed Clem's drum, and the newspapers made him famous as "Johnny Shiloh."

A year later, in the chaos of retreat from Chickamauga, Clem carried a shortened rifle as well as his drum. A Confederate colonel called for his surrender at one point. John shot and wounded him and then took the colonel prisoner, becoming the "Drummer Boy of Chickamauga."

Clem was taken prisoner himself shortly after the incident. He spent two months in prison. But the experience didn't put him off fighting. He returned for the Battle for Atlanta and was wounded twice.

John Clem went on to make the army his career. He retired as a major general just before World War I.

These young Confederates were typical of the inexperienced troops who fought at Shiloh. The battle left thousands of them—as well as their Yankee opponents—in their graves.

before dusk. The brave stand stopped the Rebel advance for six hours and probably saved Grant's army.

As evening drew on, though, the Union situation was still desperate. Pushed back against the Tennessee River by the headlong Confederate attacks, Grant's tired men tried to bolster themselves for another assault. But it never came. The Confederates were spent. General P. G. T. Beauregard, who had replaced Johnston, decided he would finish off Grant's army in the morning.

> *"Some cried for water...God heard them, for the heavens opened and the rains came."*
>
> —*A Union soldier at Shiloh, 1862*

Darkness brought no peace. Union gunboats shelled the Rebel camps. Broken and dying, men cried out for water. General Grant could not bear the screams from the wounded and slept off in the damp woods under a tree.

During the night Buell's troops from Nashville began to arrive. In the early morning of April 7, Grant—now reinforced—counterattacked. Now outnumbered, the Rebels tried to strike back. In the face of fresh Federal troops, though, they were sent crashing back over ground taken at such terrible cost the day before.

The wounded and dead lay everywhere. A Union officer came across a blood-soaked Rebel lying across yet another shattered body. "Why did you come down here?" the dying man asked the Northerner. "We would have never gone up there."

BEGINNING OF A NIGHTMARE. The Confederates simply could not hold on anymore. They retreated to Corinth; but that city's key rail depot was doomed. Within two months, it would fall. With it would go Memphis and Tennessee's resources: its industry, people, and supplies. These were losses the South could scarcely afford.

Shiloh's violence shocked North and South alike. Grant's army of 62,000 had lost over 13,000 men—wounded, killed, or missing. The Rebels had lost fewer men, but a larger percentage of their total: nearly 12,000 casualties out of an army of 44,000. No one had dreamed that the "little war" would come to this.

The fighting at Shiloh was the closest and most brutal yet seen in the Civil War. The wild savagery turned one writer into a dark prophet of the nuclear age. Just a few days after the bloodshed ended, Henry Adams wrote:

"I firmly believe that before many centuries more, science will be the master of man. The engines he will have invented will be beyond his strength to control. Someday science shall have the existence of mankind in its power, and the human race commit suicide by blowing up the world."

DEFENDING RICHMOND

While the Western armies mauled each other at bloody Shiloh, Union forces in the East moved out under a new commander. He was thirty-six-year-old General George B. McClellan, the hero of several small victories in western Virginia. McClellan, a master organizer, had quickly built his army of recruits into a powerful, well-trained force—the Army of the Potomac, more than 100,000 strong.

ON TO RICHMOND. Prodded into action by Lincoln, McClellan set his sights on Richmond, Virginia, the Confederate capital. He loaded his new army aboard ships in late March 1862 and came ashore on the Virginia peninsula. The Rebels, under General Joseph E. Johnston (no relation to the Albert Johnston killed at Shiloh), marched quickly from northern Virginia to block McClellan's move toward Richmond.

The Union army outmanned Johnston's force: 100,000 against 56,000. McClellan, though, was cautious by nature, and his inept spies convinced him that the Confederates really outnumbered the Yankees.

The Union general, advancing at a crawl, took a month to surround the Rebel defenses at Yorktown. By the time McClellan was ready to attack, the Rebels had escaped from his trap and pulled back to Richmond. There Johnston would try to scrape together a force big enough to face McClellan on more equal terms.

JACKSON'S PLOY. A hundred miles northwest of Richmond, Confederate General Stonewall Jackson was thinking of ways to pull Yankee pressure away from Richmond. He hoped to lure a chunk of McClellan's troops west into the Shenandoah Valley. His first attack, in March 1862, got McClellan's and Lincoln's attention. By early spring, 40,000 Union soldiers slated for the Richmond campaign were off chasing Stonewall's army in the valley.

Leading a wild goose chase, though, wasn't enough for Jackson. With his 16,000 men, he whirled around to meet his Union pursuers, winning five of six battles in the Shenandoah. Jackson's turnaround victories earned him a place as one of the ablest field generals in military history.

In mid-June, Jackson broke away from his pursuers and headed for the peninsula. Now he would help the Rebels take on the Army of the Potomac.

FAIR OAKS/SEVEN PINES. By late May 1862, McClellan's army had forced General Johnston's Confederates back into Richmond. Union soldiers could see the capital's steeples and rooftops. Sixty thousand Rebels faced McClellan's 100,000, but the Union general still believed he was outnumbered. As McClellan inched forward, he divided his army on either side of the rain-swollen Chickahominy River. Johnston saw his chance. On May 31, he moved to destroy the Union army's southern wing.

The attack, though, was a disaster. Johnston's confusing orders and the inexperience of his generals left his soldiers in chaos. A Rebel private recalled: "Men screamed…. The officers shouted out unmeaning cries. The flag went down."

In just five minutes, seventy-four soldiers of the Virginia 17th Regiment fell. Johnston, too, was stricken. Just before dark, he was wounded in the chest and shoulder.

By the next morning, the shaken Rebels were back inside their own lines near Richmond. But, amazingly, the fierce attack had once again convinced McClellan that he was outnumbered.

McClellan did have something real to worry about, though. The Rebel forces were about to get a new commander. Confederate President Jefferson Davis was

Confederate currency printed by various states replaced U.S. money in the South. Toward the end of the war, however, it was practically worthless.

Union troops guard a key bridge over the Potomac River at Washington, D.C. Lee's army soon threatened the capital.

about to replace the wounded Johnston with his personal military adviser, a general whose dazzling skills on the battlefield would make him a legend—Robert E. Lee.

LEE AND THE SEVEN DAYS.

Lee acted quickly—he reorganized the Confederate troops into the new Army of Northern Virginia. He sent his dashing young cavalry commander, "Jeb" Stuart, on a daring ride around the Union army. Stuart's horsemen discovered that McClellan's right flank north of the Chickahominy was unprotected. With help from Stonewall Jackson's hard-marching troops, Lee planned to surprise the Union right flank and crush it.

> *"It was not war, it was murder."*
>
> —*Confederate General*
> *D. H. Hill on the attack*
> *at Malvern Hill*

On June 26, Lee launched three divisions into the jaws of the strong Union line at Beaver Dam Creek. But the Yankees, under General Porter, drove off the attacks, inflicting severe casualties on some Rebel regiments.

BREACHING THE LINE.

Though he had won the battle, McClellan was still worried. He pulled some of his men back to Gaines' Mill. There, on the afternoon of June 27, the Confederates attacked again, losing heavily. Try as they might, they could not budge the Union line.

Finally, though, Stonewall Jackson appeared. His extra troops gave Lee the strength he needed to plow through General Porter's line. With General John Bell Hood's Texans charging the center, the Yankee barricade was breached.

Lee's victory at Gaines' Mill was dear: 8,000 Confederates were killed or wounded in the attack, while the Union defenders lost 4,000.

McClellan, however, was now truly rattled. He abandoned the advance on Richmond, thinking only of getting his army safely to a new base on the James River.

MALVERN HILL.

Lee had other plans. He came after McClellan, determined to destroy the Yankee army before it could reach the James. Pulling up atop the low crest of Malvern Hill, the Army of the Potomac turned to make a stand against the Rebels.

From the hilltop, the Union cannoneers stood to their guns, waiting for the gray lines to come within range. The result was a slaughter. The Union guns loosed a terrible rain of "canister" ammunition—tin cans full of lead balls that ripped open just after leaving the guns' muzzles. Each cannon was like a giant sawed-off shotgun, spraying death down the slopes into the packed ranks of infantry.

In the assault, Lee lost over 5,300 men, against 3,200 Union killed, wounded, and missing. The Seven Days battles were now over. McClellan's Army of the Potomac was safe, but so was Richmond, thanks to Lee. But the cost to the Confederates was staggering. Lee had lost one fourth of his army—over 20,000 men—trying to destroy McClellan's Army of the Potomac.

Second Manassas/ Bull Run

McClellan kept asking President Lincoln for massive reinforcements before facing Lee again. But the president was determined not to leave Washington, D.C., unguarded. Instead of sending more troops south to the cautious McClellan, he created a new army of 45,000, the Army of Virginia. The new commander, General John Pope, was a somewhat skilled officer but believed he was even better. Pope quickly marched south from Manassas, aiming to destroy Richmond's supply lines.

Cedar Mountain.

Robert E. Lee was determined to keep the Yankees out of his homeland of northern Virginia. Pope "must be suppressed," he told his staff. With one eye on McClellan, Lee sent Stonewall Jackson with 12,000 men to block Pope's advance. Jackson, being Jackson, was anxious to attack, but the Yankees struck first. At Cedar Mountain 8,000 Union troops sent Jackson's left flank reeling back in confusion. But Stonewall rallied his men, personally leading them in a counterattack that drove the Federals from the field. It was clearly Jackson's victory, but the fighting tipped off Pope that he'd stuck his neck out too far. Before Lee could trap him, the Union general retreated skillfully north across the Rapidan River.

Jackson Becomes the Bait.

Lincoln was worried about Pope's exposed army. He ordered the Army of the Potomac back north to help. McClellan, though, was jealous of Pope's command and was in no hurry to rush to his aid. Lee sensed a chance to smash Pope before McClellan could arrive. With General James Longstreet and the rest of the Rebel army, he rushed to join Jackson.

On August 25, 1862, Lee sent Jackson circling to Pope's rear, aiming to cut him off. Despite the summer heat, Jackson's "foot cavalry" marched fifty-four miles in two days. Dead tired and covered with dust, they arrived squarely behind the Yankees. Jackson captured Pope's supply dump, even bagging the Union general's dress uniform.

The real treat for the Rebel soldiers, however, was all the food. For a whole day, Jackson let his weary soldiers feast on the mountains of provisions—canned peaches, fine wines, lobster salad. His refreshed troops grabbed all they could carry, including pairs of new shoes, then marched away with bulging haversacks.

Pope, though surprised, thought he could still trap and destroy Jackson. He ordered his army north to Manassas to surround Stonewall's three small divisions. When the Federals converged on the smoking ruins of their depot, though, the Rebels were gone. Stonewall Jackson had vanished, hiding his army in a nearby woods.

The Fox Turns.

Pope couldn't find Jackson, but he was sure the Confederates were fleeing, trying to rejoin Lee's army. In fact, Jackson was doing anything but retreating. Knowing that Lee would join him the next day, Stonewall no longer needed to hide. Near sunset on August 28, Jackson moved to attack, ambushing a Yankee division near Brawner Farm. The Yankees, though outnumbered three to one, refused to run. These Union troops were just as brave as Jackson's men.

For the next hour and a half, the two battle lines slugged it out, firing into each other from a distance of

THE FIRST IRONCLADS

When Union forces abandoned the Norfolk, Virginia, naval base in 1861, they burned and sank their powerful wooden warship, the USS *Merrimack*. Confederate Navy Secretary Stephen Mallory saw an opportunity. He had the ship raised and refitted as a ten-gun ironclad, and rechristened her the CSS *Virginia*.

The ship had a slanting fortress on its deck. It was wrapped in sheet iron so thick it could deflect the largest naval cannon shells. The *Virginia* soon made her name at sea. She rammed and sank the USS *Cumberland*, burned and sank the USS *Congress*, and forced the USS *Minnesota* aground.

The *Virginia* planned to finish off the *Minnesota* the next day. But the following morning, a surprise awaited the Confederate ship. Standing by the crippled *Minnesota* was a strange, flat-decked vessel with a round turret amidships. It was the USS *Monitor*, a new Union ironclad. Built in just four months, the *Monitor* housed two powerful cannons in her rotating iron turret.

The *Monitor* was nimbler and used her turret guns to hit the *Virginia* at will. But she could only crack, not pierce, the Rebel warship's thick armor. One lucky shot from the *Virginia*, however, struck the *Monitor*'s pilothouse. The explosion blinded the *Monitor*'s captain, but the ship continued to fight. The "cheesebox on a raft" fought the *Virginia* to a draw.

A wagon park at Brandy Station, Virginia. Supplying their huge armies was the first order of battle for North and South.

no more than seventy-five yards. The impact of this concentrated rifle fire was terrible. One Confederate private, fighting behind an old fence, remembered the wooden rails splintering into fragments. Men, more fragile than wood, were knocked out of line by the dozens. Still the survivors continued to stand and fire into the clouds of flickering battle smoke. The fight sputtered out in the darkness, neither side gaining the upper hand.

> *"Some were struck in the act of eating. One poor fellow still held a potato in his grasp."*
>
> —*A nurse at Cedar Mountain*

SECOND BULL RUN. Next morning, Pope threw his arriving troops across fields and wooded lots on the old Bull Run battlefield, certain of catching Jackson's "retreating" men. Far from running, the Rebels were actually ready and waiting, crouching behind an unfinished railroad bed nearly two miles long. Pope foolishly attacked one brigade at a time. His tactics did nothing but waste brave soldiers against stiff Rebel defenses, even though, at points, the Yankees did manage to punch through.

In the heat of the afternoon Lee arrived with Longstreet's men. While Jackson hung on, Lee told Longstreet to get ready for a counterpunch on Jackson's right flank. The next day, August 30, still believing that Jackson was pulling out, Pope attacked Stonewall's lines again, unaware of what Lee had in store.

When the Confederates opened fire on one charging Union column, the first line of Federal soldiers "looked as if it had been struck by a blast from a tempest." One Union soldier remembered the slope being "swept by a hurricane of death, and each minute seemed twenty hours long."

REBEL TIDAL WAVE. At 4 P.M. on August 30, Lee unleashed Longstreet's 30,000 fresh men against Pope's weak left flank. A Union private remembered the sound of the bullets as a "continual hiss and sluck," the last sound telling that the bullet had gone into some man's body. The 5th New York Regiment was virtually wiped out—the fleeing survivors shot down as they ran into the ravine of a little creek called Young's Branch.

One Rebel private later wrote: "Young's Branch ran blood. The Federals completely dammed it up with their dead and dying bodies."

The Confederate success brought such disorder among the attacking brigades and divisions that Longstreet had to pause to regroup. Pope managed to hold off Jackson's attack on his right, while shifting men to the left for a last-ditch defense on Henry House Hill. As darkness fell, a patched-together Yankee line on the hillcrest turned back Lee's final attack.

Pope retreated toward Washington, lucky to have escaped at all. His army's losses were almost 16,000, including more than 4,000 taken prisoner. The Rebels had lost fewer than 10,000. Lee had left the sluggish McClellan behind and whirled north, thoroughly trouncing Pope. With two victories under his belt, Lee decided to carry the war into the North, across the Potomac.

ANTIETAM/ SHARPSBURG

Robert E. Lee was hoping to force a battle on Northern territory. With a victory on Northern soil, the British and French might start actively supporting the South. He also believed sympathetic young men in border states might join the Confederate cause.

INTO THE NORTH. After bloodying Pope, Lee led his ragged army across the Potomac into Maryland. Farmers watched as the underfed and weary men trudged up the roads. They were, according to one Maryland woman, the dirtiest men she'd ever seen. It was hard to believe that these shoeless ragamuffins were the same ones who had been thrashing the Union army.

With Lee practically on his doorstep, Lincoln was worried. He relieved General Pope from command and put McClellan back in charge of the Army of the Potomac. The president knew McClellan was not a fighter, but he needed to stop Lee, and only "Little Mac" could pull the Union army together in time.

McClellan was not eager for battle, but he now had an advantage. Confederate soldiers had left behind a copy of Lee's orders at an abandoned campsite. A Union corporal had stumbled on this precious piece of intelligence. Now McClellan was cocky. "Here is a paper with which, if I cannot whip Bobbie Lee, I will be willing to go home."

Tipped off by a Southern sympathizer, Lee began to realize that his forces were in trouble. He pulled his divided army back to the ridges outside the town of Sharpsburg. His back was against the Potomac.

McClellan caught up with him on September 15, but, as usual, he wasn't in a hurry to attack. The Union general, commanding no fewer than 87,000 troops, feared, as always, that he was outnumbered. Though he could not see them, he was sure Lee had more than 100,000 men waiting on the banks of Antietam Creek. He wasted all of September 16 worrying about it before deciding to attack.

MILLER'S CORNFIELD. It was nearly the end of the Maryland summer. Green corn was growing tall in the fields surrounding Sharpsburg. The weather was still humid and hot, with just a hint of autumn in the stands of trees between the fields.

A mist covered those fields at dawn on September 17. As the sun rose, Union General "Fighting Joe" Hooker sent his corps of 15,000 surging south toward the small white Dunker church. This high ground was guarded by Stonewall Jackson's men.

Hooker's troops met the Rebels in the lines of corn. Both sides blasted each other with cannon through the stalks. The rifle and canister fire ripped bodies apart. Whole regiments fell. Union soldiers finally reached the church. But as they turned to look behind them, they saw the cornfield was carpeted with dead and dying; 8,000 men lay killed or broken on the bloodied stalks.

THE SUNKEN ROAD. At midmorning, a Union attack rolled toward the center of Lee's forces. There, Confederate troops sheltered in a sunken road that formed a natural trench. As the Union soldiers approached the trench, the Confederate riflemen aimed their weapons. Colonel John Gordon waited until the Yankees were just twenty yards away, then yelled "Fire!"

CLARA BARTON

The wounded—those lucky enough not to be killed outright on the battlefield—faced an ordeal that made some wish for death. Many lay on the field for hours or even days. Those who survived faced agonizing amputations and lingering infections.

Clara Barton saw the misery of the war's soldiers and wanted to do something about it. A five-foot-tall Massachusetts schoolteacher, she wasn't exactly a choice candidate for the battlefield. But Barton overcame her natural shyness. She went first to Washington and began collecting food and donations. Through her organization, she was able to get needed supplies to the wounded.

In 1862, she headed for the fighting. She explained that her business was "stanching blood and feeding fainting men."

Barton was always the first nurse on the battlefield, beginning with the battle at Second Bull Run. At Antietam, she was giving a drink to a wounded man on the field when he was struck by a Confederate bullet and killed. The same bullet ripped a hole in her sleeve.

The soldiers she cared for named her "the Angel of the Battlefield," and she stood by them under fire, even when their officers fled in panic. In 1881, Barton founded the American Red Cross.

Union dead near Miller's cornfield, Sharpsburg, Maryland. The battle was the bloodiest day of the war.

Hundreds of Union soldiers, shot at close range, staggered and fell. Said Gordon: "The effect was appalling.... The entire front line, with few exceptions, went down in the consuming blast."

The Yankee charge at the trench was followed by another and another for two sickening hours. Thousands of soldiers seemed to melt in the musket fire.

BLOODY LANE. Finally a Union regiment maneuvered onto a little knoll. From here they could fire down on the Confederates at a slight bend in the road. The fire from above so shocked the Rebels that one whole brigade tried to escape the trench. They were shot down by the hundreds. The sunken road became the Bloody Lane. Bodies tumbled back into the trench and covered the roadbed, in some places two or three deep.

BURNSIDE'S BRIDGE. A fresh push from McClellan's reserves would have punched through Bloody Lane and split Lee's army. But McClellan held back, still thinking Lee outnumbered him. The center of the Confederate line still held—by the thinnest of threads. Now the fighting shifted to the Union left flank.

The Union corps led by Ambrose Burnside was ordered to strike Lee's right flank, across Antietam Creek. Instead of fording the shallow creek, Burnside's 11,000 men tried over and over again to capture a narrow stone bridge that crossed it. The span was defended by just 550 Rebels on the heights above. Charging Yankees drove into the teeth of the Confederate rifles. Only after three

bloody tries did Union troops scatter the defenders.

Burnside was now set to destroy Lee's weakened right flank. At three o'clock in the afternoon, he pushed toward Sharpsburg. But just as he was closing in, Confederate reinforcements arrived from Harpers Ferry. This Rebel division fell upon Burnside's men and broke the Union attack. By sunset the fighting was over. Two days later Lee's army retreated across the Potomac. McClellan had stopped Lee's invasion, but at terrific cost. The 22,726 casualties from both sides made September 17, 1862, America's bloodiest single day of combat.

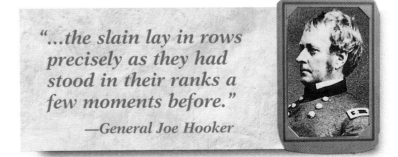

"...the slain lay in rows precisely as they had stood in their ranks a few moments before."

—General Joe Hooker

The North called the terrible field of war Antietam, while the South named it Sharpsburg. Perhaps no other battlefield was a clearer symbol of the tragedy of the Civil War. Fought practically on the border between North and South, Antietam cost both sides terribly in dead and wounded sons. In the end, no one really won the battle.

FREDERICKSBURG, CHANCELLORSVILLE

In the aftermath of Antietam, Lincoln had issued the Emancipation Proclamation. The fight to rid the land of slavery was now linked with the North's resolve to save the Union.

PURSUING LEE.

McClellan had forced the Confederates back to Virginia, but to end the war, Lee's army had to be destroyed. McClellan did not have the heart for the kill. He had shaped and polished his great Army of the Potomac and could not bear to risk it. Lincoln gave the job of finishing Lee to Ambrose Burnside, one of McClellan's subordinates.

The Confederate general had dug in on the hills over Fredericksburg on the road to Richmond. Burnside would have to come to him. From behind a stone wall at the base of Marye's Heights, four lines of Rebel infantry waited for the Union attack. Their guns were sited to fire over their heads and sweep the plain in front of them.

A cannoneer told Lee, "General, a chicken could not live in that field when we open on it."

MARYE'S HEIGHTS.

After crossing the river into Fredericksburg, Burnside attacked on the dank, cold morning of December 13, 1862. He sent his troops into the grinder of Lee's defenses, despite warnings from his fellow generals. The result was a long day of needless slaughter. A Union officer watched brigade after brigade take their turn against the Confederate storm of iron. The lines seemed to melt, he said later, "like snow coming down on warm ground."

The Confederates beat back fourteen separate charges, shooting down 12,700 Union men with bloody ease. No Union soldier got closer than twenty-five yards to that fatal stone wall. That night, many wounded froze to death in the bitter December wind.

TURNING TO HOOKER.

Lincoln despaired of finding a good commander. After the Fredericksburg disaster and another failed march in January, he replaced Burnside with General Joseph Hooker. "Fighting Joe," at least, had an aggressive streak. Right away he got the men fresh food, fixed up their camps, and restored the army's spirit. In late April 1863, he set off to outfox Lee.

Hooker meant to force Lee out of his strong position at Fredericksburg, catch the Rebels in open country, and crush them. In all, it was a good strategy.

The Union general jumped most of his army across the Rappahannock upstream of Lee's defenses. The Yankees got well behind the Confederates before Lee knew what was happening.

The Union soldiers were jubilant—their commander had Lee reacting to their movements. But just as the Yankees began to pick their way out from the tangled, scrubby growth, Hooker panicked, ordering his men onto the defensive.

SPLITTING THE ARMY.

The day that held so much promise for Hooker now gave Lee the opportunity to

---

THE EMANCIPATION PROCLAMATION

Even during the second year of the war, the North was still fighting for, and only for, the restoration of the Union. Doing away with slavery was not the objective. Lincoln, though firmly against slavery, refused to free the slaves themselves. He was too afraid of driving the border states into the Confederacy. If that happened, many Union soldiers might quit the ranks, and the war would be lost.

Another reality was that the slaves were beyond Lincoln's reach. He really couldn't "free them" until Confederate forces were driven from the field.

Still, many in the North urged the president to strike at the heart of the rebellion. Freedom for the slaves—emancipation—would strike at the Confederate economy and win support for the Union overseas. Gradually, Lincoln decided he would act to free those slaves held captive in the rebellious states, gutting the Confederate economy. By freeing slaves only in the Rebel states, he kept slave owners in the border states loyal.

Lincoln didn't want his act to seem one of military desperation. He decided to wait until the Union had a real victory on the battlefield. Lincoln got his "victory" at Antietam. With Lee driven from Union soil, the president acted. On September 22, just five days after the battle, the president ordered that, as of January 1, 1863:

"...all persons held as slaves within any State or designated part of a State, the people whereof shall then be in rebellion against the United States, shall be then, thenceforth, and forever free...."

A Confederate caisson, victim of a Union shell at Fredericksburg, Virginia. The Rebels would soon turn the tables.

craft his greatest victory. On the first night of May 1863, Lee and Stonewall Jackson sat on a pair of cracker boxes beside a small fire and plotted a daring attack. Lee would take a gamble and split his army. The next morning Jackson set off with 25,000 men. His aim was to pounce on Hooker's right flank. Lee was betting that he could hold off Hooker's 70,000 troops with the 15,000 Rebel soldiers he had left.

> *"...all persons held as slaves...shall be then, thenceforth, and forever free."*
> — *Emancipation Proclamation*

As the sunlight faded on the evening of the following day, German immigrant recruits, part of Hooker's infantry, were cooking their supper. Suddenly deer and small game came bounding from the tangled wood to the west. Bugles blared, then hordes of Rebel infantry rolled out of the forest.

Jackson's attack sent the Yankees tumbling back more than two miles. Only darkness and some stubborn men in Union blue, scratching together a defense, finally halted the Confederate advance.

Under a full May moon, Jackson tried to organize his now scattered troops for a night attack. He was riding in front of his own lines when Confederate infantry mistook him for a Yankee. Gun blasts spat into the darkness, and Jackson and two of his staff fell. His aides were dead on the ground; Jackson was alive, but his left arm was shattered. Surgeons amputated it the next morning.

BATTLE ON FIRE. Hooker was now completely on the defensive. So Lee reunited the two wings of his army and struck hard. The fierce fighting in the Wilderness set dry leaves and underbrush on fire, choking the battle lines with smoke. The wounded were burning alive in the rush of flames. One wounded Union soldier remembered the horror of it: "We were trying to rescue a young fellow in gray. The fire was all around him. The last I saw of that fellow was his face.... His eyes were big and blue, and his hair like raw silk surrounded by a wreath of fire."

When General Hooker finally pulled his battered army back across the Rappahannock on May 6, he had lost 17,000 men. Lincoln was crushed by the news of the defeat. "My God," the president grieved, "what will the country say?"

Lee had lost fewer—13,000 men, but that was a quarter of his army. The Confederacy, though, was crushed with grief. Stonewall Jackson died on May 10 of pneumonia brought on by his wound. The Confederacy would soon miss his battlefield skills dearly.

GETTYSBURG

The Confederate army had failed in 1862 to get a foothold in the North. But it was June 1863 now, and Robert E. Lee's Army of Northern Virginia was at its fighting peak.

HIGH HOPES. The men were deadly in battle now, and their commander had firm hopes that they could defeat the Army of the Potomac on Union soil. Lee was still holding onto the hope that France and Britain could be convinced to come to the aid of the Confederacy.

Behind the mountain screen of the Blue Ridge, Lee's men marched down the Shenandoah Valley and crossed into Maryland. Now that he was across the Potomac River, the fingers of Lee's three corps could reach out and threaten Harrisburg and Baltimore.

Lee's cavalry commander, Jeb Stuart, was instructed to keep an eye on Hooker and his Yankees and warn Lee if they started moving north. However, Stuart lost track of the Union army and let Lee advance blindly.

The Army of the Potomac was marching quickly to intercept Lee, but he didn't know it. He was shocked when he found out that the Yankees were already in northern Maryland and coming on fast.

THE FIRST DAY. Lee ordered his scattered army to concentrate at Cashtown near the crossroads of Gettysburg in Pennsylvania. Early on July 1, a Rebel brigade, hunting for desperately needed shoes, blundered into two Yankee cavalry brigades holding the town. The chance meeting was about to turn into the fiercest battle of the entire war.

In charge of the Yankees was General John Buford. He wasn't about to let go of this corner of high ground. He ordered his men to get off their horses and fight the Rebels on foot. This they did all morning, stubbornly holding off the Southerners until help arrived.

By midafternoon Lee brought up reinforcements and had broken the Union lines west and north of the city. Blue infantrymen streamed back through the streets of the town. Hundreds were captured, trapped in alleys and yards. But most rallied on Cemetery Hill, a strong defensive spot.

During the night, Lee tried to get General Richard Ewell to attack and seize Cemetery Hill. But Ewell failed to act. His caution allowed Union reinforcements to set up a strong line along the ridges during the night.

THE SECOND DAY. Union General George Meade, Hooker's replacement, had formed a fishhook line of men southeast of Gettysburg. These 60,000 men were anchored at Culp's Hill. The curve of the hook was at Cemetery Hill, with the shaft running down Cemetery Ridge (see map on page 55).

Lee's right flank commander, General James Longstreet, looked at the situation and advised Lee to leave the Yankees on the ridge alone. An assault on those strong positions might well be a disaster. Longstreet suggested that Lee move the men south and let the Yankees come after them. But Lee overruled him. "No," he said. "I am going to whip them [here], or they are going to whip me."

CEMETERY RIDGE. Lee aimed Longstreet's men at the Yankees' left flank. Ewell was ordered to charge the far right. Lee hoped to crush the Union line in a pincer movement.

At 4 P.M., sweltering in the July heat, Longstreet's divisions surged to attack in the face of heavy fire. The men smashed headlong into a stray Union corps and

FREDERICK DOUGLASS

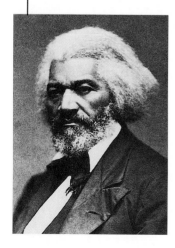

Frederick Douglass began life as a Maryland slave and ended it as the country's greatest black leader. Taught to read and write by his owner's wife, Douglass escaped to freedom in the North at the age of twenty-one. In 1841, he joined the Massachusetts Anti-Slavery Society and became one of its most effective speakers. Six years later he founded his own newspaper, *The North Star*, to spread his abolitionist arguments. Once war broke out, he insisted repeatedly that it was about slavery. "This war," he said, "disguise it as they may, is [about] perpetual slavery against universal freedom."

Once Lincoln issued the Emancipation Proclamation, Douglass campaigned loudly for the right of free blacks to fight for the cause of the Union and freedom. "The arm of the slave [is] the best defense against the arm of the slaveholder. Who would be free themselves," said Douglass, "must strike the blow…I urge you to…smite to death the power that would bury the Government and your liberty in the same hopeless grave."

Perhaps Frederick Douglass' greatest insight was that blacks—whether former slaves or freemen—were not a separate society.

"We are Americans," he reminded the country during the war, "and shall rise and fall with Americans."

Sunlight filters over the fields at Gettysburg. This battle, the bloodiest of the war, claimed over 51,000 American casualties.

shattered it, capturing a boulder-topped ridge known as Devil's Den.

The fighting there and in the wheat field was a whirl of confusion and carnage. One New York officer looked down onto the battle and was horrified: "The wild cries of charging lines, the rattle of musketry, the booming of artillery and shrieks of the wounded [created] a scene like very hell itself."

> *"The world will little note, nor long remember what we say here, but it can never forget what they did here."*
>
> —Abraham Lincoln, Gettysburg Address

LITTLE ROUND TOP.

Overrunning Devil's Den, the Rebels surged up two rocky hills, Big and Little Round Top. Rebel cannons sitting on top of Little Round Top would be able to blast the whole Union line. It was the key to the day's battle.

But a Union general saw what was happening. In the nick of time he rushed a brigade onto Little Round Top. The 20th Maine Regiment found itself alone at the far end of the Union line. Crouching down among the boulders,

they threw back five separate charges by the 15th Alabama. Colonel Joshua Chamberlain remembered the tangled fighting like the landscape of a nightmare: "At times I saw around me more of the enemy than my own men."

Chamberlain and his men bravely held on—Little Round Top was saved. Lee's two flank attacks had almost succeeded. The Rebels had broken the Union line on Cemetery Ridge and Cemetery Hill. Neither charge, though, had forced the Yankees off the hills for good. Meade's army had been terribly mauled. But he and his generals decided to stay and fight it out.

THE THIRD DAY.

Lee guessed that Meade had used men from the center of his line to plaster the holes the Rebels had punched in his flanks. On July 3, the Confederate general decided to smash that center. He planned an infantry assault, helped by massive artillery fire. A fresh division, led by General George Pickett, would lead the charge.

General Longstreet, once again, cautioned Lee against attacking this way. The men, he explained, would have to cross a mile of open ground. They would be under fire the whole way. "General," Longstreet pleaded, "I have been a soldier all my life…. It is my opinion that no 15,000 men ever arrayed for battle can take that [Union] position."

But Lee had reached his own crossroads. There was no turning back now. "The enemy is there," he said, "and I am going to strike him."

GETTYSBURG– PICKETT'S CHARGE

At 1 P.M., on July 3, in the then unknown town of Gettysburg, the Confederates opened the biggest artillery bombardment ever heard in North America. One hundred and seventy cannons concentrated their fire on the clump of trees that marked the center of the Union line. The storm of shot and shell dismembered horses, blew up ammunition wagons, and cut men in half.

PICKETT'S CHARGE. The Federals returned fire, but they knew an infantry attack was coming, so they conserved their ammunition. When the Union guns reduced their firing in the middle of the afternoon, the Confederates thought the Yankee artillery had been put out of action. Longstreet ordered Pickett to attack.

Long ranks of sweaty infantry stepped out of the trees along Seminary Ridge and headed for the Union lines. But the Federal guns on Cemetery Ridge began immediately to bark. Sometimes as many as ten men were killed and wounded by a single shell burst. One Union gunner wrote, "We could not help hitting them at every shot."

The Rebels were taking a terrible pounding, but they pulled themselves up the slope. When they closed to 200 yards, the Union lines opened up in a blaze of rifle and canister fire. "Arms, heads, blankets, guns, and knapsacks," remembered one Federal officer, "were tossed into the clear air."

Even through the storm of the battle, the terrible moan from the field could be heard.

OVER THE WALL. The surviving Confederates herded toward the clump of trees at the stone wall. The crossfire was now hitting them from three sides.

Finally, a few hundred Rebels led by General Lewis Armistead managed to break the Union line at an angle near the trees. They vaulted over the wall into a mass of Yankee defenders. Armistead was killed by a rifle bullet, but his men fought the surprised Yankees hand to hand.

LINCOLN'S GETTYSBURG ADDRESS

It took workers months to collect the debris of battle after the fight at Gettysburg. The Union dead were finally collected from their temporary graves and moved to a new site atop Cemetery Hill. Confederate dead were left in the mass graves where they'd been buried just after the battle.

The Union Cemetery was to be dedicated on November 19, 1863. President Lincoln was asked to attend, although he was not to be the main speaker. That honor was given to the distinguished orator Edward Everett. Lincoln was only to add a few "appropriate remarks."

Everett's speech before the crowd of 6,000 lasted an hour and fifty-seven minutes. By the time Lincoln rose to the podium, the audience had probably heard enough for one day. But Lincoln only had a few words to say.

"Fourscore and seven years ago our fathers brought forth on this continent a new nation, conceived in Liberty, and dedicated to the proposition that all men are created equal.

Now we are engaged in a great civil war, testing whether that nation or any nation, so conceived, and so dedicated, can long endure. We are met on a great battlefield of that war. We have come to dedicate a portion of that field, as a final resting-place for those who here gave their lives, that that nation might live. It is altogether fitting and proper that we should do this.

But, in a larger sense, we can not dedicate—we can not consecrate—we can not hallow—this ground. The brave men, living and dead, who struggled here, have consecrated it far above our poor power to add or detract. The world will little note, nor long remember what we say here, but it can never forget what they did here. It is for us the living, rather, to be dedicated here to the unfinished work which they who fought here have thus far so nobly advanced. It is rather for us to be here dedicated to the great task remaining before us— that from these honored dead we take increased devotion to that cause for which they here gave the last full measure of devotion—that we here highly resolve that these dead shall not have died in vain—that this nation, under God, shall have a new birth of freedom—and that government of the people, by the people, for the people, shall not perish from the earth."

Lincoln spoke for only two minutes. The audience was so shocked at the shortness of his speech, no one applauded it. Lincoln confessed to a friend that he thought his effort had been "a flat failure."

Lincoln's words, however, would ring through history, immortalizing the sacrifice of his nation's sons.

Union dead at Gettysburg. General Meade's Army of the Potomac, at great cost, had turned back the Rebel invasion.

A Massachusetts soldier remembered: "Foot to foot, body to body and man to man they struggled, pushed and strived and killed.... Underneath the trampling mass, wounded men who could no longer stand, struggled, fought, shouted, and killed—hatless, coatless, drowned in sweat, black with powder, red with blood..."

Within minutes, every Rebel soldier who had crossed the wall was captured or killed.

THE COST OF FAILURE. The wounded and few unhurt survivors from Pickett's Charge streamed back toward

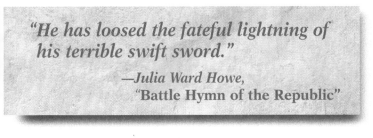

"*He has loosed the fateful lightning of his terrible swift sword.*"

—Julia Ward Howe,
"Battle Hymn of the Republic"

Lee, who tried to comfort them, but he himself was stricken. His greatest gamble had failed. Now he would lead the battered Army of Northern Virginia south again, back across the Potomac.

Lincoln urged Union commanders to pursue the Rebels, but heavy rains made it impossible. General

Meade was content to let Lee go. His own army had lost more than 23,000 men in three days. Lee had lost close to forty percent of his force; 28,000 had been killed, wounded, or captured. More than 51,000 Americans—one out of every three men at Gettysburg—had been killed or wounded. Despite the frightful losses, the War Between the States would go on.

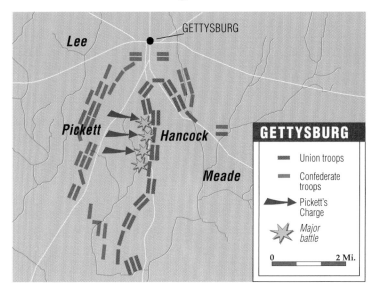

Pickett's division led the Rebels in a bloody charge that failed to crack Meade's line.

VICKSBURG UNDER SIEGE

From a bluff on the Mississippi's east bank, the big coastal guns of Vicksburg ruled a hairpin bend in the river. For two years, those cannons kept supplies flowing in from the western Confederacy to its field armies. In early 1863, Ulysses S. Grant got the job of capturing Vicksburg and splitting the Rebel states in two.

THE GAMBLE. Grant's overland march had been turned back by daring Confederate raids on his supply lines, so he moved by water instead. Grant camped his army just upstream from Vicksburg. Trouble was—he was on the wrong side of the river from the town. Its big guns and the surrounding swamps and bayous made it impossible to get to dry ground east of Vicksburg for an attack.

All winter and spring, Grant's army and the navy's gunboats tried one failed scheme after another to get at the city. Stump-clogged canals, floods, tangled forests, and Confederate gunners turned back every Yankee plan. Grant, by April, was ready to take a daring risk.

He would cross the river to dry land east and south of Vicksburg using the navy's steamboats. But first those transports had to pass by Vicksburg's bristling cannons. In the inky darkness of April 16, 1863, Admiral David Porter ran his gunboats and transports under the Rebel guns. An Iowan on one of the transports watched the Rebel gunners open up on his ship: "Their men...fire and yell as if every shot sunk a steamboat.... Down on the river it is a sheet of flame.... It was as if hell itself were loose that night on the Mississippi...."

Still, nearly all the Union ships made it through. After a quick march down the swampy west bank, Grant finally got his 41,000 men across the Mississippi. Vicksburg's commander, General John C. Pemberton, failed to attack when Grant came ashore.

Surprising the Rebels, Grant took his army inland, feeding his troops easily from the rich local farms and plantations. Pemberton couldn't cut Grant's supply lines—there were none. Instead, the Yankees defeated Pemberton twice in battles at Champion's Hill and Big Black River. Pemberton's 32,000 Confederates were soon trapped in Vicksburg's trenches.

A BLOODY STALEMATE. Grant thought he could smash through the seven-mile-long ring of Confederate defenses. On May 19, William T. Sherman's corps charged the earthworks, but the Yankees were soon pinned down under a fierce Confederate fire. One Union officer, Charles Ewing, was wounded while saving his regiment's flag. Three color bearers had been shot before him, and the banner had been shredded by fifty-five bullets.

BLACK COMBAT UNITS

For the first two years of the war, blacks helped the military efforts of both sides. In the South, many Confederate soldiers refused to do heavy manual labor. The government used slaves, rented from their owners, to build everything: trenches, roads, even prison camps. The Union, too, employed both free blacks and escaped slaves in its military work force. They drove wagons, unloaded supplies, and served on burial details.

At the start of the war, some Northern blacks formed volunteer companies and tried to enlist. But the army rejected them. It seemed that only white soldiers could fight to restore the Union and wipe out slavery. Later, though, as casualty lists lengthened and recruits evaporated, that position changed. Many Northern politicians began to call for blacks to fight in their own cause. President Lincoln authorized the full-scale recruitment of black soldiers in 1862.

After the first two regiments, the 54th and 55th Massachusetts, were organized, other units were formed in Ohio, Pennsylvania, and Connecticut.

Along the Southern seacoast, freed slaves were eager to enlist in the fight. Black troops served in all theaters of the war. They fought at Milliken's Bend, Port Hudson, and Fort Pillow in the West and outside Richmond and Petersburg in the East.

The bravery of the 54th Massachusetts, in particular, won wide praise after a battle outside Charleston, South Carolina. During hand-to-hand combat, Sergeant William Carney rescued the U.S. flag, picking it up from a fallen color bearer, saving it from capture. Hit four times and covered with blood, he still managed to crawl back to the Union lines. Thirty years after his brave act, Carney was awarded the Congressional Medal of Honor.

The Stars and Stripes flies over Vicksburg's courthouse. The Union victory put the whole Mississippi River in Union hands.

Grant lost nearly a thousand men in the futile attack. Three days later, though, he tried again. An Iowa adjutant remembered: "It was a tornado of iron on our left, a hurricane of shot on our right. We passed through the mouth of hell. Every third man fell, either killed or wounded."

A few brave soldiers made it into the Rebel trenches, but most were shot down long before they reached the defenders. Another 3,200 men were soon out of action—500 of them killed. A reporter overheard Grant say quietly, "We'll have to dig our way in."

THE SIEGE. For the next six weeks, Grant's men shoveled their way toward the Rebel lines. More than 200 Union cannons kept up a steady bombardment. The falling shells kept the Rebel soldiers crouched in their trenches, and Vicksburg's civilians had to go underground. They dug hot, cramped caves in the yellow clay hillsides, so many that Union soldiers took to calling Vicksburg "Prairie Dog Village."

With food supplies running out and his soldiers fading fast, Pemberton had run out of choices. With no hope of rescue from General Joe Johnston's relief army, Pemberton asked Grant for surrender terms. On July 4, 1863, more than 30,000 Rebel soldiers stacked arms and marched out of fallen Vicksburg.

> *"The fiery shower of shells goes on, day and night.... People do nothing but eat what they can get, sleep when they can, and dodge the shells."*
>
> —*A Vicksburg resident*

Added to the Confederate defeat at Gettysburg the day before, Vicksburg's capture struck the South a deadly blow. Grant's victory had opened the Mississippi and cut the Confederacy in two.

CHICKAMAUGA; CHATTANOOGA

Since their narrow defeat at Shiloh in April 1862, the Confederates had had mixed success in Tennessee. After being forced back out of Kentucky in October 1862, Rebel General Braxton Bragg had surprised the Union Army of the Cumberland at Stones' River, south of Nashville.

TERRIBLE CHICKAMAUGA. The attack nearly destroyed the Yankees, but they managed to regroup and throw back the Confederates, who lost 12,000 men—a full third of their army. Union troops under General William Rosecrans then captured the key rail center of Chattanooga, Tennessee.

The two armies met again on September 19, 1863, when they stumbled into a bloody fight north of Chickamauga Creek just over the Tennessee line in Georgia. One soldier described the horror of the battle: *"...in that awful roar the voice of a man cannot be heard ten feet away. Men fall to the right and left. The line stumbles over corpses as it hurries on. There are flashes in the smoke cloud, terrible explosions in the air, and men are stepped on or leaped over as they throw up their arms and fall upon the grass..."*

That night, in bitter cold, soldiers lay clutching their rifles, kept awake by the moans of the wounded from both sides. The following morning, the Confederates struck the Union left flank in a series of furious charges. Screaming the Rebel yell, Bragg's men surged up to the Yankees' log breastworks but were blown back by a whirlwind of rifle and canister fire.

Then disaster struck the Union forces. Rosecrans mistakenly ordered one of his divisions out of line to help his left flank, leaving a quarter-mile hole in the blue line. Confederate General James Longstreet chose that moment to hurl five of his divisions directly into the gap. The entire Federal right flank came apart in a panic. The few blue units that stood and fought were overwhelmed by the Confederate tidal wave.

Rosecrans and half his army choked the road back to Chattanooga in a flood of frightened men and panicked horses. But Union Major General George Thomas was not yet ready to leave the bloody slopes—his troops still hung on, grimly defending Snodgrass Hill. They fought nearly every brigade in Bragg's army that afternoon, dwindling from a force of 25,000 to fewer than 10,000. By the end of the day, George Thomas' stubbornness had saved what was left of the Federal army.

SURROUNDED IN CHATTANOOGA. The two days of fighting at Chickamauga Creek had devastated both armies. Their

GUNS AND BULLETS

The soldiers on both sides used a weapon called a "rifled musket." Older muskets from the Revolution and War of 1812 had smooth barrels and fired a round ball. Rifled muskets had longer, thinner, grooved barrels. These spun the conical bullet, or minié ball, so that it traveled farther and more accurately. The old muskets could barely hit a target at 100 yards; the new rifled muskets could shoot accurately up to 500 yards and kill out to a half mile.

Unfortunately for Civil War soldiers, their commanders' tactics did not keep up with their new weapons. In Napoleon's era, soldiers could march in solid ranks up to an enemy's line, absorb maybe just one killing volley, then rush their opponents before much more damage could be done.

Against Civil War rifled muskets, though, men in the attacking column could be killed by the defenders while still half a mile away. A trained infantryman could get off at least two shots a minute, so the attackers would be hit again and again as they tried to close the range. The result, as happened at Chickamauga, was often a slaughter, especially when the defenders fired from behind earthworks.

Cavalrymen shot their opponents from the saddle with revolvers or slashed at riders with sabers. But cavalry were most effective when they fought dismounted, using rapid-firing carbines that could be loaded from the breech, or rear, of the barrel.

Bayonets, the long steel knives attached to the end of a rifle, were used more for appearance than effect in the Civil War. Most troops never got close enough to use them on the enemy. But if a charge did succeed, the defenders would usually run away rather than face a massed bayonet assault.

Union soldiers warm themselves by a small fire. As troops moved farther into enemy territory, their living conditions grew more brutal. More died from disease than from combat.

combined losses in killed, wounded, or captured soared to more than 30,000 men. The survivors of both armies were exhausted. The Yankees staggered safely back into the trenches around Chattanooga. The Confederates rested on the surrounding hills, hoping to starve their enemies into surrender. The hungry and nearly surrounded Union troops were betting their survival on the arrival of Ulysses S. Grant. If he didn't come soon, the game would be up.

> *"...we can die but once. This is the time and place."*
>
> *— Union commander William H. Lytle, killed at Chickamauga*

It took Grant nearly a month to reach Chattanooga. By then the Rebels had choked off nearly all supplies. One reporter wrote: "I have often seen hundreds of soldiers following behind the wagon trains...picking out of the mud the crumbs of bread...shaken loose as the wagons rattled by."

Once in Chattanooga, Grant quickly ordered a surprise night attack to open a new supply route. His grateful men called it "the Cracker Line," after the boxes of "hardtack" (hard crackers) rations that it now delivered. Fresh relief troops flooded in, too, from the Army of the Potomac.

BREAKING THE SIEGE. Grant was soon ready to go after Bragg and end the siege. First, the Union commander ordered Joe Hooker to sweep the Rebels off Lookout Mountain, where their guns pointed down on Chattanooga. On November 24, 1863, Hooker's men shoved the Confederates off Lookout in a fight obscured by a thick fog.

To the east, the main Confederate army looked down on Chattanooga from the heights of Missionary Ridge, strongly held with cannon and infantry. Grant ordered Thomas' troops to create a diversion in front of the ridge. In the meantime, General Sherman could strike Bragg's flank from the right and capture the heights.

Sherman found the heights swarming with Confederates who refused to budge. They pinned the Yankees down under a hail of bullets and cannon fire. Grant ordered Thomas' 25,000 troops to charge to take some of the pressure off Sherman. And Thomas' soldiers, who had saved the day at Chickamauga, once again stunned everyone on both sides.

Their orders were to stop at the base of the ridge, but these Yankees kept on going, scrambling right up the slope of the hill, right into the hotbed of Rebel fire.

Grant protested to Thomas that his men would be slaughtered, but before they could be stopped, the wild Yankee attack rolled right up Missionary Ridge. Men clambered over rocks, grabbed bushes, and stabbed bayonets into the ground as handholds, heading for the Rebel line. The Confederates on the crest panicked, and the Yankees tumbled over the breastworks and sent the defenders flying.

Bragg himself was nearly captured by the Yankees. His army was broken in two. The Confederates had lost another 6,700 men and any hopes they had of retaking Chattanooga. General Grant now had the initiative, and he would never give it back.

The Bleeding War

Alone among Union generals, Grant had been genuinely successful. Lincoln placed him in charge of all Union armies early in 1864.

ON THE MOVE. The Union commander planned out his strategy: Federal forces would make four moves against the Confederate field armies. One Union army would attack up the James River toward Richmond. Another would advance from Harpers Ferry up the Shenandoah Valley to capture this Rebel breadbasket. From Chattanooga, Sherman would march on the rail and industrial center of Atlanta. Grant himself would join Meade for a showdown in Virginia with Robert E. Lee.

Lee's strategy was also a simple one. Since he was outnumbered, he would try to entice Grant into attacking into the teeth of the strong Confederate defenses. Lee hoped he could fight Grant to a bloody draw, inflicting so many casualties that the North would weary of the war's high human cost. If Lincoln were defeated in the upcoming November elections, Lee believed the new government might finally let the Southern states leave the Union in peace.

THE WILDERNESS. George Meade's Army of the Potomac, with Grant directing its movements, crossed Virginia's Rapidan River on May 4, 1864. Grant hoped to march quickly through the tangled, scrubby forest known as the Wilderness, site of the 1863 Union defeat at Chancellorsville. The Union soldiers camped amid the skeletons of those who died in that battle. Their bones had been washed from shallow graves by winter rains.

Lee aimed to catch Grant's 100,000-strong army in this Wilderness. Here the Yankee advantage in numbers—Lee had just 60,000—would be offset by dense woods.

On May 5, Lee's Army of Northern Virginia struck at Grant out of the tangled thickets. The Federals threw them back and counterattacked, but no general, not even Grant, could control an army in such a dense forest. The smoke from a hundred thousand rifles blanketed the thick underbrush, and muzzle flashes in the murk often were the only signs of the enemy.

Veterans remembered the Wilderness for the continuing, deafening roar of musketry—it overwhelmed orders, battle cries, and the screams of the wounded.

Soon, the heavy gunfire and shelling set the dry leaves and brush ablaze on the forest floor. The wounded

PRISONERS OF WAR

In every battle, gray and blue soldiers were left behind, cut off from friendly units or surrounded by enemies in the confusion of battle. If they were unlucky, they wound up as prisoners of war.

Occasionally, whole garrisons surrendered together. At Harpers Ferry, West Virginia, in 1862 during the Antietam campaign, Stonewall Jackson surrounded and captured 12,000 Union troops. Ulysses S. Grant took the "unconditional surrender" of more than 12,000 Confederates at Fort Donelson in Tennessee. All of these men were marched to prison camps, North and South.

Until 1864, these men were held for only a few months before being exchanged. Because most prisoners were held for only a short time, both sides failed to devote much attention to the care of prisoners. In Northern camps, the harsh weather, crowded conditions, and lack of blankets and shelter made thousands of Rebel prisoners sick. At Rock Island, Illinois, 1,800 Confederates died of raging smallpox. In Maryland, at Point Lookout, Rebel prisoners were reduced to catching rats to fill the gaps left by meager rations.

The prisoner exchange system broke down in early 1864, when Confederate authorities refused to free captured black soldiers in exchange for Southern soldiers. Instead, captured blacks were returned to slavery in the South. General Grant ordered a halt to prisoner exchanges.

The Southern camps were, in many cases, not much worse than those up North. But food shortages in the South made conditions very harsh for Union prisoners, especially toward the close of the war. Two camps were particularly infamous. Belle Isle, a muddy pen in the James River in Richmond, was a deathtrap for thousands—90 percent of the survivors weighed less than 100 pounds.

Even worse was Andersonville, in Georgia. Designed for 10,000 prisoners, by August 1864 the stockade held 33,000 Yankees. Diseases, malnutrition, and lack of medical care killed them by the thousands. One day saw Union boys dying at a rate of one every eleven minutes. By war's end, 13,000 prisoners had been buried in Andersonville's mass graves.

General Grant (leaning over bench) consults a map with officers. He now had a hold on Lee's army and would not let go.

who were able crawled desperately to escape the flames. The rest suffocated or burned to death. In the choking smoke and growing darkness, the two armies grappled for position and a little sleep before dawn reignited the fight.

HANCOCK'S CHARGE. The next morning, Union General Winfield Scott Hancock, who had turned back Pickett's Charge at Gettysburg, drove deep into Lee's right flank. The Yankees were within sight of Rebel supply wagons. Robert E. Lee was standing in his stirrups, trying to rally his men at a small farm clearing. For a moment it looked as if Hancock's men would break Lee's army, but Longstreet came up with reinforcements just in time.

Lee tried to lead the Texas Brigade into the fight personally, but the men refused to go in unless Lee pulled himself out of danger. "Lee to the rear! Go back, General Lee, go back! We won't go unless you go back."

Then the Texans charged and drove Hancock's troops back into the thickets. Soon the Yankees were backed up to their own log breastworks, hanging on against the Rebels while the wooden barricades caught fire from the burning underbrush.

Late in the day, Longstreet and Gordon swept out of the Wilderness on both of Grant's flanks, smashing the Union lines on left and right. Only darkness and the acci-

dental wounding of Longstreet (shot by his own men, like Stonewall Jackson the year before) kept Grant's army from defeat at Lee's hands.

NO RETREAT. In two days of confused but savage fighting, Grant's army lost 17,600 men, more than twice Lee's casualties. The Union toll of killed and wounded was

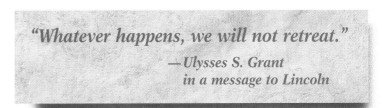

"Whatever happens, we will not retreat."

—*Ulysses S. Grant*
in a message to Lincoln

worse than either Fredericksburg or Chancellorsville. But Grant, with 100,000 men, knew he could absorb such losses. Lee could find no replacements.

In the past, the Army of the Potomac would have retreated after such a savage fight to refit and regroup. But this was a new commander. On the evening of May 7, Grant started his army not north but south, in a move out of the Wilderness and around Lee's right flank. The Union soldiers knew what this meant—they were not turning back. "Our spirits rose," one soldier recalled. "We marched free. The men began to sing."

SPOTSYLVANIA; COLD HARBOR; PETERSBURG

After the blood-letting at the Wilderness, Grant wanted to push past Lee and move on to Richmond. But Lee knew what Grant was after and moved again and again to thwart him.

SPOTSYLVANIA. First Grant marched southeast, aiming for the road junction of Spotsylvania Courthouse. Lee guessed his move and sent two corps racing ahead on parallel roads. The Confederates won the footrace and quickly dug in behind earth and log breastworks.

For the next four days Grant probed at Lee's entrenchments, while the Rebel commander hoped for a chance to smash Grant's attack. On May 12, 1864, Grant sent two army corps—nearly 20,000 men—against a salient, a part of Lee's lines that jutted forward toward the Union army. Charging out of the predawn mist, the Yankees overran the position, breaking Lee's lines wide open. But a desperate counterattack directed by Lee himself stalled the Union attack. The two sides became locked in a brutal struggle that lasted nearly until midnight. One Union general remembered huge trees tumbling to the ground, cut in half from the incessant firing. "We had not only shot down an army, we had shot down a forest...."

Between them the two armies had lost 12,000 men. Early the next morning Lee was forced to order his army to fall back. The Rebels stood ever closer to Richmond, while Grant continued to dog them.

COLD HARBOR. From Spotsylvania, Grant pressed the Army of the Potomac to the southeast, forcing Lee back toward Richmond. While Grant could never trap Lee in the open to finish him off, the Confederate general was weakening in his retreat. The Army of Northern Virginia had lost so many division and corps commanders that Lee could no longer take the offensive—even when good opportunities to defeat Grant presented themselves.

On June 1, the two armies collided again ten miles northeast of Richmond, at a crossroads called Cold Harbor. Once again, Lee had time to dig in before Grant

---

LETTERS HOME

Most of the soldiers in the Civil War were raised in rural America. Some were not formally educated at all; many others were lucky if they got through the eighth grade in a one-room schoolhouse.

It was surprising, then, how many wrote letters home and how frequently they put pen to paper. Just like today, soldiers wrote to break the monotony and to make sure that they received mail in return. Many soldiers tried to put down their most private thoughts on the eve of battle. For too many, these poignant letters became a soldier's last words to his family and friends.

The following letter was written by Major Sullivan Ballou of the Union's 2nd Rhode Island Regiment to his wife in Smithfield.

"Dear Sarah:

The indications are very strong that we shall move in a few days, perhaps tomorrow and lest I should not be able to write again, I feel impelled to write a few lines that may fall under your eye when I shall be no more....

I have no misgiving about, or lack of confidence in the cause in which I am engaged and my courage does not halt or falter. I know how strongly American Civilization now leans on the triumph of the Government, and how great a debt we owe to those who went before us through the blood and sufferings of the Revolution.

And I am willing—perfectly willing—to lay down all my joys in this life, to help maintain this Government, and to pay that debt.

Sarah, my love for you is deathless, it seems to bind me with mighty cables that nothing but Omnipotence can break; and yet my love of Country comes over me like a strong wind and bears me unresistibly with all these chains to the battle field.

But, Oh, Sarah! if the dead can come back to this earth and flit unseen around those they loved, I shall always be near you...and if there be a soft breeze upon your cheek, it shall be my breath, as the cool air fans your throbbing temple, it shall be my spirit passing by. Sarah, do not mourn me dead; think I am gone and wait for me, for we shall meet again...."

Major Ballou did not survive the campaign. He was killed on July 21, 1861.

A Confederate soldier lies dead in the trenches at Petersburg, Virginia. Lee's army held on but could no longer attack.

could strike with his superior numbers. Grant did little to prepare for battle. He simply ordered the troops to advance at dawn. Grant's generals were left to figure out for themselves a way to break through Lee's lines. The lack of a real plan left its impression on the Union ranks. The night before the attack a Union staff officer saw the men "calmly writing their names and home addresses on slips of paper and pinning them on the backs of their coats, so that their bodies might be recognized...."

In the gray light of dawn, half of Grant's army, more than 60,000 men, came pounding toward the Rebel lines, screaming as they ran. When the attackers got within rifle range, Lee's empty-looking trenches suddenly filled with black slouch hats, and muskets appeared over the parapets. All at once, the Rebel lines blazed with a solid sheet of flame. "It seemed more like a volcanic blast than a battle," one Union officer wrote.

The Yankees didn't stand a chance in that crossfire. Only a few made it to the Rebel trenches, and they were quickly thrown back. The attack was a complete failure. In the first eight minutes, 7,000 of Grant's men were killed or wounded. It was the only attack Grant would ever admit regretting.

THE SIEGE OF PETERSBURG.
Just south of Richmond, the town of Petersburg was Lee's lifeline. If Grant could capture its rail lines, he would cut off the Rebel capital and force Lee to come out and fight. Grant's failure at Cold Harbor had convinced him not to try to go through Lee's army. Now he planned yet another march around it.

Grant's army slipped away from Lee in mid-June, dropping down across the James River to come up at Petersburg. On June 15, before Lee could react, 18,000 Yankee troops were approaching the town's hollow defense lines. That evening a regiment brushed aside a few Confederates and captured over a mile of their trenches. Richmond's back door was now wide open.

But it soon slammed shut. Rebel General Beauregard managed to plug the gap, holding the line against a series of badly run Union attacks. On June 18, the lead elements of Lee's army filed into a new defense line closer to Petersburg, throwing up a wall before Grant's advance.

During the rest of that summer of 1864, the two armies dug their parallel trenches farther south and west around Petersburg. Grant tried to cut the rail lines into the city from the south. Lee counterattacked, keeping Union troops from reaching his last two railroads.

In July, Lee sent Jubal Early on a raid into Maryland, hoping to draw Grant off to defend Washington. On July 12, "Old Jube" and his 10,000 gray infantry were inside the District of Columbia, testing the strength of the Union defense lines around the city. Early's men were turned back by reinforcements rushed north by Grant.

Rebels did succeed, however, in bringing President Lincoln under fire as he stood on the walls of Fort Stevens, observing the attack. "Get down, you damn fool!" a Union officer scolded Lincoln as the bullets whizzed by, hitting a man not three feet away.

THE MARCH THROUGH GEORGIA

In early May, General William Tecumseh Sherman moved his 110,000-man army out of Chattanooga into Georgia. There he would take on General Joe Johnston's 45,000 Confederate troops. Sherman's goal was to take the vital rail and industrial center of Atlanta, the Gate City of the South.

SOUTHERN REVENGE. Sherman outnumbered Johnston two to one, but the Confederates were counting on the Southern landscape to aid their defense. The rivers and mountains of northwest Georgia and its blistering heat would pose mean barriers to Sherman's advance. Johnston hoped to bleed the Union army badly enough that Lincoln would lose his bid for reelection. If that happened, the North might agree to talk.

As Johnston had hoped, the Union advance into the deep South was no Sunday picnic. The heat was exhausting. The dust turned blue Union coats to a uniform gray. Even the insects were savage. One Illinois soldier complained in his diary: "They will crawl through any cloth and bite worse than fleas." Desperate soldiers rubbed bacon grease on themselves to keep the pests away.

Still Sherman pressed on, and after a series of indecisive but bloody battles, Johnston's back was to Atlanta. Confederate President Jefferson Davis was never a believer in Johnston's military skills, and he'd had enough of the general's constant retreat in front of Sherman. Davis decided to remove Johnston from command, replacing him with John Bell Hood. Hood was a proven fighter, but he had never commanded a whole army. Now he would have to learn his trade while trying to stop the grim-faced Sherman.

DEFENDING ATLANTA. Hood, who had lost an arm at Gettysburg and a leg at Chattanooga, wasted no time. He immediately attacked the Yankees east and north of the city. Though Hood's forces stunned the Union troops, his bloody frontal attacks were failures. In the battle for Atlanta, Hood lost 12,500 men. He barely had enough to defend the trenches around the city.

Sherman slowly surrounded Atlanta, choking off vital roads and railroads. On September 1, the defeated Hood was forced to abandon the city. He burned the military and rail offices and marched south. The city was now a ghost town. Sherman sent a telegraph to his president: "Atlanta is ours...." The capture of the Southern jewel practically assured Lincoln's reelection.

CIVIL WAR FILMS

In 1915, the War Between the States was the subject of one of the first "epic" movies, a three-hour-long silent film. *Birth of a Nation*, directed by D. W. Griffith, brought the drama of war-torn Northern and Southern

families to the screen. The battle scenes achieved a realism unlike anything seen before. They remain impressive to this day.

But the film was, and is, controversial. D. W. Griffith was a Southerner. He focused on specific Southern attitudes to the war, the South's defeat, and its aftermath. The abolition of slavery, then, is seen as a tragedy. Southern whites are shown suffering under the control of newly freed slaves. Ku Klux Klan members are portrayed as heroes who come to the rescue of defeated white Southerners.

When first released, *Birth of a Nation* aroused serious controversy, but disapproval was tempered. The film's technical and dramatic achievements were stunning. Even those who disagreed with some of the film's content were impressed with its artistic achievement.

In 1939, another Civil War film, *Gone With the Wind*, became one of the most popular Hollywood pictures of all time. Another epic, this film focused on the trials of a selfish Southern woman who survives the Civil War, though most everyone around her keels over. As Atlanta burns and the Confederate army flees, a camera passes over a huge sea of dead and wounded Southern soldiers. After the war, former slaves don't become the enemy. But poor whites do, lording it over the former Southern aristocrats.

It wasn't until 1990 that Hollywood produced another epic on the Civil War. *Glory* (see photo) focused on the true story of the formation of the first all-black regiment in the United States Army. The effects of slavery are plainly seen in the former slave soldiers, but the film celebrates their courage and sacrifice. Here the institution of slavery is seen as the tragedy, the war to end it—righteous.

Atlanta bristled with barricades and guns. But Sherman would crack its defenses and bring Georgia to its knees.

TOTAL WAR. In taking Atlanta, Sherman had destroyed much of the South's ability to supply its soldiers. The Confederacy was now wide open for Sherman's next move—a march across Georgia to the Atlantic.

The general was determined to cut the heart out of Southerners' support for the Confederacy. By scorching their rich farmland and plantations, Sherman also aimed to teach Georgians a lesson they wouldn't forget. "We can make war so terrible," he declared, "and make them so sick of war that generations [will] pass away before they again appeal to it."

With Hood's army no longer a threat, Sherman promised "to make Georgia howl." He began by burning all military buildings within Atlanta. On the night of November 15, he left the rich Gate City of the South in flames. Atlanta, in Sherman's words, was now "a thing of the past."

SACKING GEORGIA. Sherman split his 62,000 troops into two columns. They marched on parallel routes southeast through Georgia. Sherman gave up his supply lines—they would slow him down too much. Instead, he gave his troops permission to "forage liberally on the country."

His men took him at his word, scavenging for food, looting every plantation in their path. "We had a gay old campaign," one Union private recalled. "Destroyed all we could not eat, burned their cotton and gins, spilled their sorghum (molasses),...burned and twisted their railroads and raised Hell, generally."

On December 20, the Union army captured the seacoast city of Savannah. The campaign across Georgia had been one of the most daring, successful, and

"War is the remedy our enemies have chosen, and I say, let us give them all they want...."

— General William Tecumseh Sherman

destructive in military history. In her diary of the war, Mary Chestnut wrote: "They say no living thing is found in Sherman's track, only chimneys, like telegraph poles, to carry the news of [his] attack backwards."

"War is hell," said Sherman, and he clearly practiced what he preached. But the bitter legacy of the general's march to the sea would be remembered for generations.

THE ROAD TO APPOMATTOX

Lee's Army of Northern Virginia spent the last half of 1864 and the winter of 1865 pinned down in trenches around Petersburg and Richmond. Grant, with 125,000 men, had Lee's 55,000 soldiers in a slow stranglehold. The armies were locked together. Grant was unwilling to waste his men in a frontal assault, while Lee didn't have the strength to try for a breakout.

BREAKING THE DEADLOCK.

Grant was trying to curl around Lee's southern flank and cut off his supplies. The Rebels kept fending him off, but their lines were thinning.

All over the country, Southerners were losing battles. The soldiers in the trenches couldn't help but lose heart as they read reports of losses in the Shenandoah and Tennessee—not to mention Sherman's advance through Georgia. Lee's army was tired and sick. Men were deserting. Fewer supplies were making it to the front lines.

With spring coming Lee knew that he had to act. His plan was to break away from Grant's grip and march south to join Joe Johnston, now facing Sherman in North Carolina. Lee hoped the combined Rebel armies could smash Sherman's force. Then they could wheel north to deal with Grant. It was the only hope Lee had.

THE GAMBLE FAILS.

On March 25, Lee launched an attack against the Union Fort Stedman. He hoped to divert Grant long enough to get a running start south. The breakout failed, though, and a week later Grant had cut off Lee's last rail supply line. Lee let Jefferson Davis know that he'd better take his government out of Richmond.

Lee now raced to keep his army alive. He drove his battered troops, now down to 25,000, westward toward Lynchburg, Virginia, and the rail line to North Carolina. His men had little food. They were weak from months in the trenches. Now they were desperately trying to escape the Federals closing in from the south and east.

Grant sent Philip Sheridan's cavalry to get ahead of Lee. The fast horsemen captured Lee's wagon train and scooped up railcars filled with the food the Rebels so desperately needed.

Trying to buy time, half of Lee's army tried to beat the Union infantry back at Saylor's Creek on April 6. All but a few of the barefoot, hungry, and exhausted Rebels were fought out. The Rebel lines collapsed. More than 6,000 Confederates were captured—a quarter of Lee's dwindling army.

Sheridan telegraphed Grant: "If the thing is pressed, I think that Lee will surrender." In Washington, Lincoln read the message, too, and replied: "Let the thing be pressed."

ROBERT E. LEE

Lee was fifty-four when the war began and widely regarded as the best soldier in the United States Army. After Fort Sumter was attacked, General Winfield Scott offered him command of all Union forces. But Lee could not bring himself to fight against his own Virginians. He resigned from the U.S. Army to command his home state's forces. The Confederacy now had the Union's best general. The South's military fortunes would soon be tied to Lee's brilliance on the field.

Lee's fame from his many victories and his deep sense of dignity made him a legend even during the war. Later, he became the lofty symbol of the South's lost cause. But, in fact, he was simply a superb general, both on the attack and in defense.

His campaign at Chancellorsville is considered a model of military field tactics. He often gambled by splitting his army, even when outnumbered, to gain the advantage. He was a good judge of just how much risk to take.

Still, Lee did make mistakes. At Gettysburg, the charge he ordered against General Meade's line turned into a disaster for the Rebels. But it was General Grant who proved to be the Union commander that Lee could not overwhelm. It wasn't that Lee didn't understand Grant. He did. But Grant also understood Lee and knew how to beat him.

Lee's greatest gift to the restored Union, perhaps, was the way he made peace. Just before Appomattox, some urged him to scatter his army to the hills. From there they could fight a guerrilla war against the Union. But Lee refused—he knew that the war was over and peace had to be made.

Lee had never wanted this terrible struggle with the North. "I can anticipate no greater calamity for the country than the dissolution of the Union," he said before the war began.

Richmond blazed as Rebel troops fled. The war had left much of the South in cinders.

END OF THE LINE. Lee brought his ragtag army into Appomattox Courthouse. Here was a quiet country village near a rail stop where rations for the troops were waiting. His men hardly looked like soldiers anymore. "Their clothes [were] all tattered and covered with mud, their eyes sunken and lusterless," one Confederate officer remembered. Yet these survivors were still willing to go on, still "waiting for General Lee to say where they were to face about and fight."

> *"There is nothing left for me to do but to go and see General Grant...[and] I would rather die a thousand deaths."*
>
> *—Robert E. Lee*

Courage alone, though, could not carry them. Sheridan had swept in front of Lee and captured their supplies. At dawn on April 9, Lee's men drove back the front line of Union cavalry. But behind them lay a solid wall of blue—it was the Union Army of the James. Lee's troops were hemmed in on all sides.

THE GENERALS MEET. Under a white flag of truce, Lee asked to meet with Grant to discuss surrender terms. The two generals met that afternoon in the home of Wilmer McLean. McLean was a Virginian who had fled his old home near Bull Run to escape the war's destruction. Now it had followed him here.

Lee arrived first, mounted on his horse, Traveller. He was wearing an elegant dress gray uniform. When Grant arrived, he was dressed in a private's dirty shirt and a plain blue coat. His trousers and boots were spattered with mud.

After some small talk about their experiences in the Mexican War, the two commanders got down to business. Grant recognized that this surrender would set the tone for the restoration of the Union—he wanted no bitterness or humiliation. He offered to let officers keep their own baggage and side arms. Confederate soldiers could keep their own horses. Grant wrote further that "each officer and man will be allowed to return to his home, not to be disturbed by United States authorities." Grant made arrangements for Lee's soldiers to be given food, then the two generals parted.

FINAL WORDS. Lee's men mobbed him after the surrender. Tears flowed down their faces. They couldn't believe the long war was actually lost. "Boys," he told them, "I have done the best I could for you. Go home now, and if you make as good citizens as you have soldiers, you will do well, and I shall always be proud of you."

The Union soldiers began to cheer the victory, and artillery began to boom salutes. Grant ordered it stopped. "We did not want to exult over their downfall," he wrote. "The war [was] over. The rebels [were] our countrymen again."

Lee's Army of Northern Virginia stacked arms and surrendered its battle flags on April 12, 1865. By the end of June, all Confederate forces had laid down their arms.

AFTERMATH

No U.S. holiday celebrates the Union victory over the Confederacy. The Civil War was too hard and complicated for that. The wounds went too deep. The victory was bought in American blood on both sides.

Even after Appomattox, the war did not end easily. The South's other armies were still fighting, though most Confederates realized that the struggle was over. Lee's army, surrendered at Appomattox, had been the best hope for their cause. The surrender sent a thudding shock throughout the South. "We are scattered, stunned," wrote Mary Chestnut in her diary. "…Only the dead heroes left stiff and stark on the battlefield escape."

SHOCK AND MURDER. The shock of surrender in the South was followed by another shudder in the North.

President Lincoln, fresh from celebrating the war's end, was shot dead by an assassin. His murderer, John Wilkes Booth, was an actor and Confederate sympathizer.

Booth and his fellow conspirators had hoped to kill both Lincoln and Ulysses Grant as they attended a play in Washington's Ford's Theater. But Grant was not able to attend, and Lincoln was Booth's sole target. Shot from behind, the president was carried across the street and died the next morning on April 15.

The conspirators, including one woman, were hunted down, tried, and hanged. Booth was shot after being cornered in a Virginia barn. He saw the assassination as his chance to strike back at the Union. "Our country owed all our troubles to [Lincoln]," Booth said. "God…made me the instrument of his punishment."

For many, Lincoln's murder was a shock beyond belief. The president's body was carried by train across the North and back to Springfield, Illinois, for burial. The funeral procession retraced the route Lincoln took to Washington for his 1861 inauguration. Lincoln's parting words before leaving Illinois were haunting: "I now leave not knowing when or whether ever I may return."

A NEW ERA. With Lincoln's death, Andrew Johnson assumed office and continued the work of bringing the South back into the Union. With the bitterness produced by Lincoln's assassination, the healing of the country was made even more difficult.

ULYSSES S. GRANT

Grant was the most successful Union general of the Civil War. An 1843 graduate of West Point, Grant didn't stand out as a cadet. During the Mexican War, though, he proved his military savvy in a variety of assignments.

Peacetime, however, brought hard times to Grant. He failed to provide a living for his family both as a farmer and a businessman and took to drinking. The Civil War, a tragedy for the nation, turned out to be Grant's salvation. Soon he was commanding volunteers on the Western rivers.

At the core of Grant's success was his steely self-confidence. He never lost his faith that he'd come up a winner in battle. After a shockingly bloody first day at Shiloh, William T. Sherman found his friend, dripping wet and exhausted, under a tree. "Well, Grant," Sherman said, "we've had the devil's own day, haven't we?" "Yes," Grant answered. "Lick 'em tomorrow." And so he did, driving the Confederates from the field.

Grant's belief in aggressive attacks was not popular with everyone. After the shocking casualties at Shiloh, Grant's commander, Henry Halleck, had him removed from command, and Grant considered resigning. But the war was Grant's destiny, and he returned to go after the Army of Northern Virginia, and its legendary commander, Robert E. Lee.

Grant refused to be rattled by Lee's reputation for chewing up Federal commanders. One historian called it "four-o'clock-in-the-morning courage—you could wake up Grant at four in the morning, tell him Lee had just turned his right flank, and he would be as cool as a cucumber."

During the terrible fighting in the Wilderness in 1864, Grant had that coolness—in spades. He pulled up a seat on a log and whittled on a stick, occasionally giving orders to direct the battle. He never retreated from Lee, just kept dogging him south, waiting for an opening.

Finally Lee had no choice but to surrender. Grant's determination to wage war to the finish, whatever the cost, made him our first general who understood and practiced modern warfare.

All across the South, the armies of the Confederacy continued to surrender, one after another. Jefferson Davis fled south into Georgia, hoping to keep some form of Rebel government alive. Union cavalry finally captured him on May 10, 1865.

He was held for the next two years in a damp cell in Fortress Monroe, Virginia. Remarkably, he was never tried for treason against the United States.

The last battle of the war was fought on May 13, at Palmito Ranch in far south Texas. Ironically, it was a Confederate victory.

A TRAGIC HOMECOMING. As if the long war had not brought enough misery, yet another catastrophe struck freed Union prisoners heading home. Crowded onto a Mississippi steamboat, most of the soldiers were asleep when the ship's boiler exploded. More than 1,700 men drowned or burned to death.

Across the South, thousands of ragged, hungry Confederate soldiers also made their way home. Veterans were often forced to beg or steal their food. Too many returned to find a burned-out chimney, a ruined farm, and their families scattered by invading Yankees.

The armies were soon gone. After a grand review through the streets of Washington in May 1865, the Union armies shrank from a million men to just 80,000 a year later. Still, the effects of war lingered for decades and were felt most strongly by the newly freed slaves.

PROMISE OF FREEDOM. The 620,000 lost lives had restored the severed Union. The national bloodletting had freed 4 million people from the cross of slavery. But that freedom took nearly a century to realize.

> *"It seems to me that I have been dreaming a horrid nightmare for four years, and now the nightmare is over."*
>
> —Abraham Lincoln, April 3, 1865, twelve days before his death

Though the 13th Amendment to the Constitution, passed in February 1865, had legally freed the slaves, the restored Southern states enacted laws after the war that took back many expressions of that freedom. Blacks, denied most legal and political rights, were forced into a separate society. It was a world of back doors, servitude, threats, and lynchings for many of those set "free." Many emigrated to the North or into Western territories.

Not until the Civil Rights struggle of the 1960s did black Americans win equal voting rights and a chance at a decent education. The fight to preserve and expand those rights continues today.

The balcony at Ford's Theater where Lincoln was shot. His death meant a harsher peace for the South, and more bitterness throughout the nation.

SOUTHERN OCCUPATION. The South saw its economy and way of life shattered by the war. Its political power was all but gone. Reconstruction, in part, a postwar occupation of the South, continued for twelve years. Congress divided the South, except Tennessee, into five military districts, and federal troops were sent in to monitor them. Though Reconstruction ended in 1877, the South did not immediately resume its former place in the political life of the country. Only in 1912 was a Southerner, Virginia-born Woodrow Wilson, again elected to the presidency.

FEDERAL CHANGES. In the victorious North, the federal government had changed forever. Prior to the war, the only federal agency that touched most citizens' lives was the post office. By 1865, the government in Washington had created a national paper currency (greenbacks) and a national banking system. It had even started the first national social welfare system—the Freedmen's Bureau, designed to aid freed slaves in the postwar South. This expansion of federal power has continued—and is argued about—to the present day.

THE INDIAN WARS

Several Indian tribes sided with the British in the American Revolution. Colonists fought bitter battles with Native Americans north and south. When the war ended, the U.S. government threw its military power against all "hostile" Indians as the frontier moved west. The conflict against Native Americans was bitter and long. It was a battle Americans would win with some of the most brutal campaigns seen on the continent.

PRELUDE TO WAR

Trouble between Indians and European-Americans began long before the United States—as a nation—was formed in 1787. The troubles, in fact, go right back to that first invader, Christopher Columbus. The Italian/Spanish explorer was the first to meet the peoples he incorrectly called "Indians."

CONFLICTING CIVILIZATIONS. Though Columbus was charmed by his encounter with the friendly Taino in the West Indies, he was also the first European to enslave Native Americans and punish those who could not meet his demands. The peaceable Taino would be driven to near extinction in a matter of years after Columbus' arrival.

Similar tragedies followed. The Spanish crushed the great civilizations of the Maya, Inca, and Aztec, then went on to decimate tribes in California and Florida.

Troubles between Native Americans and Northern Europeans began right after the first settlement at Jamestown, in 1607. Settlers turned against the Powhatan in Virginia, stealing their lands and forcing them to live on the first reservations. After a series of massacres instigated by both settlers and Powhatan, English forces massacred the entire Powhatan population in 1644.

More bad blood followed in New England. In the 1630s, Puritans killed hundreds of Pequot and took their lands. After a long war with the Wampanoag, settlers took their lands and sold the Indians into slavery.

TRADING PARTNERS. Ironically, Europeans continued to have strong trading relationships with most eastern Indian tribes. Indians traded furs for manufactured goods, especially clothing and weapons. Trade with whites changed Indian dress, weapons, diet, and even lifestyle. Trading was so prosperous that many Indians began to rely on it as the source of much of their wealth.

Europeans, too, profited much from the relationship. Indians taught settlers about native plants and how to farm in the New World. Indian medicine proved a useful tool for some New World ills. Indians served as valued scouts and guides for explorers like Lewis and Clark and others who followed them into the West. Before long, the image of the feathered Indian brave came to stand for America's spirit of freedom.

By the mid-1700s, however, New World colonists were turning against many Indian tribes. George Washington himself became famous battling them in the French and Indian War. Thomas Jefferson, who had once expressed admiration for Indian customs, labeled them "savages" in the Declaration of Independence.

The situation didn't get any better when Britain enlisted Indians to battle the colonists during the Revolution. Many eastern tribes were quite willing to lend a hand in fighting the new Americans. War brought the possibility of reclaiming lost hunting grounds from the intruders. British soldiers, at least, could be expected to go home.

For the Americans, Britain's Indian allies were a mortal enemy. And Washington's armies showed no mercy in retaliating against them.

1776–1800	1801–1820		1821–1850
War Against the Iroquois [American Revolution]	Tecumseh's Rebellion [Shawnee] Battle of Tippecanoe *(Nov. 8, 1811)*	First Seminole War *(1816–1818)*	Black Hawk War *(Sac and Fox)*
Little Turtle's War [Miami and Shawnee] *(1790–1794)*	Creek Wars *(1813–1814)*	Battle at Negro Fort *(July 27, 1816)*	Cherokee Forced March from Georgia *(1838)*
Battle of Wabash River *(Nov. 4, 1791)*	Battle/Massacre at Fort Mims, Alabama *(Aug. 30, 1813)*		Second Seminole War *(1835–1841)*
Battle of Fallen Timbers *(Aug. 20, 1794)*	Battle of Horseshoe Bend *(March 27, 1814)*		

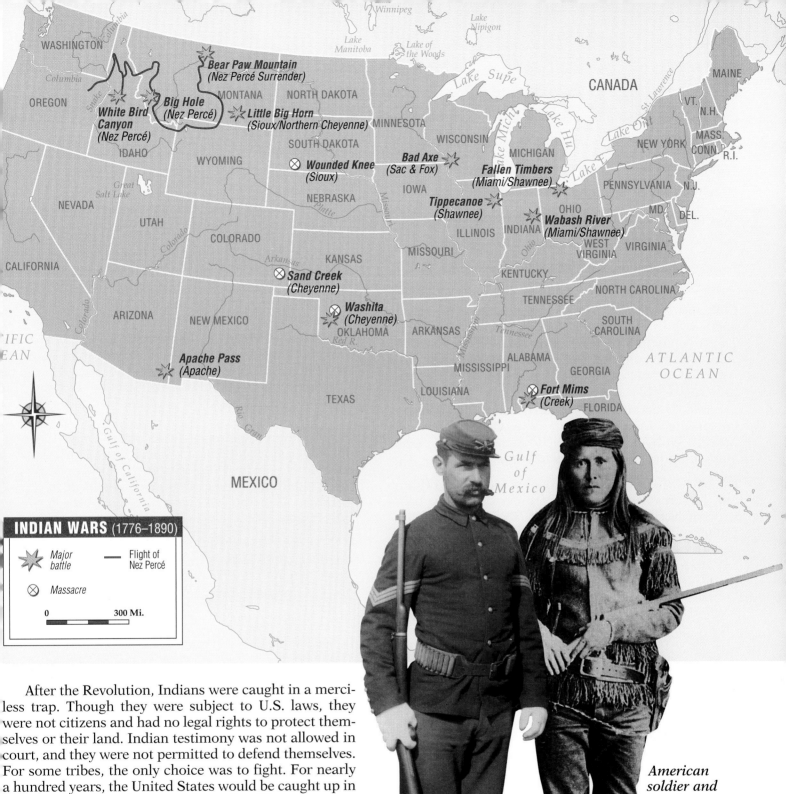

INDIAN WARS (1776–1890)

Major battle

Flight of Nez Percé

Massacre

0   300 Mi.

After the Revolution, Indians were caught in a merciless trap. Though they were subject to U.S. laws, they were not citizens and had no legal rights to protect themselves or their land. Indian testimony was not allowed in court, and they were not permitted to defend themselves. For some tribes, the only choice was to fight. For nearly a hundred years, the United States would be caught up in a series of conflicts known as the Indian Wars.

American soldier and Apache scout

1851–1870

Apache Wars *(1861–1886)*

Battle at Apache Pass *(July 15, 1862)*

Sioux-American War *(1862–1865)*

Battle at Wood Lake *(Sept. 23, 1862)*

Cheyenne Massacre at Sand Creek *(Nov. 29, 1864)*

Southern Plains Indian Wars [Arapaho, Comanche, Kiowa, Sioux, Southern Cheyenne] *(1864–1875)*

Battle/Massacre at Washita River *(Nov. 27, 1868)*

1871–1890

Sioux War [Sioux and Northern Cheyenne]

Battle of the Little Bighorn *(June 25, 1876)*

Battle of Wolf Mountain *(Jan. 1877)* Crazy Horse surrenders.

The Nez Percé Indian War and flight *(July–Oct. 1877)*

Battle of Big Hole *(Aug. 9–10, 1877)*

Apache Wars Geronimo surrenders *(Sept. 4, 1886)*

Sioux Massacre at Wounded Knee *(Dec. 29, 1890)*

THE EARLY WARS

The British turned to the Indians for help during the American Revolution because they could rely on them more than any of their other allies. When General Burgoyne put a call out for troops to help invade the colonies from Canada in 1777, only a few American Loyalists showed up. But 1,400 Indians answered the call.

IROQUOIS ALLIANCE. The strongest alliance the British had was with the Iroquois Nation in western New York. The tribe created so many problems for the American colonists during the early part of the war that Washington ordered General John Sullivan to lay waste to Iroquois settlements in 1779.

Sullivan and his men followed their orders, destroying forty-one Indian towns and savaging crops ready for harvest. Without shelter, their food supplies destroyed, many Iroquois starved to death during the winter.

BRITISH AGITATION. The Iroquois were not Britain's only Indian allies. The British army had also paid tribes in what was then the Northwest Territory (now Ohio, Indiana, Illinois, Wisconsin, and part of Minnesota) to terrorize American settlers there.

After the Revolution, most tribes in the northeast made peace. But in what was then Northwest Territory,

Tecumseh is killed at the Battle of the Thames. His death put an end to the idea of a broad alliance of native tribes.

trouble was still brewing. The British had agreed to evacuate their posts along the Ohio-Indiana border after the war. But they had not. Instead, they continued to supply arms to the Indians in the area, particularly the Miami and Shawnee. The British encouraged them to harass the Americans.

LITTLE TURTLE'S WAR. The Northwest Territory had been "federalized," or taken under U.S. control, in 1787. In 1790, its governor, General Arthur St. Clair, sent Brigadier General Josiah Harmar with 1,500 men to try and scare the Indians into submission. But the plan backfired. The Miami, led by Chief Little Turtle, along with the Shawnee, under Chief Blue Jacket, attacked and defeated the force that was supposed to "intimidate" them.

Soon another army was sent to build a fort to defend against the Indians. St. Clair brought 2,300 men up to the Wabash River about 100 miles from Cincinnati. The soldiers camped peaceably there overnight, but at dawn the Miami and Shawnee attacked. The untrained militia panicked. More than half of St. Clair's army was destroyed—637 were killed outright.

The United States was humiliated. It had succeeded in defeating the powerful British army only to be outdone by frontier Indians. President Washington had had enough. He charged Major General Anthony Wayne to form and train a competent army to challenge the forces of Little Turtle. In 1794, the general took his army up to Fort Miami, a British post built on American territory.

BATTLE OF FALLEN TIMBERS. Chief Blue Jacket and his warriors were hidden in a ravine along the Maumee River where white water flowed. Windstorms had downed trees by the ravine, giving it the name Fallen Timbers.

Wayne's army was late in arriving. Weak from hunger, some of the Indians went off in search of food. This gave the general some advantage when he finally arrived on August 20.

Wayne formed his lines along the ravine and drove forward, bayonets flashing. The Indians were forced into the open. Hundreds were speared through and left dying in the ravine. The rest were driven back. Wayne didn't pursue them into Canada, but he and his men destroyed their villages and crops on the American side.

The following year the chiefs and their warriors abandoned their resistance. They agreed to cede to the United States much of what would become the states of Indiana and Ohio. Little Turtle's war, a conflict that surprised everyone, was over.

MORE U.S. TERRITORY. In 1803, President Thomas Jefferson concluded the Louisiana Purchase, enlarging U.S. territory by one third. Jefferson began a process of relocating the Indians to the West, ignoring the fact that other tribes were already living there.

Jefferson at first believed he could relocate the

*Bring me the Scalps
and the King our master
will reward you....*

*Reward for
Sixteen
Scalps*

A cartoon shows British officials paying for American scalps. Scalping and massacres were committed by both sides.

Indians peaceably through negotiation. One of the main negotiators was the governor of the Indiana Territory, William Henry Harrison. Harrison had complete disdain for the Indians, and his negotiations with them were intimidating and possibly deceitful. Harrison "bought" much of Ohio, Indiana, Illinois, and sections of Wisconsin and Michigan—all for about a penny an acre.

> *"Is one of the fairest portions of the globe to remain...the haunt of a few wretched savages?"*
>
> —William Henry Harrison, 1810

TECUMSEH'S REBELLION. One person who opposed turning over any Indiana territory to the United States was the Shawnee chief Tecumseh. He railed at the idea of exchanging Shawnee homelands for money. "Sell a country! Why not sell the air, the clouds and the great sea?"

Tecumseh had fought in Little Turtle's uprising and his father and an older brother had been killed in battles with settlers. The chief was a powerful thinker; even Harrison called him an "uncommon genius." Tecumseh saw the swelling tide of land-grabbing Americans and knew that they could not be stopped by individual tribes. Instead, Tecumseh believed that the Indian nations must unite against the settlers. He believed it was the only chance for Indian survival.

Tecumseh traveled north to the Great Lakes and south to Florida. He gathered a host of tribes who were willing to oppose the Americans. However, Harrison wasn't blind to what Tecumseh was doing. In November 1811, at the Battle of Tippecanoe, he torched the chief's stronghold on the Wabash River, dealing a powerful blow to united Indian resistance.

BRITISH ALLIES. In 1812, the United States was once again at war with Britain. Tecumseh believed this new war might be the Indians' last and best chance. He urged his fellow Indians to ally with the British and oppose the Americans. "[They]," he said, "are our eternal foes, the hungry devourers of the country...."

Tecumseh and the British fought the Americans in the Great Lakes region from 1812 to 1814. Although there was no clear-cut victory, in the end Britain sacrificed its claims to Indiana territory. For the Indians, the War of 1812 was a dead loss. During a battle in 1813, Tecumseh was killed. The great dream of uniting Indian tribes to save Indian lands bled away in the great Shawnee chief's defeat.

THE INDIAN REMOVALS

When the War of 1812 ended in 1815, Indian tribes in the Southeast—like those in the Northeast—were at a decided disadvantage.

THE FIVE TRIBES. The Creek had long-established trading relationships with Americans. But they, too, had been pushed back from their Atlantic coastlands, and some had turned violently against the increasing waves of settlers. In August of 1813, a mixed-blood Creek led an attack on Fort Mims on the Alabama river, killing 400 settlers. In 1814, General Andrew Jackson led the Tennessee militia in a battle against the Creek at Horseshoe Bend in Alabama. The Indians were beaten decisively. Afterward they were forced to turn over 23 million acres of Creek land to the United States. Worse was to come.

The Creek were part of a group known to Americans as the "Five Civilized Tribes." This group also included the Cherokee, Chickasaw, Choctaw, and Seminole. These five tribes lived a more settled existence than some other Indian nations and relied on farming and trading for their income. They practiced and accepted many European traditions.

RELOCATION WEST. The Civilized Tribes farmed on rich land that American settlers envied. In 1825, President James Monroe suggested moving all these eastern tribes to west of the Mississippi River. This meant relocating nearly 100,000 Indians—residents of seven states—who were clearly settled on lands they owned. Moving them, said Monroe, would prevent more "wars between them and the United States."

In more than one sense, Monroe was correct. The "war" for Indian lands was already on. In Georgia the government held lotteries for Indian lands. In other areas, settlers squatted on or stole tribal lands, attacking Indians who tried to reclaim what was legally theirs. In 1829, gold was discovered on Cherokee land in northeast Georgia. The pressure to take Indian lands now became a frenzy. The Cherokee appealed to the U.S. government for protection. They received none.

Instead, in 1830, Andrew Jackson, now president, proposed the Indian Removal Act. In accordance with Monroe's suggestion, the law would move all Indians west of the Mississippi. Jackson's act was extremely popular with Southern settlers and others interested in staking claim to Indian lands. But many saw it for what it was, pure and simple theft.

Congress passed the bill by a close vote: 103 to 97. President Jackson signed the Indian Removal Act into law on May 28, 1830. The Choctaw were the first to go, abandoning their homes and farms on 10.5 million acres of ground. Thirteen thousand made the 400-mile journey accompanied by U.S. soldiers (see map). Some rode on wagons; others walked. Trudging from the early winter into the spring, some froze to death. Others survived the bitter cold only to be stricken with deadly cholera and smallpox in the spring.

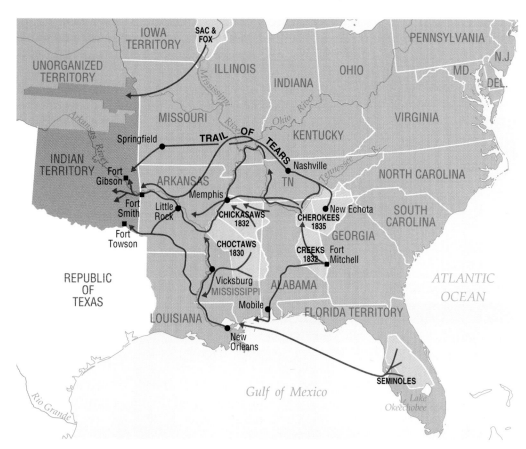

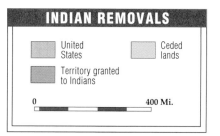

INDIAN REMOVALS

United States	Ceded lands
Territory granted to Indians	

0   400 Mi.

A cartoon shows the "body" of the Cherokee nation being taken apart. Indian tribes were being pushed into the West.

CHEROKEE DEFENSE. Both the Chickasaw and the Creek migrated west after giving up much of their land. But the Cherokee resisted relocation—and theirs was a strong case. Cherokee rights in Georgia were protected under a series of treaties. An agreement signed in 1785 made

> "We have crowded the tribes upon a few miserable acres of our Southern frontier; it is all that is left to them of their once boundless forests; and still,...our insatiated cupidity cries, give! give! give!"
>
> —A New Jersey senator

Cherokee lands off-limits to non-Indians. Two later treaties signed in the 1790s reaffirmed the boundaries of the Cherokee lands.

In a major Supreme Court decision, the Cherokee claim was upheld by the Court in 1832. In 1838, however, President Martin Van Buren ordered the tribe removed from Georgia. United States soldiers rounded up 17,000 Cherokee and placed them in concentration camps. A few weeks later the Cherokee began a thousand-mile journey to their new home west of the Mississippi. Like the Choctaw and Chickasaw before them, many would die along the journey. Others would only wish for death as they struggled along the "Trail of Tears."

SEMINOLE DEFEAT. The Seminole, another of the Civilized Tribes, also found themselves threatened with removal during the 1830s. These Indians, along with large numbers of escaped slaves, had battled U.S. forces in Florida in 1816–1818. At Negro Fort on the Apalachicola River, 300 blacks allied with the Seminole were attacked by American forces. Negro Fort was destroyed and almost all of its defenders killed.

In 1835, a long guerrilla war between the Seminole and U.S. forces began. Led by Osceola, the Indians again allied with runaway slaves to battle the Americans. Though the war was long, most of the Seminole were defeated and removed to Oklahoma. However, quite a few managed to retreat into the impenetrable Everglades and were never captured.

BLACK HAWK WAR. The Civilized Tribes were not the only Indians to resist the law. In 1832, the Sac and Fox, led by Chief Black Hawk, returned to their former hunting grounds east of the Mississippi in Illinois. The Sac and Fox had been removed from these lands in the 1820s. Now they were starving and searching for food.

State militia and U.S. Army troops were called in. Black Hawk and his Sac and Fox were chased across the Mississippi. The following year, the Sac and Fox ceded (gave up) 6 million acres of land and were moved to Indian Territory.

WAR FOR THE PLAINS

When Indian nations like the Cherokee and Creek were relocated across the Mississippi, they were not moving onto uninhabited lands. The American Plains were home to many other tribes, including the Cheyenne, Arapaho, Kiowa, Comanche, Crow, and Lakota.

ROAD TO THE WEST. The Plains Indians now faced battles with relocated tribes as well as their traditional enemies. In addition, their lands were now being encroached upon by more and more settlers.

In 1851, the United States had promised to pay yearly fees to tribes that allowed settlers to pass through their territories. Soon after, the U.S. divided the Nebraska Territory and encouraged new settlement there. The multiplying numbers of migrating Americans were coming now from both the far West and the East. Some had even tried to take land within Indian Territory (see main map on page 74).

Tensions reached fever pitch after gold was discovered in the Rocky Mountains in 1858. Miners poured in. In 1859 alone, 100,000 new settlers arrived. The unending river of immigrants was more than some Indians could take. Cheyenne and Arapaho warriors took to raiding white settlements in the dark of night.

The raids were swift and brutal. Miners and ranchers

Custer's scout, Curly. The U.S. Army relied heavily on Indian scouts for intelligence and tracking. Indian cooperation was a factor in Indian defeat.

were killed and scalped. Women and children were often captured. Men who were taken alive fared the worst. Plains Indians, according to their custom, almost always tortured male victims to death.

SETTLEMENT REACHED. Indian raids, particularly the incidents of kidnapping and torture, led the Plains settlers to plead for help from the government. But U.S. soldiers were soon too busy battling the Confederates in the Civil War.

In the summer of 1864, Indian raids reached a brutal peak. Stagecoaches were routinely ambushed. Settlers could not even collect their crops from the fields. Colorado Governor John Evans appealed for help from the U.S. Army but was turned down. Instead he received permission to form a volunteer regiment. Most of his Colorado volunteers were hard-drinking miners. They were determined to make all Indians—even innocent ones—pay for the suffering of settlers.

In the late autumn of 1864, Governor Evans met with Black Kettle, a Cheyenne leader who was interested in negotiating a settlement. With Evans was Colonel John M. Chivington, commander of the Colorado Volunteers. Evans insisted that the Indians cease their raids, surrender their weapons, and move onto a reservation.

Black Kettle and his band agreed to the provisions. The Indians were told to report to Fort Lyon. This the Cheyenne did, along with a few Arapaho. Once at the fort, they were told to make camp at Sand Creek, a short distance away.

SAND CREEK MASSACRE. The Cheyenne believed that their agreement with Evans would protect them. Colonel Chivington, however, hated all Indians and didn't believe that they would keep their promise. Now that he was in control, Chivington would make sure they wouldn't get a chance to try.

On November 29, 1864, Chivington, along with 700 troops, rode out to Sand Creek. Perched on the banks above the Indian village, they immediately began to set up howitzers to fire into the camp. The Cheyenne, seeing the soldiers and their guns, were struck with terror. But Black Kettle, believing the camp was safe, tried to calm them. The Cheyenne chief even raised a white truce flag and the Stars and Stripes from his tepee. No flag of truce, however, could stop Chivington's murderous rage. He ordered his men to attack, instructing them to take no prisoners.

Rifle and howitzer fire poured down on the helpless Cheyenne, most of them women and children. Chivington's cavalry overran the camp. Goaded on by the colonel, the regiment slaughtered the Cheyenne. Troops gutted women and crushed the heads of infants with their rifle butts. The pitiful victims were then ritually scalped.

Chivington was openly proud of the murdering spree. The scalps of his hapless victims were put on display in Denver. Not everyone, though, thought the offi-

A soldier relaxes in his tent. After the Civil War, the U.S. Army turned its attention to the total defeat of the Indians.

cer's work was a triumph. Even Kit Carson, who had been in his share of Indian battles, was shocked: "And ye call these civilized men and the Indians savages?"

After an investigation by Congress, Chivington was forced to resign from the military. His principal target, Black Kettle, managed to escape the massacre.

PUNISHED FOR SOUTHERN SYMPATHY.

In 1865, the Civil War ended. One of the first moves of President Andrew Johnson's government was to punish Indians who had sided with the South. The Five Civilized Tribes had supported the Confederacy. In retaliation, the U.S. government took away half of their lands in Indian Territory.

> *"The Government of the United States desires peace, and its honor is hereby pledged to keep it."*
>
> — *Fort Laramie Treaty*
> *signed in April 1868*

The United States was now free to turn its full attention to the other Indian conflicts, especially those with the Cheyenne. The Cheyenne, along with the Sioux, Arapaho, Comanche, and Kiowa, had been staging massive attacks and raiding settlements in Kansas and Colorado since 1864. A treaty had been signed with the Cheyenne at Fort Laramie in 1868, but Cheyenne "dog soldiers" continued to raid. The Civil War's end freed the U.S. Army's most experienced generals for plains duty. One of these was Philip Sheridan, who had studied warfare among Plains Indians. He knew that tribes seldom waged war in winter. During these bitter months on the prairie, their supplies were lowest and their animals weakest. Sheridan determined to strike the Indians when they were most vulnerable.

BATTLE AT WASHITA RIVER.

Lieutenant Colonel George Armstrong Custer was ready to test Sheridan's idea. Late in November 1868, Custer brought 800 soldiers of the 7th U.S. Cavalry into the Oklahoma Panhandle. Riding all night through deep snow, they arrived at the banks of the Washita River where Black Kettle camped with his Cheyenne.

Just before dawn, the cavalry pounded into the Cheyenne village. Sleepy and shocked, the dazed warriors tried to defend their families. But Custer's men slashed them with sabers and rifle fire. The banks of the Washita were soaked in blood.

Chief Black Kettle was killed along with more than 100 of his tribe. Custer burned the Cheyenne blankets and food and destroyed what was left of the camp.

By summer of 1875, the tribes of the Southern Plains had been rounded up and herded onto reservations. Many were placed on land in Indian Territory taken from the Five Civilized Tribes. Soon, even portions of these lands would be taken away and sold to settlers.

THE LITTLE BIGHORN

The Lakota, or Sioux, people arrived on the plains of South Dakota around the time of the American Revolution. The land was used by the Arikara, Kiowa, Cheyenne, and Crow. The forceful Lakota pushed back the other tribes and carved out a home for themselves. By the 1860s, though, new settlers were putting pressure on the Lakota for their land.

SANTEE SIOUX REVOLT. More and more conflicts developed between the Indians and the European settlers. Cheated by traders and given spoiled food rations, the Sioux had been pushed to the limit. The Santee leader Little Crow had tried to maintain peace, but he, too, had grown furious watching his people being cheated and starved. In August 1862, Santee Sioux in Minnesota massacred hundreds of settlers. Throughout September, Sioux attacked forts and towns in both Minnesota and Iowa. The U.S. Army finally crushed the Sioux revolt at the Battle of Wood Lake on September 23.

In 1868, a major treaty was signed between the Lakota and the United States. Millions of acres, including the sacred Black Hills, were offered as a Great Sioux Reservation. The U.S. government promised that, if the Indians moved, they would no longer be harassed by the "people of the United States." Many Lakota, though, including the great war leader Sitting Bull, refused to move to the reservation.

BLACK HILL'S GOLD. In 1874, the U.S. Army confirmed a rumor that there was gold in South Dakota's Black Hills.

Hoping to strike it rich, miners poured into the area. The Indian holy lands were overrun by prospectors. The U.S. government offered to buy, or even rent, the Black Hills from the Sioux. But the hills were sacred territory to the tribe and they refused.

Sioux who had moved onto the reservation thought all this prospecting violated the U.S. treaty. In anger, many left to join other Sioux living outside reservation lands.

The following December, the U.S. government insisted that all Sioux must return to the reservation by the end of January or be considered "hostiles." Most Sioux paid little attention, moving north instead to the Powder River area in Montana.

The U.S. Army came after them. Three columns of troops, about 2,000 soldiers, moved into southeastern Montana. About 600 of those troops were in General George Custer's 7th Cavalry.

On June 17, one of the columns, led by General George Crook, was attacked on the Rosebud Creek. Crazy Horse, with a large force of Sioux and Cheyenne warriors, battled the U.S. troops for a good six hours and then withdrew. Crook's weakened soldiers limped back to Fort Fetterman, leaving the rest of the expedition to fend for itself.

THE LITTLE BIGHORN. Late in June, George Custer and two other officers met on a steamer to decide what to do. They had information from scouts that the Sioux were now gathered along the Little Bighorn River. The officers decided that Custer and his soldiers would push south into the Bighorn Valley. The other columns would then move in to block any Indian retreat. Custer would either attack the Indians or simply round them up.

On June 22, 1876, Custer's troops moved south into the valley. Two days later he was at the bottom of the Bighorn Valley. Hills curled around the lowland, making surveillance a problem. Custer couldn't see his enemy very well. He didn't know how many Indians were there. But he was sure the Indians would flee from his "Incomparable 7th Cavalry" as soon as he attacked. What Custer needed to do was find the Indian village before the

THE GATLING MACHINE GUN

One major warfare innovation did come from the Indian Wars—the machine gun. Developed during the Civil War, only a few of Richard Gatling's rotary guns saw service in that conflict. They did, however, see action during the Indian Wars. Troops hauled them along over the often roadless frontier, and the cavalry used them on long campaigns. The Gatling usually had six barrels, each firing a .50 caliber (half-inch

wide) bullet. Turning a crank at the side of the gun rotated the barrels, fired the bottom one, and loaded a fresh bullet into the one at the top. The Gatling could pump out 300–400 shots per minute.

Custer left his Gatlings behind in his final campaign in the summer of 1876, not expecting any heavy fighting. Had he brought them along, at least some of his command may have escaped from the Little Bighorn.

Custer's 7th Cavalry crosses the plain. A disaster awaited them at the Little Bighorn.

Sioux had a chance to escape.

Two days passed before an army lieutenant, perched on a high hill, spotted rising smoke. From its position, he believed he could tell the location of the Indian village.

Earlier that morning, army scouts had run into some Sioux warriors. The Indians now knew that the army was here. Although Custer was scheduled to make his move on June 26, he pushed the schedule up a day.

Anxious to publicize his role in the campaign, Custer had brought a journalist with him to report the action. Arriving on the Little Bighorn River, Custer ordered one battalion, under Major Marcus Reno, to attack the village just upriver. But when the soldiers moved down the valley, a large Indian force fell upon them. They had to fight their way back up the high bluffs behind the river to escape.

Custer then circled the camp on the north, and at last saw how big it was. He sent for three companies of men left with Captain Frederick Benteen. The instructions were taken by an army trumpeter. It was the last time he would see Custer alive.

CUSTER'S LAST STAND. Scouts had informed Custer that there were about 800 warriors in the village. But when the warriors struck, the general likely faced twice that many. Surrounded, Custer's force was wiped out. Not a single man under Custer's immediate command survived.

Fighting continued the next day until half the 7th Cavalry was dead or wounded. Indian losses, by comparison, were slight.

The victory for the Sioux was short-lived. The death of George Custer angered whites across America. It gave them yet another reason to force all Indians, especially the Sioux, onto reservations.

The victory at Little Bighorn, accomplished by an alliance of tribes, may have worried the army. A united Indian front would pose much more serious problems than scattered isolated tribes. Just weeks after Little Bighorn, the army attacked and defeated a large group of Cheyenne, about to join Crazy Horse and Sitting Bull. In November, U.S. troops destroyed another Northern Cheyenne camp.

"Benteen. Come on. Big Village. Be Quick...."
— Custer, before the Battle of Little Bighorn

More Sioux defeats followed. After the Battle of Wolf Mountain in January 1877, the great chief Crazy Horse surrendered. Sitting Bull led his people, the Hunkpapa Sioux, into Canada. They stayed there until 1881, when they returned once more to the Standing Rock Reservation in the Dakotas.

The troubles were far from over for the Sioux, however. In 1890, their massacre at Wounded Knee (see Aftermath) would mark the bitter end of the Indian Wars.

WARS IN THE SOUTHWEST

The U.S. government's policy was to concentrate Indian tribes onto parcels of land—usually land that other Americans didn't want. In the Southwest, however, that policy met with violent resistance.

RAIDING TRIBES. During the 1600s, the Spanish had established settlements in the territories of Arizona and New Mexico. Here several tribes shared the stark shelves of land between the fingers of the Rocky Mountains. The Hopi, Zuni, and Pueblo Indians managed to survive using techniques of "dry farming"—growing crops with very little water.

The Apache, however, were hunters and raiders, and other tribes feared them. The Apache nation did not live as one tribe but was spread out in smaller bands that were named for their home area. White Mountain, Chiricahua, Mescalero, Jicarilla, Mimbres, and Navajo were some of the main bands. The Navajo eventually grew so large that they became a separate tribe. Unlike the rest of the Apache nation, they turned to shepherding and growing crops such as corn and melons.

WAR WITH MEXICO. The Apache and Navajo had a long history of raiding the frontier settlements in Arizona and New Mexico. Since these territories belonged to Mexico, the raids were the problem of the Mexican government. In 1846, however, the United States declared war on Mexico, and the U.S. and the Apache nation became allies.

The cooperation, though, did not last long. In its peace with Mexico, the United States agreed to keep the Apache on their side of the border. The Apache were unhappy with this idea. They had always gone on raids in Mexico and were not about to stop now.

The Apache also wanted the Americans to leave after the settlement with Mexico, but that didn't happen. Instead, more settlers and miners flowed into Apache territory, eager to take advantage of whatever riches the Southwest had to offer.

Those riches, sadly enough, included Apache scalps. The Mexican government was now offering bounties for these macabre war trophies. Scalp hunters savaged entire villages, collecting scalps of men, women, and children. Not a few of the famous gold rush Forty-Niners paid their way to California with the bounty from Apache heads.

CONFLICT CONTINUES. Despite the scalping frenzy and the hatred it generated, relations between whites and some Apache groups were relatively peaceful during the 1850s. Chief Mangas Coloradas (Red Sleeves), who had offered to collaborate with the Americans in an invasion of Mexico, managed to bridge the gulf between the races—at least for a short time.

In 1860, though, a group of miners captured Coloradas, tied him to a wagon wheel, and whipped him. They were laughing as they struck blow after blow, but Coloradas was not. For an Apache to be beaten was the

---

GUERRILLA TACTICS AND GERONIMO

U.S. soldiers owed a long-standing debt to the Indians. Using native guerrilla tactics against the British helped win the Revolution for the Americans.

During the Indian Wars, however, those guerrilla tactics were turned back on them. Few of the battles between the army and Native Americans were fought in a conventional way—with large numbers of soldiers out in the open. Indians were far more likely to conduct lightning-fast raids and deadly ambushes with small parties of warriors.

The Apache specialized in such techniques. Their warriors could disappear after an attack faster than anyone. They were nearly impossible to capture. The U.S. Army experienced this phenomenon when it tried to round up Geronimo and his band of renegade Apache who were resisting being confined to a reservation.

The U.S. Army, led first by General Crook and then by General Howard, chased Geronimo's band for more than ten years through the stark landscape of Arizona and New Mexico. Geronimo was captured three different times only to slip through the army's grasp.

Only after a decade of hide-and-seek were the brilliant Apache and his band caught and confined in Florida.

Left to right: Geronimo, the son of Mangas Coloradas, and Natchez. The Apache kept the U.S. Army at bay for a decade.

most terrible insult. From that day on, Mangas Coloradas fought a bitter war against all whites. It would last, on and off, for twenty-five years.

APACHE ALLIANCE. Coloradas was joined in his war by the great Chiricahua Apache chief Cochise. Cochise had long been a friend and trader with the whites. But an experience with a treacherous army officer had changed his mind. He now thought the whites were cheats and murderers, and he meant to get revenge. Cochise's rampage through the Southwest left behind ghost towns and dead settlers. An Arizona newspaper reported: "Within six months nine-tenths of the whole male population have been killed off...."

In 1862, 2,000 volunteers from California were marching east to join the Union forces in the Civil War. But first they were sent to Arizona to try to stop the Apache rampage.

Coloradas and Cochise combined forces and planned to ambush the U.S. soldiers at Apache Pass. After their long haul across the desert, the troops needed water, and the pass was the only place to find it. Seven hundred braves surprised the soldiers, but the army fought back. It brought in cannon and shelled the Apache hideouts on the cliffs.

The Apache force was eventually defeated, and the following years were hard ones for them. Coloradas was captured and slain, and an order was given that any Apache man should be killed on sight. Cochise, however, continued his fight against the treacherous "White-Eyes." The Chiricahua continued to hide out in the unmapped southern Rockies, coming out only to raid white settlements.

The army made several attempts at peace with Cochise and his Apache. In 1872, General O. O. Howard offered to create a reservation out of the lands that now belonged to the Apache. Cochise agreed. "Hereafter, the white man and the Indian are to drink the same water, eat the same bread, and be at peace."

> "Let those come with me who would dare help drive [the Whites] out, so that Apache lands will belong to Apache people!"
>
> —Geronimo

By 1874, almost all Apache living in Arizona and New Mexico had moved onto the reservations. There were some holdouts, however. One of them was the great warrior Geronimo, the leader of the Apache bands along the United States and Mexican border.

It would take a decade and two generals to end Geronimo's revolt (see sidebar).

WARS IN THE WEST/FLIGHT OF THE NEZ PERCÉ

Indian tribes in the West had suffered at the hands of Spanish conquerors centuries before American settlers began arriving. Spanish soldiers behaved with indifferent cruelty toward the Indians, while Spanish missionaries often used intimidation to convert them to Christianity.

CRUSHED IN THE GOLD RUSH. The arrival of new settlers from the East began yet another episode of conquest. In 1848, when the California gold rush began, the Osage as well as other Indians were forced off their lands at gunpoint. Some were killed outright, but European diseases brought in by miners and settlers killed many more. At the dawn of the gold rush, about 100,000 Indians lived in California. When it was over, the native population had dropped to around 30,000.

But that wasn't the end of the Western Indian saga. To the north, in Oregon, the army led a senseless campaign against the Cayuse, who had massacred a settlement after their tribe was devastated by a measles epidemic. The crusade against the Cayuse roused the ire of other local tribes, including the Walla Walla, Umatilla, Palouse, and Nez Percé. Between 1869 and 1872, more than 200 separate Indian battles were fought in the far West. Though the results of individual battles varied, the Indians were now completely outnumbered. The tide began to flow powerfully against them.

THE LONG CHASE. One of the tribes who had tried to stay out of the way of the chronic warfare was the Nez Percé. These Indians lived on the good grazing lands where Idaho, Oregon, and Washington now meet. In 1855, the Nez Percé agreed to establish a reservation. It would comprise most of the land they then held.

> *"Bullets were singing through the tipis, splintering the poles... shouts and war whoops mingled with the firing and children and women were crying."*
>
> —*Two Moons, Nez Percé*

The treaty was kept until the 1860s, when local ranchers, settlers, and miners began demanding more open land. The U.S. government, under pressure, reduced the territory of the Nez Percé reservation to one fourth its original size. Many of the Nez Percé refused to sign the treaty, though those living in the new reservation area did.

Those refusing to sign were led by Chief Joseph. In 1877, Chief Joseph's people were ordered to move onto the new reservation. The chief tried to negotiate with U.S. Army General O. O. Howard, but the general had strict orders. He gave the Nez Percé thirty days.

By the deadline almost all of the nontreaty Nez Percé had moved onto the new reservation. The issue seemed to have been put to rest. But then three young Nez Percé killed four settlers in revenge for past murders of members of their families. Chief Joseph feared there would be serious army retaliation for the killings. With 800 other nontreaty Nez Percé, he decided to flee. Taking with them what animals and belongings they could, the refugees went north toward White Bird.

Hearing of the Nez Percé flight, General Howard sent Captain David Perry after them. Perry caught up with them at White Bird Canyon. Chief Joseph sent a peace delegation to the army lines, but some untrained volunteers jumped up and shot them. A battle began, and Perry's tiny force was decimated.

Looking Glass favored continuing the fight against the United States, but Chief Joseph overruled him.

Chief Joseph of the Nez Percé surrendered to the U.S. Army not knowing his people would never see their homeland again.

On July 11, Perry was joined by General Howard, who brought with him 400 fresh troops. He battled the Nez Percé warriors with artillery but without much success. Eventually Chief Joseph's forces withdrew, but Howard's troops were too exhausted to pursue them.

INTO MONTANA.

Chief Joseph realized that his people could not escape the army in their own Idaho territory. He decided to travel east to Montana, where he could join up with the Crow nation. By August, the Nez Percé had crossed the border over the Bitterroot Range into Montana. On August 8, they reached the Big Hole Valley.

At this point, their war chief Looking Glass believed they were safe for the moment and needed to rest. The U.S. Army, though, had not given up the chase. They attacked the next morning. After the attack, Chief Joseph gathered his band together. Many had been injured; eighty had been killed. But there was no time to care for the casualties. The army would soon be in pursuit. They had to run—and fast.

The Nez Percé turned east. They hoped to reach Yellowstone Park, where they might find protection with the Crow. But soon their hopes were dashed. The Crow had allied with the army. The Nez Percé turned north instead—to Canada and the protection of the Sioux chief Sitting Bull.

THE ESCAPE FAILS.

Just thirty miles from the Canadian border, the exhausted Nez Percé stopped to rest on September 30. Only a single day from safety, the tribe was attacked by Colonel Nelson Miles and 400 U.S. soldiers. The fighting and negotiating continued for five days. In the interim, fifty women and 100 warriors managed to escape over the Canadian border.

Chief Joseph had no choice but to surrender to Colonel Miles. Afterward, the chief sent the colonel this message from Bear Paw Mountain:

Tell General Howard I know his heart. What he told me before I have in my heart. I am tired of fighting. Our chiefs are killed. Looking Glass is dead. Too-hul-hul-sote is dead. The old men are all dead. It is cold and we have no blankets. The little children are freezing to death. My people, some of them, have run away to the hills, and have no blankets, no food; no one knows where they are—perhaps freezing to death. I want to have time to look for my children and see how many I can find. Maybe I shall find them among the dead. Hear me, my chiefs. I am tired; my heart is sick and sad. From where the sun now stands I will fight no more forever.

On October 5, the remaining Nez Percé surrendered at Bear Paw Mountain. Eight hundred people had begun the 1,700-mile journey—only 480 were left.

Joseph had been assured that his people would be allowed to return to their homes in Oregon. Although General Howard had agreed to this, he was later overruled. Joseph's Nez Percé were forced to move onto a reservation in Washington. Their chief spent the rest of his life mourning the loss of his home in the Walawala Valley and trying desperately to find a way to return. He was never allowed to go back. In later years he insisted that he would have never surrendered if he knew the Nez Percé would have to leave their homes forever.

AFTERMATH

In 1881, Helen Jackson published a book called *A Century of Dishonor*. Jackson's work chronicled a hundred years of disgraceful treatment of Indians by the U.S. government.

WOUNDED KNEE. Even as the full horror of the Indian experience was being revealed, however, another shameful chapter was being added. Before the end of the decade, one of the most savage attacks against the Indians was committed in South Dakota.

In late December 1890, an entire camp of unarmed Sioux, mostly women and children, were set upon by the American 7th Cavalry (Custer's old regiment) at Wounded Knee. The attack was hardly a battle at all—the army used howitzers against mainly unarmed Indians. In its aftermath, about 200 frozen Sioux littered the Dakota landscape. Of the army's seventy-three casualties, many were felled by friendly fire during the killing rampage.

A poster advertises lands for sale in Indian Territory. Even lands allotted by treaty to the Indians were sold out from under them.

NO PLACE FOR THE INDIAN. By the end of the nineteenth century, about 250,000 Indians lived in the United States—compared to the approximately one million who had lived there before Europeans had arrived. Confined mainly to about 200 reservations, they continued to suffer abuse and neglect from their "Great White Father" in Washington.

Representatives from the Bureau of Indian Affairs presided over the reservation Indians, treating them as wards of the government. But many of the BIA personnel were corrupt, others completely uninterested. Said one Indian commissioner: "There is no question of national dignity involved in the treatment of savages by a civilized power."

That "civilized power" now oversaw the welfare of Indians who were more or less powerless. By the end of the nineteenth century, Indian nations had no sovereignty and could no longer negotiate treaties with the U.S. government. This was, perhaps, less of a loss than it appeared. The United States had already violated nearly all of the 400 treaties it had made with Native American tribes.

Most Indians living on reservations had fallen into a spiral of poverty and despair. Watching their downfall, some whites believed the Indians' only possible salvation was to adopt white ways. The federal government, along with some well-meaning volunteers, set up day and boarding schools to teach Indian children to live like other Americans. They were taught farming and mechanical skills and forced to speak English. In a clear violation of the principles of the Bill of Rights, Indians were even denied the right to practice their religions or to wear traditional dress or hairstyles.

DAWES ACT. In 1887, another Indian civilizing scheme arrived with the Dawes Act. This bill's purpose was to turn reservation Indians into self-sustaining family farmers. To do this, reservation land was divided into parcels, which were distributed among tribe members. "Excess" land was disposed of by the U.S. government, usually sold to non-Indians. Other traditional Indian lands were taken for national parks.

That wasn't the end of Indian land grabbing. At the end of the 1880s, large parcels of the Indian Territory, now known as the Oklahoma Territory, were given away in a series of land rushes. In 1907, when Oklahoma became the forty-sixth state, the Indian Territory ceased to exist.

Continuing land pressure and changes in the Dawes Act allowed more and more white access to Indian land. Native American holdings continued to dwindle to just 52 million acres in 1934. This represented a huge drop from the 138 million acres Indian tribes called their own as late as 1887.

ATTEMPT AT REFORM. The passage of the Snyder Act in 1924 gave American Indians citizenship and the right

An Absaroka woman collects firewood. In just decades, the Indian way of life would be a memory.

to vote. Ten years later, during Franklin Roosevelt's presidency, the tide against Native Americans began to turn.

Roosevelt appointed John Collier as the new Commissioner of Indian Affairs. Collier began a complete overhaul of the U.S. government's Indian policies. His Indian Reorganization Act stopped the allotment policies instituted by the Dawes Act and strictly regulated the sale of Indian lands. In addition, the act called for the purchase of surplus lands so that they could be restored to Indian tribes.

> *"Our Indian life, I know, is gone forever."*
> —*Buffalo Bird Woman, Hidatsa*

Collier also initiated the building of schools and roads on reservation lands. Tribal control within individual Indian nations was strengthened, as was Indian economic development. Collier also succeeded in getting the ban on Indian religious ceremonies lifted. Indian languages could now be taught on the reservation and traditional rituals practiced.

Finally, in 1946, Congress passed a law that allowed Indians to claim damages from the U.S. government for illegal land losses. Through the next decade, Indians received more than $500 million in compensation for lands taken from them during the nineteenth century.

A SHAMEFUL PRECEDENT. In the 1940s, when Adolf Hitler was planning his extermination of Europe's Jews, he expressed admiration for the way the United States had destroyed its Indian population. Today the Indian Wars remain the hardest conflict to reconcile with a sense of the United States as a free and fair nation. Like the Civil War, the Indian Wars were fought against other Americans. There could be little satisfaction in the victory.

In spite of the tragedies that befell the Indian nations, many tribes did survive and continue to grow. Today the number of Indians in the United States may actually equal the number that were here before the Europeans arrived and the wars against them began.

Spanish-American War

T he Cubans rose up against their Spanish colonizers in 1895. Americans sympathized with the revolutionaries, whose cause echoed American principles of liberty and freedom for all. But war with Spain would eventually pit America's desire for control against its own revolutionary ideals.

PRELUDE TO WAR

The Cuban revolution coincided with the emergence of a new force in American politics, the press. In the late 1800s, most newpapers were not nearly as accurate as they are today. Two sensationalistic papers—William Randolph Hearst's *New York Journal* and Joseph Pulitzer's *New York World*—were waging a circulation war. In an effort to outsell each other, the two papers began competing to see which could drum up more support for the Cuban rebels.

YELLOW JOURNALISM.

Hearst claimed that "newspapers control the nation because they represent the people." Newspapers, he believed, even had the right to "declare wars." So Hearst and Pulitzer started tainting the reports coming out of Cuba and turned them into horrific tales meant to shock readers.

However, sympathy for the Cuban revolution alone could not produce a war. By 1897, President William McKinley began to pressure Spain to loosen its extremely harsh hold on the Cubans. During the previous year, the Spanish had set up concentration camps in which tens of thousands of Cubans had died. Spain was anxious to avoid war with the United States and gave in slightly, even allowing Cubans a share in running their country. The Cubans, though, encouraged by the prospect of an American intervention, demanded full independence.

In January 1898, the mood in Cuba turned ugly. McKinley ordered the battleship *Maine* to anchor in Havana harbor to keep a check on the hostilities. A month later, on February 15, the *Maine* blew up while at anchor, killing 262 sailors. The next morning the newspapers demanded the United States take action against Spain. The *Journal* read, "Remember the Maine! To hell with Spain!"

The United States accused Spain of a deliberate attack. Spain denied the charges, claiming an explosion aboard the ship caused it to sink. But Theodore Roosevelt, the Assistant Secretary of the Navy, said, "The *Maine* was sunk by an act of dirty treachery on the part of the Spaniards." Others, too, were quick to blame Spain, even though no one had proof of wrongdoing. To this day, experts are unsure of what caused the explosion.

To prove their innocence, the Spanish gave in to all the U.S. requests—except complete Cuban independence. The American public, however, was unwilling to let the issue drop. In the end, McKinley, who desperately wanted to avoid war, was too weak to stand against those in favor of fighting. On April 11, 1898, he reluctantly asked Congress to authorize the use of force. By April 21, Spain had severed diplomatic ties with the United States. Congress officially declared war just four days later.

WAR WITH SPAIN

Even before war was declared, Teddy Roosevelt had sent a fleet south. Under the command of Commodore George Dewey, the naval force was instructed to prepare for an attack against the Spanish fleet in the Philippines. By May 1, 1898, Dewey had defeated the entire Spanish fleet in Manila Bay with only eight American casualties.

THE ROUGH RIDERS.

Meanwhile Roosevelt quit his post at the Navy department and formed a cavalry unit of volunteer soldiers. Roosevelt's men, known as the Rough Riders, arrived in Cuba on June 21. Upon landing, they headed inland toward the San Juan Ridge.

The Spanish had set up their main defense along the ridge, with key positions on San Juan Hill and Kettle Hill. By July 1, the Rough Riders were poised at the bottom of Kettle Hill ready to attack. Meanwhile, another force was stationed at the bottom of San Juan Hill. The Americans faced a formidable enemy at the top of the hills, but nonetheless they charged ahead.

On horseback and armed with a pistol, Roosevelt led the way up Kettle Hill. His men charged after him, and when they reached the top, the Spanish army raced down the other side in retreat. The Americans also succeeded in securing San Juan Hill.

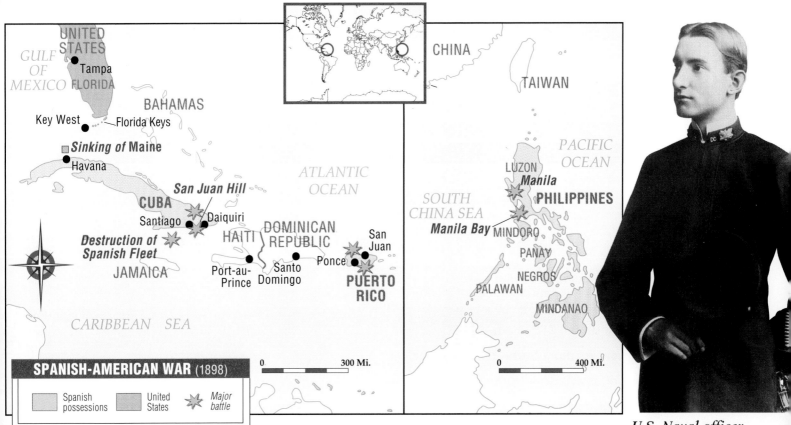

SPANISH-AMERICAN WAR (1898)

Spanish possessions

United States

Major battle

U.S. Naval officer, Spanish-American War

TAKEOVER IN THE PHILIPPINES. U.S. forces now headed toward the city of Santiago, where the Spanish had 10,000 men ready to counterattack. The Spanish, though, were too weak to defend the city and decided to abandon it.

With the defeat of their fleet at Santiago, the Spanish were ready to surrender, and war in Cuba came to an end.

Dewey, however, was still in the Philippines, facing a somewhat different situation. Filipino rebels, who were also battling it out with the Spanish, had surrounded Manila and were eager to fight for their own independence.

Manila's Spanish governor wanted to make a deal with the Americans. He proposed that if the United States would protect his men from the Filipino rebels, he would give up the city. On August 13, Dewey took Manila without Spanish resistance. Dewey's men hoisted the U.S. flag above the city, signaling the end of the war, but also dashing Filipino hopes of self-rule.

The war had lasted only 113 days and was one of the most popular wars in U.S. history.

AFTERMATH
The warring countries signed a peace treaty in Paris in December 1898. Cuba was granted independence, but in fact remained under U.S. military rule, and Spain surrendered Guam and Puerto Rico to the Americans. In exchange, the United States agreed to buy the Philippines for $20 million.

Teddy Roosevelt returned from Cuba a hero. He became McKinley's vice president in 1901, and less than a year later, when McKinley was assassinated, he assumed the office of president. In 1901, the Platt Amendment gave the United States the power to veto most of the decisions made by the new Cuban government. In addition, the United States refused to acknowledge the Philippine Republic. As a result, war eventually broke out, and the United States had to crush the rebellion. It would be another forty-six years before the Philippines would win their independence.

1895–1897	1898		
Insurrection against Spanish rule begins in Cuba *(1895)*. Spanish set up concentration camps in Cuba *(1896)*.	U.S. battleship *Maine* explodes and sinks in Havana harbor *(Feb.15)*. American media blames Spain. U.S. declares war on Spain *(April 25)*.	American seaborne army attacks Santiago *(July 1)*, which surrenders *(July 17)*. American forces invade and take Puerto Rico *(July–Aug.)*.	Treaty of Paris signed *(Dec. 10)*. Spain leaves Cuba. U.S. takes Puerto Rico, Guam, and (with payment of $20 million) the Philippines.

WORLD WAR ONE

More than 100,000 American soldiers lost their lives in World War I. That number was large, but, compared to other countries, the United States got off easy. World War I was a global conflict more brutal than any that came before it. Senseless attacks into the face of machine guns bought graves for millions.

The Great War began in Europe in August 1914. The United States, however, didn't enter the conflict until the middle of 1917. American forces didn't arrive in Europe in large numbers until 1918. Given the scope of the conflict, the United States hardly participated at all. Still, the American entry was decisive and helped end the war.

World War I was a milestone in U.S. history. While winners and losers in Europe came out of the war crippled, the United States, in many ways, gained in stature. The nation, at last, had become a world power, with all the pride and hardships that role brought with it.

American ambulance driver, World War I

ATLANTIC OCEAN

GREAT BRITAIN

Londor

Lusitania sunk

Pa

Bay of Biscay

FR

PORT.

SPAIN

ALGERIA

1914

Austro-Hungarian Archduke Francis Ferdinand assassinated in Sarajevo by Serbian nationalists *(June 28).*

Germany invades Luxembourg, Belgium, and France, beginning World War I *(Aug.).* President Wilson declares U.S. neutrality *(Aug. 19).*

1915

German submarine sinks the *Lusitania,* killing American passengers *(May 7).*

First use of poison gas by Germans at Ypres *(April 22).*

Turks mass murder 800,000–2 million Armenians.

1916

President Wilson reelected *(Nov. 7).*

Battle of the Somme costs 1.25 million casualties *(June).*

Battle of Verdun results in 1 million French and German casualties *(Feb. 21–Dec. 18).*

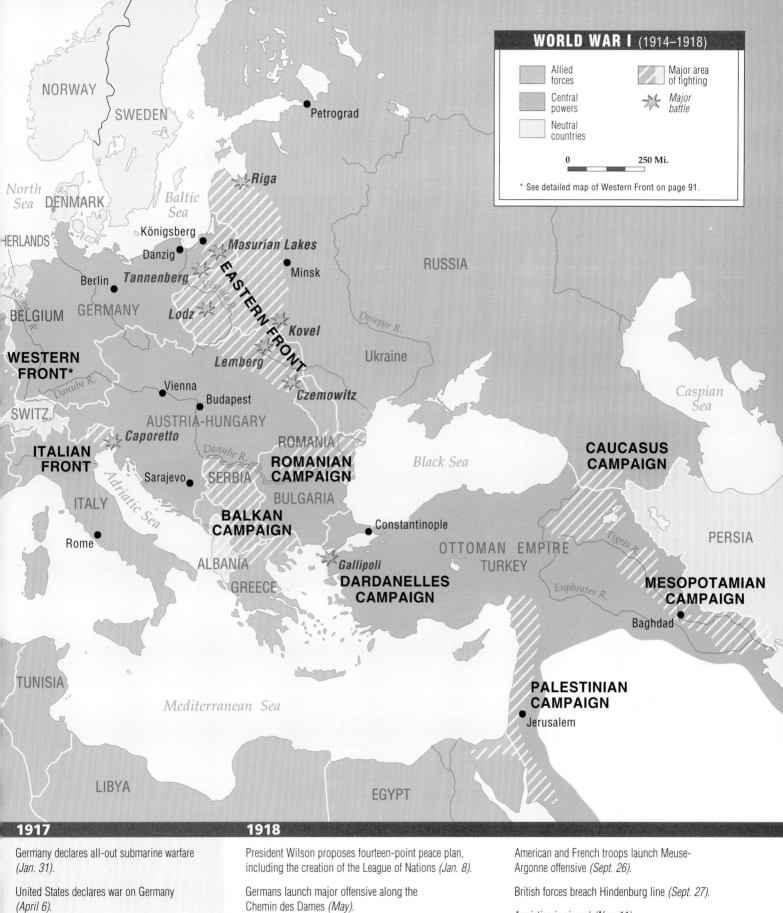

WORLD WAR I (1914–1918)

Allied forces

Central powers

Neutral countries

Major area of fighting

★ Major battle

0   250 Mi.

See detailed map of Western Front on page 91.

NORWAY

SWEDEN

Petrograd

North Sea

DENMARK

Baltic Sea

Königsberg

Danzig

Riga

Masurian Lakes

Minsk

RUSSIA

HERLANDS

Berlin

Tannenberg

GERMANY

Lodz

EASTERN FRONT

Kovel

Dnieper R.

BELGIUM

Rhine R.

Lemberg

Czernowitz

Ukraine

Caspian Sea

WESTERN FRONT*

Danube R.

SWITZ.

Vienna

Budapest

AUSTRIA-HUNGARY

ROMANIA

Black Sea

CAUCASUS CAMPAIGN

ITALIAN FRONT

Caporetto

Danube R.

ROMANIAN CAMPAIGN

PERSIA

Sarajevo

SERBIA

BULGARIA

Tigris R.

ITALY

Adriatic Sea

BALKAN CAMPAIGN

Constantinople

OTTOMAN EMPIRE TURKEY

MESOPOTAMIAN CAMPAIGN

Rome

ALBANIA

Gallipoli

Euphrates R.

Baghdad

GREECE

DARDANELLES CAMPAIGN

TUNISIA

Mediterranean Sea

PALESTINIAN CAMPAIGN

Jerusalem

LIBYA

EGYPT

1917

Germany declares all-out submarine warfare *(Jan. 31)*.

United States declares war on Germany *(April 6)*.

First U.S. troops arrive in France *(June)*.

Revolution in Russia

1918

President Wilson proposes fourteen-point peace plan, including the creation of the League of Nations *(Jan. 8)*.

Germans launch major offensive along the Chemin des Dames *(May)*.

Americans defeat Germans at Belleau Wood *(June)*.

American and French troops launch Meuse-Argonne offensive *(Sept. 26)*.

British forces breach Hindenburg line *(Sept. 27)*.

Armistice is signed *(Nov. 11)*.

PRELUDE TO WAR

After the end of the Franco-Prussian war in 1871, both France and Germany entered into alliances to protect themselves. Germany, the victor, united with Italy and Austria-Hungary (then one nation). France, to guard against Germany, formed an alliance with Russia, and eventually with Great Britain. Though these alliances were designed to protect the peace, they helped to provoke the largest and most destructive conflict the world had yet seen: World War I, known at the time as the Great War.

RISING NATIONALISM. The war was made possible, and maybe even inevitable, by the great rush of nationalism that went before it. Most of the countries of Europe had their hopes set upon improving their national status. Some sought to mark their own national boundaries; others wanted to add more land to their territory. A few nations wanted both.

What started as national greed grew into a worldwide conflagration. World War I would eventually involve thirty-two nations, destroy four empires, and cost the lives of 17 million people.

The Great War began with a relatively isolated incident. During a visit to Sarajevo in 1914, the Austro-Hungarian Archduke Ferdinand was assassinated along with his wife, Sophie. They were shot to death by a terrorist as they rode through the streets of Sarajevo.

The terrorist, Gavrilo Princip, was a member of a small band of Serbian nationalists called the Black Hand. They resented the Austro-Hungarian Empire's treatment of Serbia. Austria, wary of Serbia's desire to expand, was protective of its own Slavic lands near Serbia. The empire was determined to keep Serbia from becoming any more powerful than it already was.

The archduke's assassination, at first, did not raise the prospect of war. But within a month, a series of threats and counterthreats put forward by several different European countries, including Austria-Hungary and Germany, triggered a virtual avalanche of hostility. In the frenzied nationalistic atmosphere, Germany, France, Russia, and Austria-Hungary made their huge standing armies combat ready.

In August 1914, the Austro-Hungarian Empire declared war on Serbia. Germany, as Austria-Hungary's ally, was now committed to the conflict. Russia, Serbia's traditional protector, was forced to its defense. France, then allied with Russia, joined in the fray. The French-English-Russian alliance became known as the Allied Forces. Germany and Austria-Hungary formed the Central Powers.

THE FAMILY WAR

In 1914, as war threatened, an urgent message from Russia came to Kaiser Wilhelm in Germany: "I beg you in the name of our old friendship to do what you can to stop your allies from going too far."

The letter was signed simply "Nicki." Nicki (Nicholas) was the kaiser's cousin, but he was also ruler of Russia. The two men were about to lead their countries into war against each other. The cousins' touching but futile communication was a last-minute attempt to try and stop it.

One of the strangest aspects of World War I was that it was fought between countries whose rulers were related. King George V of England was the first cousin of the German kaiser and Russian Czar Nicholas. Most of the other European monarchs were close relatives or in-laws. The royal cousins controlled Europe and sizable parts of Africa, Asia, Australia, and the Americas.

Queen Victoria, the grandmother to all these royal children, was a determined matchmaker. She believed that the international marriages of her children and grandchildren would secure world peace in the twentieth century.

About that she was wrong. Her extended family feuded. The cousins bickered over African and Asian colonies. The German kaiser, Wilhelm, was determined to have as large and sophisticated a navy to command as his English cousin, George. Together, the royal monarchs individually oversaw the creation of huge standing armies ready to mobilize quickly against each other. In the tense summer of 1914, that mobilization began. Declaring war against each other, the cousins inaugurated the bloodiest melee the world had yet seen. The political firestorm that accompanied it would dethrone many of Europe's monarchs and send Nicholas to an early grave.

An English regiment advances. Filled with romance about the war, farmers and shepherds joined the ranks.

GERMANY INVADES BELGIUM.

In early August, the war began as the German Army smashed through neutral Belgium, defeated its small army, and invaded France. By early September the Germans had gotten within fifty miles of Paris. The French government was so alarmed, it packed up and fled the city.

The combined efforts of the French and British armies managed to stop the German advance at the Battle of the Marne. The price, though, was higher than anyone could have imagined. A million and a half soldiers clashed at the Marne. Casualties were shockingly high. Infantrymen rushed forward in waves, only to be cut down by machine-gun fire. Suffering horrifying casualties, both armies realized they needed protection from the ferocious machine-gun fire and heavy artillery. Both sides quickly developed elaborate trench systems (see sidebar, next page).

During the next four years (1914–1918), the Great War was fought on land in several different areas. The Western Front extended from Belgium's North Sea coast through France and to the Swiss border. The Eastern Front ran from the Baltic Sea through Russia, Poland, and the Ukraine to the Black Sea. More combat took place on the Balkan Front, countries on or near the Balkan Peninsula. The Italian Front stretched along the Alps at the border between Italy and Austria. Other fighting took place in the Caucasus and Mesopotamia and in and around Palestine (see main map on pages 88–89).

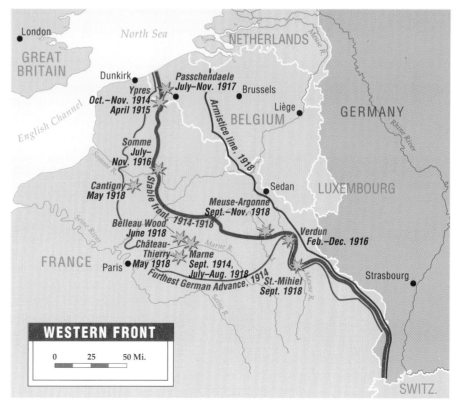

WESTERN FRONT

0   25   50 Mi.

WAR ON THE FRONTS

The Allies desperately needed to hold the French ports of Dunkirk and Calais on the English Channel for resupply. In the Marne's aftermath, a race for these ports began. To stop the Germans from getting there first, Belgium flooded the northern Yser River region as the German Army tried to get across it. The Belgians' quick thinking worked, and the Allies got to the ports first.

THE WESTERN FRONT.

The huge armies and heavy fortifications used in the race for the ports became part of a defensive line known as the Western Front. The Belgian Army occupied the northern third of the front. The British held the midsection, and the French took the southern part ending at Switzerland (see map on page 91).

The opposing forces faced each other—sometimes at shouting distance—across a deadly no-man's-land. The combined trenches of both sides eventually stretched to about 25,000 miles, long enough to circle the earth.

In October 1914, the first major trench offensive began in Flanders (in Belgium) near the village of Ypres. For a week the Germans attacked, and the British and French counterattacked. Seven days later, a shocking quarter of a million soldiers were dead.

Casualties were made even worse because troops on both sides were packed close together when they attacked. As soldiers panicked and retreated on the sodden ground, they frequently trampled their own dead and wounded.

POISON GAS.

At the end of April 1915, the Germans introduced a powerful new weapon. After a bombardment near Ypres, they began dispersing poison chlorine gas over the British and French trenches. Even though the attack lasted only fifteen minutes, 15,000 men were gassed. The French soldiers were completely unprepared. Many panicked and ran. Others died where they stood, literally coughing to death.

The Germans didn't fully understand what a lethal effect the gas would have. As a result, they didn't use those precious minutes of panic to launch a full-scale attack. The stalemate continued. Both sides, however, now began using gas before their ground assaults.

The victims of these first rounds of chemical warfare had little protection. They wet handkerchiefs and tried to cover their faces. Gas masks eventually provided some protection. Many victims, though, were permanently blinded by the chemicals. Others had difficulty breathing for the rest of their lives.

TRENCH WARFARE

Though the trenches did provide some basic protection against enemy fire, they also created a "stationary front." In other words, the soldiers didn't move or, at least, not very far. Not only was it dangerous

for the troops to come out from their trenches, but once they climbed out, more trouble lay ahead. The area between the trenches was

so ripped up by shell fire that it was nearly impossible to move across it.

Things were made even worse because the land was naturally wet. The excess water created a landscape of bogs and mud.

If a soldier did manage to claw through the muddy craters to the enemy's trenches, he would likely face barbed wire and bullets. The image of a machine-gunned soldier tangled in barbed wire became a symbol of the tragedy of trench warfare.

Though the trenches were built for protection, they were often not safe at all. Even when guns were silent, soldiers had to worry about "trench raids." Groups of enemy soldiers would sneak into the trenches at night and capture or kill sleeping soldiers.

Staying healthy was an even bigger problem. Because the bottoms of the trenches were

covered with several inches of muddy water, soldiers couldn't keep their feet dry. Many developed a condition called "trench foot." Penicillin and other antibiotics didn't exist yet, and even small cuts could disable or kill a soldier. Troops also waged a constant war with lice that lived in the seams of their clothes. Worse were the rats, which fed on dead flesh and were a particular hazard to the wounded.

Yet the World War I soldier did have moments of respite. Relieved from front-line duty, soldiers spent their free time in some of the most beautiful countryside of Europe. Surrounded by tranquil farms, fed on fresh vegetables and cheese, troops at the rear had a chance to really rest. But it never lasted long enough, and returning to the dismal trenches was made doubly hard by having spent a few days on the "other side."

A German aviator aims a bomb over the Western Front. Early bombing attempts usually missed their mark.

THE EASTERN FRONT.

One German army was deadlocked on the Western Front. Another, commanded by General Paul von Hindenburg, was successfully battling the Russians at the Battle of Tannenberg in East Prussia. The Russians suffered yet another massive defeat at the Masurian Lakes. At both battles two Russian armies were nearly completely encircled by German forces. Like the fights on the Western Front, these battles were slaughterhouses for soldiers. Russian losses in the combined defeats were close to 250,000.

Russian troops in Austria, however, advanced westward through the winter of 1914. By March 1915, they had reached the Carpathian Mountains on the Hungarian border. By then, though, the Russians were overstretched and running into trouble. A combined Austrian-German force began to drive them back. Over the summer, the Russians were pushed completely out of Poland and most of the Baltic countries.

In November, Russian armies attacked west once again, toward East Prussia and Silesia. But German forces stood them off. It would be the last time Russia would seriously threaten Germany during the war.

THE BALKAN FRONT.

By October 1915, Turkey joined Austria and Germany. In response, Russia declared war on Turkey. That act shut Russia off from its major sources of trade and access to vital Black Sea traffic. Though no one recognized it, this event would help bring on Russia's economic collapse and the Russian Revolution a year later.

The war gave Turkey the opportunity to attack its ethnic Armenians. Throughout 1915–1916, groups of Turks set out to exterminate Armenian Christians, killing an estimated one million. Many of the victims died from famine and diseases as they were held in concentration camps in Syria. Another million Armenian refugees fled north with Russian soldiers retreating after battling the Turks.

GALLIPOLI AND SALONIKA.

Through Turkey ran the Dardanelles, a strategic waterway that connected the Mediterranean, the Sea of Marmara, and the entrance of the Black Sea. The Allies believed that if they could seize the strait they could aid their Russian allies.

In the spring of 1915, a combined British, Australian, and New Zealand force attempted to land at Gallipoli, a peninsula that bordered the Dardanelles. The troops managed to get ashore but, because the terrain was so rugged, they were caught along the shoreline.

Despite the men's hopeless, trapped position, the offensive continued. By the end of July, more than 50,000 had died. By August, another 40,000 graves were filled, all for a mere 500 acres of ground. Meanwhile, British forces had also landed at Salonika in Greece. Like Gallipoli, Salonika was a gateway to the Balkans. Greece was not in the war yet, but it nevertheless allowed the Allies to land.

The Allies were expecting Bulgaria to declare war on Serbia. They needed Salonika as a jumping-off point for an advance into Serbia. In October 1915, Bulgaria did declare war on Serbia and sent armies in to defeat the advancing Serbian and Allied forces.

At the same time, the Germans sent an army of 250,000 into Serbia from the east. To avoid being completely trapped, the Serbians retreated into Albania in the dead of winter. Thousands of women and children refugees trudged along with them. By the end of 1915, the Serbians, who had fired the first shot of the war, were out of it for good.

THE CONFLICT SPREADS

By 1915, both sides were discouraged by the stalemate that trench warfare had produced. With no end to land warfare in sight, they turned their attention to the seas.

BLOCKADE. England's sea power had virtually halted German shipping. This created problems for the United States, which had been supplying food and arms to both sides in the war. England's progressive blockade, however, first barred war shipments, then food supplies, to Germany.

As Germany's supply routes closed off, its people faced starvation. The German Navy began to use submarines—called U-boats—to torpedo ships supplying England. That included U.S. ships. Germany warned that the waters around the British Isles were now a war zone.

U.S. President Woodrow Wilson was alarmed by these developments. The United States had prospered from the sale of war goods to the warring countries. Now those sales were disappearing. Wilson was also determined that the United States stay neutral. Even though many Americans sided with the Allies after the invasion of Belgium, most of the country was inclined to agree with the president. Americans still remembered the terrible carnage of the Civil War. They wanted to keep far away from the fighting.

GERMANY SINKS THE *LUSITANIA*. In April, the Cunard liner *Lusitania* was preparing to leave New York harbor. The German embassy posted a notice in the paper warning passengers that the ship would be at risk of attack. Only one of the passengers canceled his ticket. On May 7, the ship was passing Ireland on its way to England when the German submarine U-20 attacked it. The *Lusitania* went down with 1,198 people aboard. Among those who died were 128 Americans.

Germany asserted that the *Lusitania* had been carrying munitions. Though the United States denied it, there were, in fact, small arms aboard. But the passenger ship was clearly unarmed and defenseless. The attack on the *Lusitania* enraged most Americans, but the president was still determined to keep the United States out of the war. Most Americans echoed his feelings.

THE WESTERN FRONT—1916. Verdun was a great French fortress town. The Germans felt its capture was the key to breaking the French line. The Germans began their attack on February 21. While they succeeded in capturing several other forts, they were unable to take

---

POETS IN WORLD WAR I

If any war can justly be called a writer's war, it would be World War I. Many well-known poets and novelists fought and wrote about the Great War, including Ernest Hemingway (*A Farewell to Arms*) and the German novelist, Erich Maria Remarque (*All Quiet on the Western Front*).

English poets were probably best represented. They included Rupert Brook, Edward Thomas, Wilfred Owen, Edmund Blunden, Ivor Gurney, David Jones, and Siegfried Sassoon (see photo). What happened to these poets gives a good sample of what happened to the entire generation that fought in the Great War.

Brooke, one of England's Romantic poets, died of blood poisoning before the landing at Gallipoli. Thomas died in the trenches. Owen was machine-gunned to death on the Western Front. Gassed and shell-shocked at Ypres, Gurney spent the rest of his life in a mental institution. Blunden, Jones, and Sassoon survived the war but could not forget it.

Siegfried Sassoon's story is especially interesting. He was a junior officer in the Royal Welsh Fusiliers. He performed bravely as a soldier, winning the Military Cross at one point. But as the war ground on he became convinced that continuing the fight was useless. He eventually made a statement condemning the war and refused to continue fighting.

Sassoon expected a court-martial but was instead sent to a mental hospital. He felt so guilty about not being punished that he returned to the trenches. He was seriously wounded in July 1918. Below is Sassoon's poem on the idealization of warfare.

GLORY OF WOMEN

You love us when we're heroes, home on leave,
Or wounded in a mentionable place.
You worship decorations; you believe
That chivalry redeems the war's disgrace.
You make us shells. You listen with delight,
By tales of dirt and danger fondly thrilled.
You crown our distant ardours while we fight,
And mourn our laurelled memories when
    we're killed.
You can't believe that British troops "retire"
When hell's last horror breaks them, and
    they run,
Trampling the terrible corpses—blind
    with blood.
O German mother dreaming by the fire,
While you are knitting socks to send your son
His face is trodden deeper in the mud.

Soldiers, blinded by gas, walk holding onto each other for guidance. Poison gas was used as a weapon by both sides.

Verdun. The battle raged on for ten months. More than 2 million men fought to gain just two miles of territory. The casualties were horrific; France and Germany each lost half a million soldiers.

At the same time, the Allies were building up a force along the Somme River. Before the war began, the area had been a peaceful wildlife refuge. By the end of the war, the Somme would be witness to the most wrenching and deadly battle of all time.

> *"Humanity is mad! It must be mad to do what it is doing. Hell cannot be so terrible."*
>
> — *French lieutenant Alfred Joubaire at the Battle of the Somme*

On July 1, a million and a half rounds of Allied artillery fire exploded on the soft green landscape. In the smoke from the bombardment, British and French soldiers advanced toward the German lines. As they came forward, enemy machine-gun and artillery fire cut them down in rows. By the end of the day, 60,000 British soldiers were either dead or dying. The attack had been a

disaster. The English poet Siegfried Sassoon summed it up. "I am staring," he said, "at a sunlit picture of hell."

The events on the Somme, like so many of the battlefield nightmares of the Great War, showed a failure of command. On both sides, the generals in charge had wasted the blood and lives of millions of soldiers in repeated senseless assaults. Nevertheless, the slaughterhouse methods continued. The French general Joseph Joffre ordered his troops to keep fighting. He was convinced that the war could be won by attrition, or bleeding the other side to exhaustion, so he pressed the battle into early November. In five months, the British managed to take forty-five square miles of terrain. More than 415,000 men lost their lives in the grinding battle.

THE EASTERN FRONT—1916. In June, the Russian Army staged its last and strongest offensive. Flattening the Austrians, they pushed deep into Poland, Galicia, and Hungary. Stranded deep in the mountains, the Russians soon ran out of supplies and were reduced to fighting with their bare hands. A full million soldiers, the best force the Russians had to offer, had been lost in the advance.

The Austro-Hungarian Empire was shattered from trying to hold the Russians back. Nearly 400,000 of its soldiers had fallen into captivity.

THE U.S. ENTERS THE WAR

In 1916, President Wilson ran for and won reelection on the slogan: "He kept us out of war." On the radio, Americans listened to a popular tune called "I Didn't Raise My Boy to Be a Soldier." The sinking of the *Lusitania* had brought the war home to the United States, but America still kept its distance from Europe's struggle.

THE RUSSIAN REVOLUTION.

Russia's terrible losses in the Great War in 1916 caused panic, rioting, and finally desertion among its troops. It also brought calamity to the Russian Empire, where millions had lived in grinding poverty for centuries.

The Revolution began in March 1917 when factory workers began to strike for higher wages. The unrest worsened, eventually forcing Russia's leader, Czar Nicholas II, to give up his throne. (The Czar, his wife, and children were murdered by the Communists a year later.)

A provisional government formed, headed by Alexander Kerensky. Kerensky promised to keep Russia in the war. In November, however, a group of Bolsheviks, led by Vladimir Lenin, overthrew Kerensky. The Bolsheviks disbanded the Russian assembly and executed anyone who opposed them. They also put an end to Russia's participation in the war.

More than any other single event, the Russian Revolution—and the Bolshevik formation of a Communist state—would shape the history of the twentieth century.

ALARMS IN EUROPE.

As Russia braced for the aftershocks of revolution, the German command gave orders for vigorous unrestricted submarine warfare. The German military believed that all-out use of the submarine could defeat Britain in six months. President Wilson had warned the Germans against such a move and was finally forced to break off diplomatic relations with Germany. During a speech to Congress, Wilson suggested that if American ships were sunk, he would be forced to act. He didn't have long to wait.

AN OFFER TO MEXICO.

The break in United States relations did not stop German aggression. Instead Germany sent out an offer to Mexico in a secret telegram. If the United States should declare war, the message said, Germany would offer Mexico an alliance. In return for its help against the United States, Germany suggested that Mexico could win back lost territory in Texas, New Mexico, and Arizona. The telegraphed message was intercepted and made public.

This secret offer was bound to provoke the U.S. Just a year earlier, the Mexican revolutionary Pancho Villa had

ANTIWAR ACTIVISM IN THE UNITED STATES

Although the majority of representatives in Congress voted for war with Germany, there were exceptions. One was Jeanette Rankin, a representative from Montana, who would also cast a lone vote against World War II years later.

Resisting the rush to war was not an impulse just confined to Congress. In small towns in the South, many draftees stood in their doors with rifles at the ready, willing to shoot, but only at the enlistment officers.

Some war resistance actually led to violence. In Montana, Frank Little, a labor leader, was hanged by a mob after delivering a speech denouncing the war. In Tulsa, Oklahoma, a pacifist preacher was tarred and feathered after delivering antiwar sermons.

One of the most notable antiwar activists was a Lithuanian-born woman named Emma Goldman. Goldman was a professed anarchist who urged

young men to resist the draft. She considered the war in Europe "unjust" and spent her time distributing antiwar literature. In July 1917, she was accused of conspiracy and brought to trial with a coworker, Alexander Berkman.

Goldman defended herself during the trial, insisting that her right to free speech was constitutionally guaranteed.

Said Goldman: "We love America. But that must not make us blind to the social faults of America.... That cannot make us inarticulate to the terrible wrongs committed in the name of patriotism and in the name of this country."

Goldman and Berkman were convicted and sentenced to two years in prison and $10,000 in fines. Following her release, Goldman was deported to Russia.

U.S. troops march to training camp. Americans brought little expérience, but lots of confidence, to the war effort.

raided a fort in New Mexico, killing fifteen people.

President Wilson was enraged. As the German telegram made headlines across the country, preparedness parades became the fashion. Marchers carried banners that read: "Kill the Kaiser!" and "Let's Get the Hun!" On March 16, German U-boats torpedoed two American ships, the *Illinois* and the *City of Memphis.*

WILSON ASKS FOR A DECLARATION OF WAR. On April 2, thousands assembled outside the Capitol building. Wilson finally spoke: "…we will not choose the path of submission…. The world must be made safe for democracy. Its peace must be founded upon the trusted foundations of personal liberty."

> *"It is a fearful thing to lead this great peaceful people into war, into the most terrible and disastrous of all wars, civilization itself seeming to be in the balance."*
>
> —*Woodrow Wilson, April 2, 1917*

When he finished his speech, Wilson received a tremendous ovation. The applause shocked him. He turned to his secretary and said, "Think of what it was they were applauding…a message of death for our young men."

The United States was hardly ready for war, but it did have a leader in mind. General John Pershing had led the force that gave chase to Pancho Villa after the raid in 1916. He was the natural choice to command the American Expeditionary Force (AEF) in Europe.

Pershing's job was already laid out for him. Unlike the European countries, the United States did not have a large standing army ready to fight. Nor did it have planes, ships, and other military equipment in large supply. The first step was to set up a draft system to gather the men needed for the army. A major effort would be needed to assemble the troops and outfit them. While most of the country was ready to go to war with Germany, there was some stiff resistance (see sidebar).

MUTINIES SPREAD. The Italians had switched sides in the war in 1915 and joined the Allies. During the first eight months of 1917, Italian forces tried to break through the Austrian line along the Isonzo River. Their hopes were pinned on pushing through to Trieste. At the end of the year, however, the Austrians were reinforced by six new German divisions. These combined forces broke the Italian lines near the town of Caporetto and pushed Italy's troops back. The Italian losses were crushing. Hundreds of thousands of soldiers dropped their arms and abandoned the battle entirely.

The Italians were not the only soldiers who were sick of the war. For three years, the Allied and German armies had been trying to break through each other's trench lines. During that time, the Western Front had not moved more than ten miles in any direction.

In the late spring of 1917, the Allies made several more desperate attempts at a breakthrough. In April, the casualties were so great and so little ground was gained that some French troops revolted. Fifty-four divisions of the French Army, nearly half the total number, threw down their rifles, got drunk, or just stubbornly refused to obey orders.

YANKS IN EUROPE—1917

At the end of 1917, much of the Allies' hope of ending the war was pinned on the use of tanks (see sidebar) and American soldiers. By June 1917, nearly 200,000 U.S. troops were training in France. For the Allies, the Yankee landing didn't come a moment too soon.

THIRD BATTLE OF YPRES. Ypres in Belgium had seen some of the worst fighting of the Great War. The town itself had been all but smashed to the ground. For two years, the British had been working on an idea for a major offensive on one of the ridges outside the town. Tunneling under the ground between the trenches, British "sappers" had burrowed under German positions and planted a million pounds of explosives. Before dawn on June 7, the switches were thrown and nineteen mines went off. The explosion created craters 100 feet deep and killed or wounded 20,000 German soldiers. In the panic and confusion, British troops moved forward, taking some German positions.

On the last day of July, another major attack was launched to take the Passchendaele Ridge on the outskirts of Ypres. In the midst of violent thunderstorms, British soldiers waded through waist-high mud while dodging shell fire. Thousands of wounded men were trampled in the fierce fighting. Many literally drowned in the mud. Others were trapped for days during the storm and went mad. The campaign continued into the autumn. Only when the mud fields froze solid did the battle end. Nearly 245,000 Allied soldiers had been killed or wounded in the taking of just 9,000 yards of ground.

U.S. TROOPS IN TRAINING. Soldiers from the States had no idea of the kind of fierce warfare they would face in Europe. And they were little prepared for it. But they did have a few very important assets. Unlike the European troops, they were not exhausted. And they believed they could win the war.

Allied generals wanted to use the American troops as replacements in the French and British armies, but President Wilson would not hear of it. He ordered General Pershing to preserve the identity of U.S. troops and keep them under his own command. That independence fostered a pride in the troops and their work. On the other hand, U.S. soldiers had to rely on the skills of American military officers who knew as little about the war as they did.

American troops did get the opportunity to train at some of the tasks at hand, however. Specialists were sent off to learn about poison gas, hand grenades, and demolition. They learned how to build and stay alive in trenches and about the weapons that they would face. It was all fairly daunting for the "doughboys," especially because they did not speak French. But they soon learned the important phrases, and their confidence inspired the now desperate French nation.

FIRST FIGHT. The German army decided to test the resis-

TANKS

The miles of defensive trenches created a desperate problem. Soldiers could hold the trenches but were powerless to attack against them. What was needed was an armored attack vehicle. But that vehicle needed to be able to cross shell-pocked ground and barbed wire. A possible answer: the tank.

In late 1914, a British staff officer came up with the idea of a "landship." Built like a warship and carried on caterpillar-type tracks, the tank, as it came to be known, was an ingenious military development. It was not, though, a total success story.

The first tanks were lumbering beasts, unbelievably hot and uncomfortable. Crews, stripped down because of the intense heat, shared space with a giant engine. Fumes from the engine and from hot shell cases made the air nearly unbreathable. The first tanks could only move about three or four miles an hour and tended to break down every five to ten miles.

Still, despite its problems, the new tank scared the enemy to death. One German infantryman described the experience of seeing the first tanks. "Panic spread like an electric current…. (Men) were shot down or crushed, while others threw up their hands in terrified surrender…."

Tanks first went into battle in force in 1917. The British used nearly 400 in the Battle of Cambrai in November. Though casualties reached 4,000, the British were able to advance six miles in six hours. For World War I, that was a bargain.

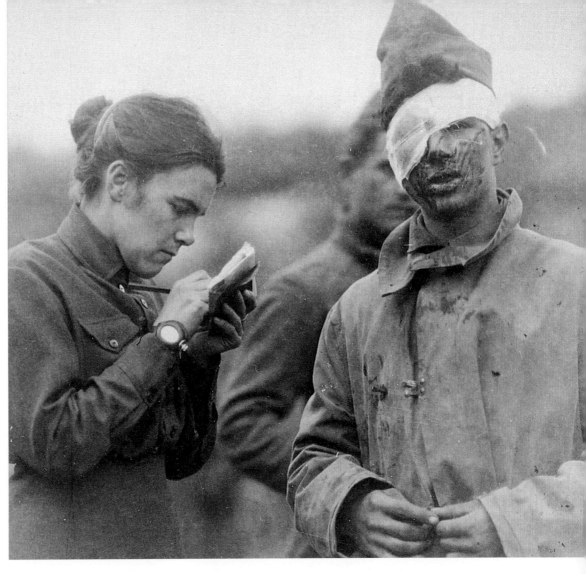

A Salvation Army worker writes a letter for a wounded soldier. Americans were put to the test by battle-hardened German troops.

tance of U.S. troops in April near Seicheprey, a quiet section of the French trenches. In the early morning hours German guns blasted the American lines. Then more than 3,000 German shock troops attacked a trench manned by 470 soldiers from Connecticut. Though the Americans were vastly outnumbered, they didn't panic but fought hard against their attackers. The odds, however, were against the doughboys. One hundred and sixty were killed outright; most of the rest were taken prisoner.

By afternoon, though, the battalion's survivors had taken back the lost ground. Seicheprey was hailed as the first Yank victory. It wasn't quite that, but it did prove to the Germans that U.S. troops would not break and run.

More victories—and hardships—would follow as American troops would be called upon to help hold the tide against Germany's last great offensive.

NURSING THE WOUNDED

As soon as the call came for troops to serve in Europe, another call went out for nurses to take care of the wounded. The casualties in Europe had been overwhelming. There was little doubt that American doughboys would suffer their share.

The nurses in World War I had some of the toughest medical duty ever. They faced the worst military casualties of all time without electricity or antibiotics. They dealt with men and boys riddled with bullets and blinded and scorched by poison gas. Few, if any, were paid for what they did.

Perhaps the best known Allied nurse of the Great War was Vera Brittain. Brittain lost not only her fiancé, but her brother and two friends in the fighting. From a French hospital in 1917, she wrote to her mother:

"I wish those people who write so glibly about going on no matter how long the War lasts and what it may mean, could see a case—to say nothing of 10 cases—of mustard gas in its early stages—could see the poor things burnt and blistered all over… with blind eyes—sometimes temporarily, sometimes permanently…stuck together, and always fighting for breath, with their voices a mere whisper, saying their throats are closing, and they know they will choke."

THE TIDE TURNS

In 1918, the Germans were pushing forward in the north, and the British and French had their hands full. They turned to the Americans to take the small village of Cantigny to gain an observation point of the German front. On the morning of May 28, American troops took Cantigny in less than an hour. Sixteen hundred U.S. troops went down in the fight, in a real, but costly, victory for the Americans.

CHEMIN DES DAMES.

A hard-thinking U.S. Army major who worked under General Pershing had spent considerable time studying German strategy. He felt that the next major attack on the Allied lines would come at the end of May along the Chemin des Dames Ridge. French soldiers occupied this zone. Their commander wasn't convinced an attack was forthcoming, so he did nothing to improve French defenses.

The Germans, however, had gathered nearly 4,000 guns along the forty-mile front. Fifteen new German divisions had been brought up to support the line. On May 27, German artillery erupted, raining shells and gas on the French troops. The attack left the soldiers sick and stunned. They were hardly ready when German soldiers poured out of their trenches and attacked.

The Germans were able to push through the French front remarkably swiftly. Twenty-four hours later, they were on the road to Paris. Once again the French government prepared to evacuate.

HELP FROM PERSHING.

Allied leaders begged Pershing to use some of his troops to stem the tide of Germans heading toward Paris. Although Pershing wanted to keep American troops together, he gave in and offered his soldiers to help hold the French lines.

The U.S. Second Division was brought northward to block the tip of the German advance. As they moved up along the Paris-Metz highway, they met mobs of French refugees on the run from the German guns. French soldiers, their uniforms in shreds, trod the road behind them. Beyond panic and often drunk, the soldiers shouted to the American troops: *"La guerre est finie."* "The war is over."

One French major even ordered an American captain to retreat. He refused: "We just got here," he said.

BELLEAU WOOD.

The Second Division was made up of two brigades. The first was a regular army brigade. The second was composed of two regiments of marines. The marines—seaborne soldiers—were out of place in the French countryside, but Pershing considered them his best fighters.

The Second Division's mission was to capture the small hunting ground, Belleau Wood, where the Germans had dug in. As the American troops approached their target, they were barraged by large-caliber shells. Flying low, German Fokkers strafed the troops with

---

THE AIRPLANE AS WEAPON

The Wright Brothers flew their first airplanes in 1903. Just a dozen years later, military planners were trying to figure out how to use this transportation miracle to make war.

Zeppelins (hydrogen-filled airships) were the

first aircraft to be used for warfare. The Germans dropped bombs from them onto civilian targets in 1915. Airplanes gradually were used for bombing raids on the fronts. But results were generally "hit and miss." A pilot had to hand-toss his bomb from the plane. Bombing tactics improved slowly but surely. Pilots also learned how to "strafe," or fire on, troops from the air.

Strafing was a real problem for soldiers on the ground. They had limited defenses against it, since moving planes were hard to hit from the ground. Aircraft were easier to shoot down from the air by another plane.

That's how aerial "dogfights" began. These battles pitted pilot against pilot, and plane against plane. Allied pilots flew Spads, Nieuports, and Sopwith Pups and Camels (see photo). Germans fought back in their Albatrosses, Pfalzes, and Fokkers.

The Fokker was the favorite plane of the greatest ace of the war, Baron Manfred von Richthofen. Richthofen's own Fokker triplane was painted bloodred. Although the Allies had a number of aces (pilots who had brought down five planes or more), Richthofen had bested them all. When he was finally shot down, the baron had racked up eighty kills. Allied pilots considered him the scourge of the sky, and pilots sweated whenever they saw a crimson plane.

An American gun crew fires on enemy positions. U.S. doughboys had proven that they would not break and run.

machine guns. Though they were at the mercy of the planes, by nightfall the division managed to dig in just north of the road that passed through the wood.

To get at the wood, the Americans needed to take a hill overlooking it where German spotters kept watch.

> *"COME ON!... Do you want to live forever?"*
> —*Sergeant Daniel Daly to his troops, leading the Marine charge into Belleau Wood*

Just before dawn, the marine brigade started for Hill 142. Amid bursts of machine-gun fire, the marines charged the hill and finally took the spotters' position. But the Germans wanted it back. Over and over, they went at the hill and were repulsed by marine fire. At this point the Germans coined a name for the Yankee troops: *Teufelhunden*—the Hounds of Hell. A letter found on a German private read: "The Americans are savages. They kill everything that moves."

DEADLY APPROACH.
By the evening of June 6, U.S. Marines were on the west and southern sides of Belleau Wood. On the west a long buckwheat field stood between the marines and the wood. It had to be crossed.

The marines formed a line and began to wade through the field. The Germans began firing. Machine-gun bullets slashed through the wheat, smashing into some soldiers and pinning the others down. The battalion had struggled about 200 yards when the line collapsed completely. Only a few troops had made it to the edge of the trees.

On the south side of the wood, the other marine battalion managed to get into the trees, crawling on their stomachs and heaving hand grenades as they went. Once inside they realized that a tight grid of German machine-gun nests covered the ground. The woods were strewn with large boulders giving the Germans extra protection for their guns. Taking the position would be like searching a hornet's nest with bare hands.

ARTILLERY SUPPORT.
On June 11, American commanders pulled the brigade back to just outside the wood. Then U.S. artillery hit Belleau with everything it had, ravaging the stand of trees and shelling and gassing the Germans. As the Germans reeled in shock, the marines pushed back inside the trees, capturing 300 enemy soldiers.

It was not over yet. On June 13, after a fair amount of hand-to-hand fighting, the Germans counterattacked. The marines once again proved their skill with rifles, beating back the Germans. By June 25, Belleau Wood, or what was left of it, had been cleared. The marine brigade, though, had lost half of its men. The French people renamed the wood in their honor: *Bois de la Brigade de Marine.*

THE MEUSE-ARGONNE

The Allied armies were now steeled with the addition of more than a million U.S. troops. More were arriving daily. Thus armed, the Allies believed they could push the Germans back beyond the Hindenburg line—their main line of resistance. The Allies also aimed to cut the Germans' main rail supply route.

CROSSING THE LINE. The German Army had had four whole years to fortify the Hindenburg line. Bunkers were reinforced with concrete; trenches bristled with machine-gun nests. Towns in the area had been cleared and turned into virtual forts. Pushing through the Hindenburg would be tough, but the Allies figured they could do it if they hit the Germans all along the Western Front at once.

The battle began on September 12, 1918. More than 200,000 U.S. troops, aided by another 48,000 French soldiers, moved forward. Overhead the sky was filled with Allied planes. French, Italian, U.S., Belgian, Portuguese, and Brazilian pilots provided air support.

The Germans couldn't match such an impressive lineup. American gunners fired hundreds of thousands of phosgene gas shells, stunning the Germans and leaving many unable to fight. After two days the Americans

THE LOST BATTALION

During the congestion and chaos of the battle of Argonne, one U.S. battalion went "missing" for a week. Under orders, a battalion of New York City infantrymen pushed forward and got separated from the rest of their division.

The battalion, commanded by Major Charles Whittlesey, became separated, and then were surrounded—they found themselves at the bottom of a steep ravine with woods on either side. Whittlesey soon figured out that he and his men had slipped through a gap in the German lines. An entire German regiment knew, too, and had completely encircled them, taking the high ground. The doughboys were outnumbered at least five to one.

Whittlesey told his men to dig in. In the morning he sent out patrols to try to find an opening in the German lines. There were none. In the afternoon, the Germans attacked, tossing grenades into the hunkered-down battalion. The Americans, crouched in their foxholes, waited until the Germans were on top of them, then hit back with rifle fire. Their resistance was enough to send the Germans scurrying back into the woods. They would hit the Yankees with shell fire and snipers from a safe distance.

The German shelling continued till sunset. At night each cry of pain from a wounded man brought down a rain of sniper fire. Hit in the knee himself, a captain crawled from one wounded soldier to another. "Everything is practically okay," he would say, trying to console them.

It wasn't close to the truth. The troops were running out of supplies and had virtually no medicine to take care of the wounded. They did, however, have two carrier pigeons. Whittlesey taped a message with the battalion's position onto the leg of one of the birds. He asked for supplies and, most of all, help. He wanted some big guns to cut a path through the circle of Germans around him.

The next day the battalion's hope soared with the carrier pigeon. Someone sighted a spotter plane with red, white, and blue insignia. It dropped a flare near the troops. Suddenly the men were being hit with more shell fire—U.S. shell fire. The spotter plane had dropped the flare too close to them.

Whittlesey wrote another message: "We're along the road parallel 276.4. Our artillery is dropping a barrage directly on us. For heaven's sake, stop it." The message was taped to the last carrier pigeon, Cher Ami. The bird lifted into the air and then faltered, perhaps out of fear of the shell fire. The soldiers threw pebbles to get her airborne again.

As she flew into the sky, German gunners spotted her and rattled bullets up at her. She arrived at her home loft with a shattered breastbone and missing an eye and a leg. But her message was intact. The shelling ceased.

After three more nightmare days, the battalion was rescued. Of 600 men, only 194 were able to walk from the woods. Medics nursed Cher Ami back to health and fitted her with a new leg. At the close of the war, she received the French Croix de Guerre for her bravery.

Buy Your Victory Bonds

A German plane downed by U.S. machine-gunners in the Argonne. The air war heated up as the conflict wore on.

had captured 13,000 prisoners and hundreds of big guns. One particularly lucky sergeant rounded up 300 Germans with an empty pistol.

TO THE ARGONNE. From San Mihiel, an American army of half a million men moved fifty miles northward to help break the Hindenburg line. It started off easily enough. Surprised by the initial attack, which included tanks and air support, the Germans backtracked the first few miles along the Meuse River. The Americans had faced only some intense machine-gun fire directed at them from the thickets.

As they moved into the Argonne Forest, however, the situation worsened. The forest was thick, bouldered terrain, and the Germans, though outnumbered, had the advantage in holding off the attack. The offensive bogged down. The huge number of troops was difficult to supply and even more difficult to manage. In addition, Spanish influenza had arrived in Europe; the doughboys were not only exhausted—many were seriously sick with the deadly flu.

The Americans continued to slog ahead through the

month of October. Every square mile of terrain was fought over. At the end, U.S. troops had cleared the Argonne Forest. In terms of the Allied strategy, it had been a victory. But the cost had been unbelievably high. The Germans had 100,000 casualties. The American toll had reached that number and gone beyond it: 26,000 had been killed and 100,000 wounded. For the Americans, the battle was the largest and costliest engagement of the war.

THE FIGHT FOR YPRES. Along the Belgian lines, things had progressed a little better. The heavily fought-over Passchendaele Ridge near Ypres had been taken from the Germans on the first day of October. German troops had been pulled from the Belgian lines to cover the attack of French and British forces farther south. The Allied plan of attacking all across the Western Front seemed to be working.

The Hindenburg line was broken on the fifth of October. The Germans were in retreat all along the front. In just over a month, the worst war the world had ever seen would be over.

AFTERMATH

The official armistice, or cease-fire, of World War I came on November 11, 1918. The end of the war brought relief to the exhausted Allies. A million U.S. soldiers who had slugged their way through the Argonne Forest could finally come home.

POSTWAR MISERY. The joy of the Allied victory was short-lived, though. The deadly influenza that had struck during the Meuse-Argonne offensive was now spreading with a vengeance. More than half a million people were killed by the virus in the United States alone. Around the world, 20 million people, many already weakened by the war, lost their lives in the epidemic.

For Germany, the influenza was just one more bitter hardship to bear. Though the war had ended in November, the Allies continued the German blockade through March. The Allies were afraid Germany might assemble its forces and start fighting again. The blockade would help prevent that.

For the military, the blockade may have been a smart move. But in Germany, it made a bad situation even worse. Many were left with little food or fuel. Cold and hungry during the entire winter, many died of starvation or the raging flu virus.

PARIS NEGOTIATIONS. From January through June 1919, the Allies discussed the official peace treaty, eventually called the Treaty of Versailles.

This accord—and local conflicts in 1920—would change the map of Europe. Like a great jigsaw puzzle, nations were divided up. Nationalities changed overnight. Serbia became part of the new state of Yugoslavia. Polish people had their country back once again. Germany lost large pieces of territory, mostly to France and Poland. Russia had to give up the Baltic states (Lithuania, Latvia, and Estonia) as well as Finland.

The treaty divided up the old empires. Austria and Hungary, linked in their dual monarchy, were separated. Much of their land was taken to create the new Yugoslavian, Polish, and Czech states. Nearly all of Turkey's Arab lands were taken over by the British and French.

Little consideration was given to the desires of those living in these Arab lands. In fact, the treaty makers neglected the interests of colonial nations almost entirely. This was true despite the fact that large numbers of colonial soldiers had fought bravely for the Allies during the war. Many expected that their countries would be given independence or at least a say in their destiny, in return for their service.

THE FOURTEEN POINTS. One of the treaty provisions—the formation of a League of Nations—was based on President Wilson's idea. Wilson's points, written while the world war was still being waged, rose above the strivings of individual warring nations. He was looking for a way to stop the war and achieve world justice. Woodrow Wilson, along with many others, believed that World War I could be the war to end wars. In order for that to

JOHN PERSHING

One year before he was called to lead the American Expeditionary Force to Europe, John Pershing had led 12,000 men into Mexico. Nearly the entire National Guard had been assembled to hunt for Pancho Villa, the Mexican bandito who had attacked Fort Columbus, New Mexico. The call to arms was decidedly overkill (12,000 against a small band), but it gave Pershing the chance to lead a large force.

When he heard about the approaching declaration of war, Pershing was the first to get in line to lead the troops. Speaking to reporters, he said, "We have broken diplomatic relations with Germany. That means that we will send an expedition abroad. I'd like to command it."

Like other World War I generals, Pershing occasionally found his troops unwilling to attack heavily fortified positions. On at least one occasion, Pershing ordered that stragglers be shot. His officers ignored him.

Pershing, however, was not without emotion. He had lost his wife and two children in a fire in 1916. The death and loss of the many young men who surrounded him during World War I was a replay of a nightmare he could never get over.

During the last offensive of the war, the usually steely Pershing came close to collapse. Covering his face with his hands, the general broke down in front of his driver. "My God," he said. "I sometimes wonder if I can go on."

American and British veterans celebrate the Armistice. The bitter peace would not last.

happen, though, the way nations behaved had to change. In January 1918, Wilson had outlined a series of proposals that he believed would create a just and lasting peace in the world. They included:

1) The end of secret diplomacy; open agreements between nations.
2) General freedom of the seas in peace and war.
3) Removal of world trade barriers and equality of trade conditions.
4) The reduction of armaments (weapons).
5) Settlement of colonial disputes with approval by both sides.

The last of the Fourteen Points advocated the creation of an association of nations.

STRONG OPPOSITION.
The Germans expected the treaty to be based entirely on Wilson's generous Fourteen Points, but they were disappointed. During the war, several Allied nations had made secret promises of land to other countries to get their cooperation. Now these debts were being settled at Germany's expense. The Allies presented Germany with the finished treaty. There were to be no negotiations.

In some ways this was unfair. Germany had not agreed to an "unconditional surrender" and so (legally) should have been able to negotiate a peace settlement. But the Allies were unmoved. Germany had no choice: either sign or return to war.

The Treaty of Versailles may have solved some of Europe's problems, but it created others. Many Germans were strongly opposed to the treaty provisions, especially payment of reparations to the Allies for the cost of the war and loss of lands. Revolutions broke out in Germany and Hungary in protest of the treaty. These revolts failed, but the bitterness that sparked them did not die.

LEAGUE OF NATIONS.
The initial hope was that the world would stabilize if some sort of world organization could control local conflicts. The focus of that hope became the idea of the League of Nations. That hope was dashed when the United States failed to join, but the League had other problems as well.

The main goal of the League of Nations was to keep a world war from ever happening again. Great and small nations could cooperate to keep any one country from attacking another. It was a good idea on paper, but in practice it did not live up to its promise.

The main issue was cooperation. If certain members of the League, especially large and powerful countries, refused to cooperate with the League's wishes, there was little hope of accomplishing anything. The League had no way to enforce its will. The failure of the League did not actively lead to the aggression that would overwhelm Europe in the 1930s. Given its weakness, though, the League was only able to watch as Germany kindled the flames of another world war.

WORLD WAR TWO

WORLD WAR II (1939–1945) EUROPEAN THEATER

- Germany, 1933 borders
- German Annexed and Occupied Territory, 1942
- German Allied or Dependent States
- Allied Nations, 1942
- Countries proclaimed Neutral
- ✦ Major battles

0   400 Mi.

IRELAND

ATLANTIC OCEAN

PORT.

Gibraltar (Br.)

SPANISH MOROCCO

● Casablan

MOROCCO (Vichy Fr.

Following World War I, the United States rode an economic roller coaster. The prosperous Roaring Twenties were followed by the worst economic depression the United States had ever known. Struggling to get on its feet, the nation was slowly but surely drawn into another world war.

The United States, which prided itself on independence and isolation, would now become a key player in changing the face of Europe. Although it fought hard to keep out of this Second World War, the United States would develop and use the most destructive weapon of all time to win it.

World War I had made the United States a global power, but World War II would transform the nation into a world leader. When this war began in Europe, the U.S. military ranked seventeenth in the world. By war's end, the United States had become a superpower with no equal.

Coast Guardsman, World War II

1939–1941

World War II begins in Europe as Hitler invades Poland *(Sept. 1, 1939)*.

Japanese planes bomb Pearl Harbor *(Dec. 7, 1941)*.

U.S. troops surrender in Bataan, giving up Philippines to Japan *(April 1941)*.

1942

U.S. Navy defeats Japanese fleet in Battle of the Coral Sea *(May)*.

U.S. Navy defeats Japanese in Battle of Midway, stopping their eastward thrust *(June)*.

U.S. forces invade Guadalcanal *(Aug.)*.

U.S. and British forces land in North Africa and suffer defeats at Kasserine Pass in Tunisia *(Nov.)*.

1943

Solomon Islands liberated by U.S. forces *(March)*.

German and Italian forces surrender in North Africa *(May)*.

Allied forces invade Sicily *(July)*.

Italy surrenders to the Allies though fighting within Italy continues *(Sept.)*.

NORWAY

SWEDEN

FINLAND

Leningrad (besieged)

ESTONIA

LATVIA

Moscow

SOVIET UNION

North Sea

DENMARK

Baltic Sea

LITHUANIA

Danzig

Kursk

Stalingrad

GREAT BRITAIN

London

NETH.

Berlin

GERMANY

Warsaw

POLAND

Kiev

Elbe R.

BELG.

Battle of the Bulge

LUX.

CZECHOSLOVAKIA (SLOVAKIA)

Normandy

Paris

Alsace-Lorraine

Munich

Rhine R.

Danube R.

AUSTRIA

HUNGARY

Vichy

VICHY FRANCE (occupied by Germany)

SWITZ.

ITALY

Adriatic Sea

YUGOSLAVIA (SERBIA)

ROMANIA

Black Sea

BULGARIA

SPAIN

Rome

Anzio

Monte Cassino

ALBANIA

Aegean Sea

GREECE

TURKEY

SYRIA

CYPRUS (Br.)

Algiers

Oran

Tunis

Kasserine Pass

MALTA (Br.)

LEBANON

PALESTINE (Br.)

Suez Canal

TRANSJORDAN (Br.)

ALGERIA (Vichy Fr.)

TUNISIA (Vichy Fr.)

Mediterranean Sea

El Alamein

Cairo

LIBYA

EGYPT

1944

U.S. forces invade Marshall Islands and land at Anzio Beach in Italy (Jan.).

Allied forces storm the beaches along the Normandy coast of France (June 6).

U.S. forces take the Mariana Islands (July).

Paris is liberated (Aug. 25).

U.S. forces cross German border (Sept.15).

U.S. forces return to the Philippines (Oct.).

U.S. wins major naval battle at Leyte Gulf (Oct.).

Germans launch major counterattack at the Battle of the Bulge near Bastogne, Belgium (Dec.).

1945

U.S. Marines land on Iwo Jima (Feb.).

U.S. forces invade Okinawa.

Americans and Soviets meet in Germany (April).

Germany surrenders unconditionally (May 8).

U.S. drops atomic bombs on Hiroshima (Aug. 6) and Nagasaki (Aug. 9). Japan surrenders (Aug. 15).

PRELUDE TO WAR—EUROPE

In 1919, after five years of conflict, few could imagine that in twenty short years Europe would once again be at war. The results of the Great War were everywhere: starving refugees, smashed towns, disfigured and crippled soldiers, and gashed fields filled with half-buried dead.

But the defeat of Germany in World War I had left many questions unanswered. Powerful national interests and strong ideologies were still brewing discontent throughout Europe and Asia.

CHANGES IN GERMANY. The Treaty of Versailles had stripped Germany's military of soldiers and weapons. A democratic Weimar government had replaced the German kaiser. The treaty had also scissored away a quarter of German territory and dissolved the empires that had once been Germany's allies.

Moreover, the Allies were forcing Germany to pay reparations for civilian property destroyed during the war. To the Allies, these payments seemed fair because, in their view, Germany had started World War I.

A poster exhorts Germans to "look to your colonies." The Nazis had their eyes on reclaiming territory lost after the world war.

Deutschland, deine Kolonien!

Yet other provisions of the treaty limited Germany['s] ability to produce goods and sell them. The country['s] ability to make money in the world market was part[ly] cut off. Germany had no real way of getting the cash i[t] needed to make reparation payments. As the Germa[n] economy shrank, Germans bristled at the unfairness o[f] this situation.

Germany had no tradition of real democracy. Th[e] democratic regime that took over after the war was frag[]ile and faced many enemies. The Russian Revolutio[n] had popularized the idea of communism. Some support[]ed this idea for Germany. Other Germans wanted t[o] return their country to its old traditions. They wante[d] the kaiser, Germany's old ruler, to return from exile an[d] rule Germany as before.

The democratic Weimar government was trying t[o] make Germany stable, but it faced some of the bleakes[t] financial prospects Germany had ever known. Thes[e] prospects grew even bleaker when the Grea[t] Depression began in the United States and bleaker stil[l] when financial markets collapsed around the world. T[o] avoid paying reparations, German currency was deval[]ued severely. Eventually, it took millions of marks (th[e] German unit of currency) to buy a loaf of bread.

REVOLTS AROUND THE WORLD. Germany wasn't the onl[y] country in crisis. Revolution and dissent erupte[d] throughout Eastern Europe and Asia.

Discontent after the Great War sparked a search fo[r] new leadership. Across the world, many looked to th[e] bold new workers' state being advanced in communis[t] Russia, although few realized how brutal it ha[d] become. Other countries, struggling to find security i[n] the ashes of the war, clung to ultranationalistic ideals[,] especially fascism.

FASCISM ON THE RISE. The idea of fascism had starte[d] in Italy during the early 1920s. Fascism saw the stat[e] as the ultimate power. Individuals only had worth i[f] they served the state. Fascists were antidemocratic[.] They believed in controlling society and completel[y] quashing opposition.

During the late 1920s and 1930s, fascists gaine[d] power in many European countries, including Portuga[l,] Croatia, Romania, Hungary, Spain, Italy, and Germany[.] There were small fascist parties in Britain, France[,] and Poland.

Though fascism made harsh demands, it seemed t[o] many to offer a cure for the frightening chaos that afflict[]ed Europe after WWI. Millions of Europeans lacke[d] work, food, and clothing. As conditions grew worse, the[y] became willing to trade freedoms for a steady job an[d] bread to eat. For many, unwilling or unable to see th[e] future, fascism seemed like a reasonable choice.

The German Reichstag burns. Many suspected that the fire was set by the Nazis.

THE NAZIS GAIN POWER.

The National Socialist (Nazi) Party had been gaining support in Germany since the end of the 1920s. Though it claimed to support the rights of workers, the party was strictly fascist. Its leader, Adolf Hitler, was a persuasive speaker and powerful manipulator. Throughout the 1920s, he, along with other Nazis, preached the doctrines of National Socialism to anyone who would listen.

Like Hitler himself, many of the first Nazis were bitter soldiers from World War I. They blamed their defeat on communists and German Jews. They belittled democracy, which they identified with weakness and defeat.

> *"Once we have the power, we will never give it up."*
>
> —Joseph Goebbels, Hitler's aide
> (later Minister of Propaganda)

Though it had few members at first, the Nazi Party slowly gained strength in Germany. Nazi storm troopers (uniformed strongmen) intimidated and attacked their opponents openly in the streets. Meanwhile Hitler courted powerful allies in the army and in industry.

By 1932, the Nazis wielded considerable power in the German parliament (Reichstag), but that was not what Hitler wanted. He had openly stated that he wished to crush the now weakened Weimar government. He scorned the whole idea of democracy and advised Nazi deputies to "hold their noses" while in the Reichstag.

Hitler wanted absolute power, but he wanted to get it legally. At the end of January 1933, he got his chance. With another crisis in the government, German President Paul von Hindenburg was forced to appoint a new chancellor. Because of the Nazis' powerful position, he had no real choice but to name Hitler.

Hindenburg—as well as other leaders of the Reichstag—believed they could keep Hitler under control. They were wrong. Hitler was determined to take total control of the government. To do this he would have to destroy the German constitution and abolish the civil rights it guaranteed to the people of Germany.

Hitler needed an excuse to declare an emergency and suspend the rights guaranteed by the constitution. On the night of February 27, 1933, he got his opportunity when the Reichstag building was set on fire. Many suspected that the fire had been set by the Nazis, but a Dutchman was charged. President von Hindenburg signed an emergency decree suspending civil rights.

NAZIS TAKE CONTROL.

Given a free hand by the decree, Hitler's aides terrorized Nazi opponents throughout much of Germany. In the next election, the Nazis polled over 17 million votes, more than any other party. But again Hitler and his party did not win enough votes to gain a clear majority.

More importantly, Hitler needed a full two-thirds majority to change the constitution. So he proceeded to change the percentages in his favor. Though eighty-one communist deputies had been elected, those seats were empty when the Reichstag opened. Most of the deputies had been arrested by the secret police; the rest were running for their lives.

The German Centre Party was all that stood between Hitler and dictatorship. On March 23, these deputies threw in their lot with Hitler. This allowed him to disband the constitution. The Nazis now began to take total control of Germany. The government, workers' unions, radio, and press—all were under Hitler's iron hand.

FASCISM DOMINATES EUROPE

In the 1930s political quakes shook Europe. The aftermath of World War I had given birth to two strong political movements: fascism and communism. These state-centered ideologies fought for center stage in Europe—and around the globe—as the world tilted toward another great war.

AGGRESSION IN EUROPE. Italy's fascist government was led by Benito Mussolini. Nicknamed Il Duce by his Italian admirers, Mussolini set the standard for fascist aggression that would become a staple in the world war to come. In 1935, Mussolini's troops marched into tiny Ethiopia, a nation in East Africa. The Italians terror-bombed small towns to crush the country's morale. Ethiopia's democratic allies, including Britain and France, ignored repeated pleas from Ethiopia's leader, Haile Selassie, for help.

Large anti-Jewish riots spilled through the French streets in 1934. Fascist groups there, particularly the Croix de Feu (Cross of Fire), used riots in an attempt to bring down the French democracy. In 1936, after battling fierce demonstrations and street fights, the French government banned the Croix de Feu and other fascist parties.

In Spain the conflict between republican-communists and nationalists exploded into a gruesome civil war. In 1931 Spain's king, Alphonse XIII, was deposed by Republican (procommunist) forces. In 1936 a fascist general, Francisco Franco, led a force that captured much of southern Spain and laid siege to its capital, Madrid. Germany and Italy were interested in the success of fellow fascists. They sent military supplies, and their pilots terror-bombed Spanish towns.

The Soviet Union sent aid to the procommunist Republicans. They were also helped by the International Brigade, volunteers from around the world. Many of these soldiers were not communists but were willing to stake their lives in the fight against fascism.

The writer Ernest Hemingway and thousands of other Americans served in the war. In one battle, the Abraham Lincoln Brigade attacked fascist troops as they laid siege to Madrid. More than 400 U.S. volunteers were wounded or killed in heavy fighting.

THE FÜHRER'S GERMANY. As the fascist flame spread through Europe, Hitler consolidated his power within Germany. He formed organizations to further the Nazi cause, including the *Hitler Jugend* for boys and *Bund deutscher Madel* for adolescent girls. Schoolbooks, especially history books, were rewritten to reflect Nazi values. Hitler even tried to nazify the Protestant churches.

But Hitler was not just interested in co-opting

TRIUMPH OF THE WILL

Hitler was fond of public appearances and was a master at manipulating crowds. The huge Nazi rally held in the town of Nuremberg in 1935 gave the führer an opportunity to exhibit a full range of Nazi pomp and power. Hitler hired director Leni Riefenstahl to film the rally. Her work, the *Triumph of the Will*, is still considered the most powerful political propaganda film of all time.

Through expressive camera work and lighting, Riefenstahl created a monument to Nazism. Hitler's plane is filmed descending majestically from the clouds, while crowds below receive him as heaven-sent. Riefenstahl intercuts intense close-ups of individual admirers with shots of huge Nazi crowds to show Hitler's personal as well as mass appeal.

The rally features dozens of speakers. The task of showing long speeches without boring viewers is a challenge. Riefenstahl overcame this problem in a variety of ways. When Hitler's ministers are speaking, she edits them so severely, each is only permitted a few key lines. Her technique may have been the first use of the political sound bite.

Hitler's own speeches are intercut with dramatic images—swirling swastikas, flashing belt buckles, gleaming jackboots, and awestruck faces. There is no opportunity for boredom.

Triumph of the Will made Riefenstahl's reputation as a director but destroyed her career. So powerful was the effect of her film that it was banned in Germany after the war. Many feared the movie might inspire the rise of new Nazi movements. Riefenstahl herself was also banned—she was no longer permitted to make films in Germany and much of the world. The filmmaker now insists that she never supported the Nazis and was forced by Hitler to make the film.

The debate over *Triumph of the Will* continues. Can great art serve evil purposes? Are creative artists responsible for how their work is used?

The Nuremberg rally demonstrated fascist pomp and power. Its decrees were the first step in destroying German Jews.

German minds. He wanted to change the makeup of the German people. In his vision of Germany, there was no place for the deformed, the weak, or the handicapped, or for any Jews. He particularly blamed Jews for Germany's defeat in World War I. He called communism a Jewish movement, further distancing German Jews from "loyal" Germans. He wanted to form a pure "master" race and insisted that Jews were "poisoning German blood."

> *"The supreme Court of the German people during these twenty-four hours consisted of myself."*
>
> — *Adolf Hitler, after arresting and shooting numbers of SA storm troopers*

THE NUREMBERG LAWS. In 1935, the Nazis held a huge rally at Nuremberg. During the meeting the Nuremberg Decrees were established. These laws were designed to close Jews out of German business and society. Jews could no longer marry non-Jews. They were banned from government positions. Many of their civil rights were taken away.

Jews were shocked by the laws. Though they made up less than one percent of the population of Germany, German Jews considered themselves very German. Many had fought in World War I, and not a few had been decorated. Jews had lived in Germany for generations and were strongly connected to German society. For many, the laws seemed unbelievable. Though some Germans emigrated after the Nuremberg Decrees were passed, most believed the Nazi era would not last. For many, this assumption would prove a fatal mistake.

CUTTING TIES. Under Hitler, Germany had been rearming itself, creating an air force, and increasing the number of German army troops. This, of course, was forbidden by the Versailles Treaty. But Hitler was certain that England wanted to keep the peace and would not oppose his buildup. Without England's backing, France would be almost powerless to stop him. He had already withdrawn Germany from the League of Nations, further distancing himself from the rest of Europe.

Hitler wanted to secure his power within the German state. For this he needed the loyalty of the German army. Ernst Roehm had been Hitler's friend since the 1920s and served as commander of the brutal Nazi private police force (the SA). Roehm believed he and his men could challenge and replace the old German army. Roehm thought he was a true Nazi, but Hitler saw him as a threat. On June 30, 1934, on Hitler's orders, most of the leaders of the SA were arrested and executed. Roehm was ordered to commit suicide. When he refused, he was shot.

Many thought Hitler's brutal move would undo the Nazis, but the killings just strengthened Hitler's position. A few months later, President Hindenburg died. Hitler, in a decree, combined the powers of chancellor and president. He was all-powerful now. No one within Germany could stop him.

THE WORLD WAR BEGINS

The Great War had been over for less than fifteen years when Hitler came to power. European countries, especially England and France, had lost millions of young men in the war. They were still torn by political strife, and their economies were in shambles from the worldwide depression. Hardly anyone in Europe could face the idea of more bloodshed.

EXPANDING GERMAN BORDERS. In fact, many European leaders were willing to do just about anything to prevent another war. Hitler was not one of them. The paralyzing fear of war, in fact, played into Hitler's and other fascist plans to grab territory throughout the 1930s.

Hitler, in particular, believed the German state had to expand to become more powerful. He wanted to enlarge Germany by absorbing Austria. He also had his eyes on territory that belonged to Germany before the First World War. This included the Saar region, portions of Czechoslovakia, and part of Poland, including the city of Danzig (see map on pages 106–107). These were all areas where German-speaking people lived.

In 1935, Saar citizens voted to return to Germany.

Then in early 1936, in violation of treaties, German troops occupied the Rhineland, a German territory that had been demilitarized after 1919. Neither England nor France moved to stop them.

AUSTRIA IN CHAOS. Austria had been part of the large Austro-Hungarian Empire before the war. Now it was just a small country of 6.5 million people. The world economic depression had hit the country hard. Some Austrians favored a union with Germany, if only to regain position as a world power. Others wanted to preserve a democratic state.

In early 1934, a brief civil war broke out in Vienna. Hitler had pressed Austria's Chancellor Engelbert Dollfuss to resign and let Austrian Nazis take over the government. But Dollfuss resisted. The Nazis, though, weren't to be ignored. In July, Austrian Nazis seized the main government buildings in Vienna. They broke into Chancellor Dollfuss's office and murdered him.

To nearly everyone's surprise, the takeover failed. An ally of Dollfuss took over the Austrian government and headed it for the next four years. Hitler, however, did not give up on making Austria part of the German Reich. In the spring of 1938, the German army marched into Austria and took over the government. Austria was officially annexed in what was known as the *Anschluss*. There was little opposition to the move. Immediately, intense persecution of Austrian Jews began.

JEWISH PERSECUTION. At the same time, Hitler kept up his pressure on Jews within Germany. In 1938, non-German Jews, mostly Poles, were expelled from the country.

By the autumn of 1938, Jewish shops were closed and turned over to non-Jews. Jewish men and women were

---

KRISTALLNACHT

On November 9, 1938, a German diplomat was killed by a Polish Jew in Paris. The following night, Nazi storm troopers (SA), along with other Germans, smashed and looted Jewish-owned shops in major cities throughout Germany.

There was so much scattered glass on the sidewalks and streets, that people in Berlin coined the term "*Kristallnacht*" (Night of Crystals) for the episode. This is one German woman's remembrance of *Kristallnacht*, from a book entitled *Frauen*:

"*That evening, I wrote a letter and wanted to go mail it. And I saw an enormous crowd on the streets, and the most elegant street of Wiesbaden. It's a long, wide street with very elegant shops. They were almost all Jewish-* owned. The synagogues were burning. And the SA man grabbed my arm and told me, 'Fraulein, get away. There's nothing here for you....' The next day one heard, ja, it was the anger of the Volk that caused the synagogues to burn. The anger of the Volk [German people] unloaded itself on the Jews. But it was not the anger of the Volk. It was the SA that did it all. I saw all the SA men on the streets, how they pushed the Jews together and how they threw stones through the panes of glass, and destroyed the stores, tore everything out and threw it in the street. Went up in the homes, threw all the furniture out the windows, and took the Jews away. It was horrible. One thought, 'For God's sake, what is going on?'*"

German police march into Austria. Soon Hitler's armies would be pounding over much of Europe.

barred from all professions, such as medicine or law. Jews could no longer attend German universities. At the same time the Nazis began to build more concentration camps. In November of 1938, Hitler instigated a pogrom or massacre of Jews (see sidebar), and the camps began to fill.

Some in Germany opposed Hitler's policies, but most were silent. The few who did speak out usually ended up in the concentration camps.

After the pogrom, many Jews panicked and tried to leave Germany, but foreign countries, including the United States, refused to take them in large numbers.

MUNICH AGREEMENT.
The country of Czechoslovakia had been formed by the Treaty of Versailles after World War I ended. It was composed of a variety of peoples including 7 million Czechs, as well as Slovaks, Hungarians, Ruthenes, Poles, Romanians, and Yugoslavs. It also contained more than 3 million Germans living in the northern part of the country—the Sudetenland.

Hitler wanted control over the Sudeten Germans. As war threatened in 1938, British prime minister Neville Chamberlain and representatives of France met Hitler in Munich. The leaders agreed simply to hand over this part of Czechoslovakia to Germany. The Czechs were not consulted about the agreement to dismember their country. But England and France felt that they had made the best of a bad situation and had avoided war. Chamberlain returned to Britain with Hitler's signature, saying it guaranteed "peace in our time."

That peace would prove short-lived. In March 1939, the Czech leader, President Emil Hacha, was pressured into surrendering the rest of the Czech nation to Germany. Hitler's air marshall, Hermann Göering, threatened to smash the capital of Prague if he refused.

England and France knew they were in trouble. The question was: what to do? They could no longer just watch as Hitler grabbed up Europe piece by piece. In a speech on March 17, 1939, Neville Chamberlain asked the question that was on everyone's mind: "Is this... (Hitler's) attempt to dominate the world by force?"

THE POLISH CORRIDOR.
After the First World War, the Treaty of Versailles had taken a piece of German territory and given it to Poland. This piece of land, known as the Polish Corridor, separated the still-German state of East Prussia from the rest of Germany (see map on pages 106–107). The northern section bordered the sea and included the important port of Danzig. Germans, especially Hitler, were determined to have the corridor returned.

But France and Britain now agreed not to allow Hitler to annex Polish territory by force. At the end of March, they signed a document guaranteeing Poland protection against German aggression. Remarkably, though, England and France were still open to negotiations concerning Polish territory. Hitler, however, was bent on war, and in April 1939 ordered preparations for an attack to begin on September 1.

Meanwhile, Hitler made a pact with the Russians not to oppose Germany's interests in Poland. Italy, as well, agreed to fight with Germany should it go to war. Strained negotiations continued through August 1939. Then Hitler struck. On September 1, the German Army, the *Wehrmacht*, attacked Poland. For the next two days, British and French ministers tried to negotiate their way out of war. But Hitler would not be budged out of Poland.

On September 3, France and Britain declared war on Germany. A new world war began.

BLITZKRIEG

When Hitler refused to withdraw his forces from Poland, England and France declared war on Germany. Neither Britain nor France was prepared for a major war, especially the kind of war Hitler was about to wage. During the next two years, nearly every country in Western Europe would be brought to its knees by the German *blitzkrieg*, or lightning war. Hitler's army, the *Wehrmacht*, appeared invincible.

POLAND FALLS. Germany invaded Poland on September 1, 1939. Hitler had destroyed most of the Polish Air Force while its planes were still on the ground, and the German *Luftwaffe* dominated the skies. By the end of the month, Poland was defeated.

Neither Britain nor France gave the Poles any direct help. Though the Polish Army fought bravely, it was outnumbered and outgunned by the Germans. As if that weren't enough, Russia attacked Poland from the east in the middle of September, sealing its fate.

Hitler's defeat of the Poles was followed by a brutal campaign against Polish Jews. Most of Europe's Jewish population, more than 1.5 million, lived in Poland. The country had a history of anti-Semitism (violence against Jews), and some Poles cooperated with the Nazis, leading them to Jewish families. Jews were forced to wear an armband with a Star of David. During 1940, many were killed openly and brutally, sometimes barricaded in synagogues and burned to death. Others were forced into large concentrated ghettoes in cities like Lodz and Warsaw.

SCANDINAVIA OCCUPIED. Hitler knew he would need raw materials to continue his drive through Europe. The Scandinavian countries could provide Germany with food, iron ore, aluminum, and other resources.

In the spring of 1940, Hitler's forces occupied all of Norway and Denmark. Small resistance groups, especially in Norway, would continue to work against the Nazis throughout the war.

The loss of Norway, in particular, was a nightmare for the Allies. Hitler was now in control of the Norwegian fjords. From these secure inlets, he could launch warships and submarines to prey upon Allied shipping.

THE NETHERLANDS AND BELGIUM CRUSHED. When war broke out in 1939, the king of Belgium, Leopold III, and the Dutch Queen Wilhelmina appealed to France, Germany, and England to make peace. Belgium, in particular, had suffered horribly in the First World War, and did not wish to repeat the experience.

The last-minute appeal was poignant but useless. Although Hitler promised to respect Dutch neutrality, Germany invaded the Netherlands, terror-bombing the city of Rotterdam. German forces crashed through Belgium and Luxembourg to outflank or swing around the Allied lines.

FRANCE THREATENED. The French believed they could defeat a German invasion. They relied on the Maginot Line, a series of strong fortifications built between the wars to make sure the Germans stayed on their side of the border. The line stretched from Switzerland to the Belgian-Luxembourg border and into the south of France. At the edge of the Belgian-Luxembourg frontier lay the thick

SUBMARINES

Submarines were used extensively in World War II by the United States, Britain, Japan, Germany, and Italy. Japanese subs, in particular, were very adaptable. Some were capable of carrying up to three aircraft. Other, smaller vessels held midget submarines or "human torpedoes," the seaborne counterpart to kamikaze (suicide) aircraft.

American subs were large and fast and carried twenty or more torpedoes or up to thirty-two mines. Compared to other subs, they were fast and easy to live in. Ships could stay out for as long as seventy-five days, traveling up to 11,000 nautical miles.

German attack submarines (U-boats) were the terror of the Atlantic during the early years of the war. They very nearly shut down shipments to Britain. Sleek and fast, the subs were nicknamed "Gray Wolves" and traveled in "wolfpacks" of ten to twenty. They carried roughly the same number of torpedoes as American subs but could travel up to 32,300 nautical miles. Near the war's end, they were supplied and refueled by large *Milch Cow* submarines.

To defeat the U-boats, the Allies began to use convoys to carry supplies to Britain. Heavily armed destroyers could defend against torpedo attacks. The U-boat kill rate gradually dropped off. By the end of 1943, German U-boats, beset by aircraft and radar, could hardly surface at all, even at night.

British firefighters struggle against London blazes. The Blitz killed thousands but stiffened British resolve.

Ardennes Forest. The Allies believed the Germans could not get through the Ardennes with heavy tanks.

In order to get around these defenses, Hitler's army would have to come in on the north, through Holland and Belgium (see main map on pages 106–107). The Allied armies moved up to meet them there and throw them back.

THE GERMAN SURPRISE.
The combined forces of the Allies (England, France, Belgium, and Holland) and those of Germany were roughly equal. Under normal circumstances, the Allies should have been able to fight off the Germans. Hitler, however, unleashed several surprises. In a brilliant strategy, he lined up the strongest German divisions against the weakest Allied lines and thrust through them with his heavy tanks.

At the same time, the *Wehrmacht* crashed through the Ardennes, throwing the French into complete confusion. Instead of aiming toward Paris, as it had in World War I, the German Army now pushed toward the French ports of Boulogne, Calais, and Dunkirk.

Desperate, France urged the British to throw in everything they had, especially the Royal Air Force (RAF), to defend France. But Prime Minister Winston Churchill, who had replaced Neville Chamberlain, insisted that he had to keep some forces to defend Britain.

The French government began to panic. French forces led by General Charles de Gaulle led a brief counterattack against the Germans. But it was not nearly enough to halt the enemy. On May 24, 1940, German Panzer divisions reached Abbeville on the Somme River. The French government began to collapse.

EVACUATION AT DUNKIRK.
The British Expeditionary Force was now trapped between the closing pincers of the *Wehrmacht*. In a matter of days, British soldiers were fighting with their backs against the waters of the English Channel.

The entire British force, as well as large numbers of French and other Allied troops, were now in danger of being captured by the Germans. Churchill was determined to save them, even though it would take something close to a miracle. Many in Britain's government had already given them up as lost.

An evacuation across the channel to England finally began on May 24. For the next eleven days, 338,226 Allied soldiers made their escape as brave French soldiers under ferocious German fire held the beachhead. Although a huge number of Allied troops—40,000 over the eleven days—were captured, the majority of the British Army was saved.

The evacuation was important from a military point of view, but it was also important politically. France was already asking for a separate peace with the Germans. England could hardly stand alone against Germany after losing most of its army.

Before the Dunkirk evacuation, the British Cabinet was seriously considering asking Hitler for peace terms. With their narrow escape across the English Channel, the British determined to keep on fighting.

EUROPE FALLS TO THE NAZIS

The German blitzkrieg raged over Europe throughout 1940 and 1941. Americans, though they still clung to neutrality, were hoping that Hitler might be stopped. But as the new decade began, fewer and fewer countries were left standing to oppose him.

FRANCE FALLS. In the aftermath of Dunkirk, France surrendered to the Nazis. What was left of the French Army escaped to Britain. There it would be led by General Charles de Gaulle, who was already working to form a Free French government in exile. A puppet government, based in Vichy, was set up by the Germans within France.

BATTLE OF BRITAIN. In order to invade England, Hitler had to control the airspace over southern England. From August to October of 1940, the Royal Air Force (RAF) battled incoming German bombers over England in some of the fiercest dogfighting ever seen.

RAF losses were severe—900 planes went down in three months. The life expectancy of fighter pilots was measured in weeks. German losses, though, were even heavier. Unable to achieve control over English airspace, Hitler cancelled his invasion but began to terror-bomb the British. From November 1940 to May 1941, German bombers "blitzed" British cities.

Many British city kids were sent to live out the Blitz in safer rural areas. Terrified Londoners crowded into tube (subway) stations while the bombing raged. Others sheltered as best they could, wherever they could, as German bombers droned overhead.

During the Blitz of Britain, British cryptographers were hard at work trying to break Germany's Enigma code. The German high command believed the code could not be cracked. But British intelligence got a lucky break. Before Poland fell to the Germans, Polish scientists smuggled a version of the Enigma code machine out of the country. They gave the machine to the British, who soon broke Enigma. The intelligence gathered from decoded German messages became known as ULTRA.

RESISTANCE

Though Europe's democracies were almost entirely under fascist control in 1941, their populations were not entirely silent or submissive. Every country occupied by the Axis powers (Germany, Italy, and Japan) had resisters. They collected intelligence, helped persecuted people to stay alive or escape, and sabotaged the war effort. Women, in particular, proved excellent and aggressive resistance workers.

Charles de Gaulle led the Free French forces from England, but Jean Moulin held the Resistance movement together within France. Shortly after they took over, the Nazis tried to make Moulin, a prefect, sign a report saying French troops had committed atrocities. Moulin preferred to cut his own throat. He survived the injury but lost his job.

He soon found another. As head of the Resistance movement within France, Moulin managed to combine the many, often competing, groups of workers into one force. In his position, he knew more than anyone else about the movement. He was terrified of being caught and breaking under interrogation.

Part of his fears were realized. In June 1943, Moulin was arrested by the Gestapo in Lyon. He was tortured by the Gestapo chief, Klaus Barbie, but refused to betray his Resistance comrades. He was so badly tortured that he died while being taken back to Germany by train.

France was not the only European country to have a strong Resistance movement. In Norway, the Sivorg movement organized strong civil resistance. They encouraged small defiant acts and giving a collective "cold-shoulder" to the Nazi occupiers. Subtle yet powerful, the tactic proved successful at limiting the strength of the Nazis within Norway.

In Denmark, the Resistance's escape service organized the transport of several thousand Jews across the sound to Sweden. Resistance workers in the Netherlands organized mass strikes against the arrests of Jews. In Bulgaria, mass opposition to Jewish deportation kept Bulgarian Jews from being sent to death camps. Polish resistance was particularly strong, especially considering the brutality of the country's defeat and occupation.

The Warsaw rising saw a quarter of a million Poles go to their deaths in a final act of defiance against Nazi oppression.

Even within Germany there were those who resisted the Nazis and spoke out against Hitler's terrors. Dietrich Bonhoeffer, a German Protestant pastor, was among the first to protest the Nazi influence on the church in Germany. He continued to work against Hitler during the war. Arrested in 1943, Bonhoeffer was executed at Flossenburg just before the war in Europe ended, in April 1945.

Resistance, by itself, did not win the war. But it gave the the Nazis chronic headaches which kept them from focusing all of their attention (as well as their troops) on the war effort. In that sense, it was at the heart of Hitler's defeat.

Many Resistance workers had ordinary existences before the Nazi era. They were human beings who were often afraid for their lives. Simple acts of sabotage could mean a firing squad. Yet these ordinary people steeled themselves and managed to strike a blow against fascism that, to this day, remains unforgettable.

A German poster calls all young boys to join the Hitler Youth. Nazi clubs helped shape young Germans into fascist thinkers.

One of the first pieces of information obtained by ULTRA was the plan for "Moonlight Sonata." This was a code name for an upcoming German bombing raid on the English city of Coventry. Though the British command knew about the raid in advance, they did not dare to risk notifying the population for fear that the Germans would realize their code was no longer secret.

Coventry was bombed by Germany during the night of November 14–15, 1940. Between 350 and 400 people died.

More than 43,000 civilians died in the Blitz. German incendiaries set historic cities like Bath and Coventry blazing. But Britain refused to give up. Said a defiant Churchill: "We will never surrender."

Even as Hitler blitzed English cities, he was also waging war in the waters of the Atlantic. Sleek, lethal German submarines torpedoed ships in British waters (see sidebar on page 114). Millions of tons of food and supplies drowned in salt water as Hitler tried to starve Britain into surrender.

U.S. REACTION.
The bombing of Britain and its battle in the Atlantic brought home the horror of the war to the United States. President Franklin Roosevelt looked for a way to help the British without violating U.S. neutrality. The U-boats were bringing Britain to its knees. Churchill begged Roosevelt for fifty to sixty destroyers to keep the submarines in check.

Britain had no way to pay for the ships; it was all but bankrupt. Simply sending the ships to Britain, a nation at war, would be seen as an act of war and would violate U.S. neutrality. But Roosevelt believed he had to take the risk. He sent Britain a batch of World War I destroyers, knowing he would face criticism for it.

BRITAIN STANDS ALONE.
European democracy was in a tailspin. The northern two-thirds of France were occupied. Fascists had taken power in Romania, and now that country was allied with Germany. In April, the Greek Army surrendered to Italian and German forces. The British were attempting to put out fascist fires all over the globe. They bested Mussolini's Italian forces in East Africa and defeated the Italian Navy at Cape Matapan. Now, though, they faced the German Africa Korps led by General Erwin Rommel.

LEND-LEASE.
Although most Americans still insisted on staying neutral, Roosevelt felt that the situation demanded more U.S. action. During one of his radio broadcasts, the president announced his plan for the United States to become the "great arsenal of democracy." Since the British could no longer afford to buy arms, the United States would "lend" them to Britain.

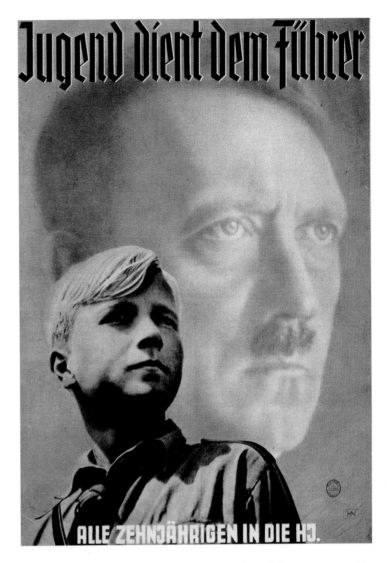

The extra arms helped the British hold out into 1941. Hitler was unable to force the quick surrender he had expected. Frustrated, he turned his attention to Russia.

HITLER TURNS EAST.
Though the Soviet Union and Germany had signed a nonaggression pact in 1939, Hitler had always had his eye on western Russia for German expansion and was now determined to attack his eastern ally. In April, paving the way, the Germans trounced tiny Yugoslavia. The Yugoslavs fought desperately; the wounded and dead approached 100,000. But within two weeks, the Nazis had control of the country.

In June 1941, in an operation code-named Barbarossa, German troops invaded the Soviet Union. Moving quickly through Minsk, Smolensk, Sevastopol, and Kiev, the Germans captured nearly one million Russian soldiers in less than a month.

Only in the north were the Germans halted as they attempted to seize the city of Leningrad. The citizens of this historic Russian city would not let go. For two and a half years, they held out against the Germans, although close to a million people died, most from starvation and cold.

PRELUDE TO WAR—ASIA

Japan had fought on the side of the Allies, including the United States, during World War I. After the war was over in 1919, Japan was given the Shantung province in China. But considering how much other countries had gained after the war, many Japanese were not satisfied. This feeling worsened when Japan was forced to give Shantung back to China in 1922.

JAPANESE EXPANSION. Japan was ruled by an emperor. But his decisions were greatly influenced by a group of powerful leaders, called *genro*. The Japanese Army, which grew much stronger between the wars, also made decisions, especially about foreign policy.

Japan's military, as well as some of the *genro*, wanted Japan to expand its empire. In 1910, it had seized Korea. In 1931, seeing chaos in China, it took control of the province of Manchuria. Early the next year, Japan terror-bombed the Chinese city of Shanghai. This was the first time airplanes had been used to bomb civilians. A horrified world watched the killing on newsreels.

In 1933, the League of Nations, while condemning Japanese aggression, sought a solution for the conflict. Japan was having none of it. It withdrew from the League, never to return. By 1935, Japan had occupied large chunks of northern China and Inner Mongolia. The Japanese would continue to interfere in Chinese affairs throughout the 1930s.

CHINESE INTERESTS. The Chinese were hardly in a position to resist the Japanese. The huge country of China was united in name only. Though the Nationalist leader Chiang Kai-shek represented China in the 1930s, he really did not control it. Much of China was still ruled by warlords. Chinese communists were also active, especially in the north (see sidebar).

The United States and, especially, Britain, had long-standing trade agreements with China. They had special rights in Shanghai and other ports. They did not want Japan to interfere with their privileged trade. Japan labeled this unfair. Said one Japanese foreign minister, "The Western powers had taught the Japanese the game of poker....But after acquiring most of the chips, they pronounced the game immoral..."

STRUGGLE FOR POWER. The Japanese believed that the world was going to be divided among great powers—and Japan wished to be the controlling power in Asia. But compared to other great nations, Japan was militarily and industrially weak. In order to increase its influence, and to acquire raw materials it did not have, Japan had to grow

---

NATIONALISTS AND COMMUNISTS IN CHINA

When Japan attacked China, it was fighting not one but two governments. Chinese Nationalists were led by Chiang Kai-shek. Chinese Communists were led by Mao Tse-tung. Both leaders had

strongholds within the country. The Nationalists held power within China's urban areas and rich ports. The Communists were

strong among peasants in China's rural areas.

Chiang Kai-shek appealed to Western nations. He was open to European trade and allowed Western teachers and Christian missionaries into China. Even though Chiang was repressive—and brutal to his enemies—Western nations, like the United States and Britain, saw him as the voice of democracy in China.

The leader of the Chinese Communists, Mao Tse-tung, sought power among the poor. He believed that converting China to a communist state was the only way to bring justice to huge numbers of desperately poor Chinese.

In 1934 Chiang launched a major attack against Mao's strongholds in the south of China. He was determined to put down the peasant uprisings and crush the Red Army. In a remarkable move, Mao, with 80,000 other Communists, set out on a 6,000-mile "Long

March" to a northern sanctuary at Yan'an. Though many did not reach their final destination, the march made a strong impression on the Chinese and the world. Mao and his Communists were not to be ignored.

In 1936, Chinese Communists captured Chiang Kai-shek and threatened to kill him. His life was actually spared by Mao Tse-tung. The communist leader had received a telegram from Joseph Stalin. Stalin believed the two groups could effectively combine to resist Japan, Russia's longtime enemy.

When Japan attacked in 1937, the two factions united. Thirty thousand troops from the Red Army joined forces with the Nationalists. But the battle for control of the Chinese nation would continue long after the war ended.

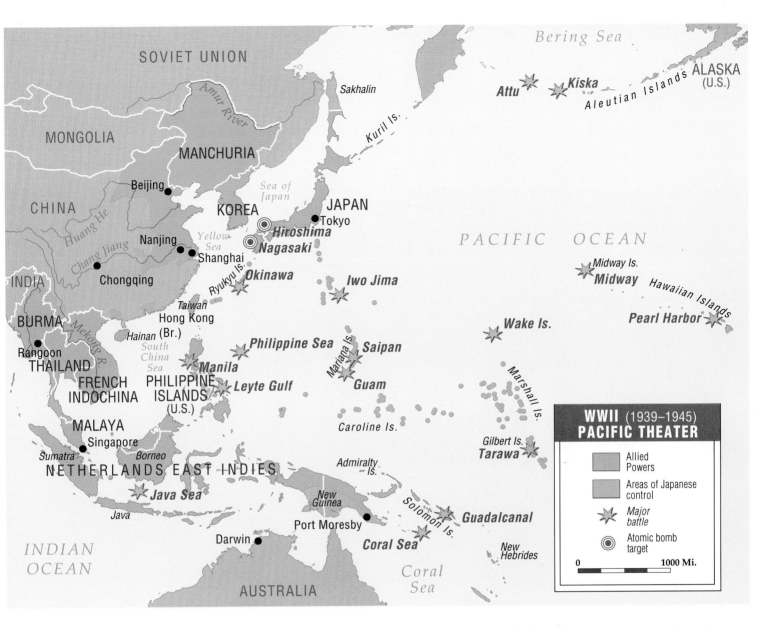

WWII (1939–1945) PACIFIC THEATER

Allied Powers

Areas of Japanese control

Major battle

Atomic bomb target

0   1000 Mi.

Because it was a small country, the Japanese felt their only choice was to colonize or seize other parts of Asia.

Throughout the 1930s, a fierce nationalism grew in Japan, just as it had in Germany. Schoolchildren were dosed with heated patriotism. Democratic and liberal thinkers were repressed. Japan's Emperor Hirohito was worshiped as both leader and god.

As Japan grew more nationalistic, it set its sights on taking over territories in Asia. And it found an ally in fascist Germany. In 1936, the two countries signed the Anti-Comintern Pact an agreement to oppose Soviet communist expansion. The pact caused concern in the United States and alarmed the British. But Japan insisted the pact would only protect against communist influence in Asia.

The United States and Britain continued to look for ways to keep the Japanese under control. But Japan bristled at such attempts to dictate its behavior. Japanese, like other Asians, had typically been treated as "inferior" by Western countries like Britain and the United States. Japanese resentment deepened further when U.S. immigration laws closed the doors to Japanese immigrants in 1924.

WAR WITH CHINA. The Japanese had hoped to gradually take over control of China and its resources. But Chiang Kai-shek resisted. In the autumn of 1937, Japanese forces again attacked Shanghai. By the end of the year, they had overwhelmed the capital city of Nanking.

Casualties in these battles were breathtaking. The Chinese alone had 370,000 killed or wounded. Atrocities committed by the Japanese, including rapes, looting, and massacres, were condemned throughout the world.

By 1938, nearly a million Japanese were battling both Chinese Nationalists and Communists (see sidebar) for control of China.

Most Americans sided with the Chinese Nationalists led by Chiang Kai-shek. The United States, though, was determined to stay neutral. Though Roosevelt sought a way to stop Japan's aggression in China, there was little real action he could take.

PEARL HARBOR

As the 1940s began, war raged in Europe. But it wasn't the only hot spot on the globe. The Japanese had occupied northern Indochina in Southeast Asia in 1940 (see map on page 119). They were still on the offensive in China itself, which was teetering toward civil war between Nationalists and Communists.

AXIS ALLIANCE. Roosevelt wanted to contain the Japanese. But with all of Europe threatened by fascism, he needed to keep the United States out of a war in Asia.

Still, the two conflicts were rapidly moving closer together. In September 1940, Japan signed the Three-Power (Tri-Partite) Pact with Italy and Germany. The three countries agreed to help each other in case of a war with another power. The power was understood to be the United States. Japan hoped the pact would keep the U.S. from interfering in Asia. Germany believed it would deter the United States from joining forces with Britain.

Roosevelt interpreted the pact as a pointed threat, but Japan was, in fact, bluffing. The Japanese were not yet keen to confront the United States. They already had their hands full in China.

Roosevelt increased support for the Nationalist Chinese to prevent Japan from dominating China. But many Japanese felt the United States was denying Japan its proper rights in Asia.

ECONOMIC EMBARGO. The Japanese-U.S. commerce treaty had expired in January 1940 and had not been renewed by the United States. In July, President Roosevelt struck another blow against Japan's economy. He ordered restrictions on the sale of certain kinds of fuels and metals to Japan. At the same time, he insisted he was still willing to negotiate.

Talks continued through the summer of 1941. Roosevelt asked Japan to pull its military forces out of China and Indochina. The Japanese did not answer directly. Privately, they were preparing for war.

Throughout November, U.S. intelligence intercepted a number of secret messages to the Japanese ambassador (see sidebar). These messages led the State Department to believe that the Japanese would soon launch an attack somewhere against the United States. The question was where. Almost everyone thought the Japanese would hit islands such as the Philippines that were close to Japan.

SECRET FLEET. On November 26, a secret Japanese task force steamed out of Hittokapu Bay. Six aircraft carriers, two battleships, and their escorts were on their way to Pearl Harbor. They were instructed to deal a "mortal blow" to the U.S. fleet in the Pacific.

Heavy clouds obscured the ships' movements for nearly the entire journey. The fleet maintained strict radio silence. On the morning of December 7, squadrons of bomber and fighter planes took off beneath the clouds. Fixing on a radio broadcast from Honolulu, they homed in on their target.

AN INTELLIGENCE CATASTROPHE

...we here highly resolve that these dead shall not have died in vain...

REMEMBER DEC. 7th!

After the attack at Pearl Harbor many people wondered how such a surprise raid could have happened. The surprise was especially hard to understand since U.S. intelligence had been reading Japanese diplomatic messages for years. The Japanese PURPLE code had been broken in the 1930s. The decoded messages were known as "MAGIC."

U.S. Army and Navy intelligence shared MAGIC information. On alternate days the Army or Navy would decode whatever messages came in. The method created confusion and may have hampered detection of the planned Japanese attack. Military intelligence was extremely cautious about MAGIC falling into the wrong hands. Only a very short list of people,

including the president, were allowed to review MAGIC intercepts. When a decoded MAGIC message was found in the president's waste can, he was briefly taken off the list.

The Japanese decided to attack Pearl Harbor on November 5. MAGIC messages then began to heat up. The Japanese ambassador to the United States was instructed that all negotiations had to end by November 29. After that, the message said, "things are automatically going to happen."

Few thought the Japanese were capable of launching a large-scale attack as far away as Pearl Harbor. None of MAGIC's messages gave any clue that the port was in danger. The real clues may have been in Japanese naval messages. But that code had not yet been broken.

The USS Shaw explodes during the Japanese raid on Pearl Harbor. The next day, the United States declared war.

As the Japanese attack force—183 planes in the first wave—roared in over Oahu, most U.S. Navy personnel were enjoying a relaxing Sunday. Sailors and officers were eating breakfast or on their way to church. They weren't expecting Japanese bombers. When the raiding planes were spotted, almost everyone thought they were U.S. aircraft.

> *"Yesterday, December 7, 1941—a date which will live in infamy—the United States of America was suddenly and deliberately attacked by naval and air forces of the Empire of Japan..."*
>
> *—FDR, asking Congress for a declaration of war*

A radar installation had even picked up the blips from the Japanese attack force early that morning. The men on duty reported the sighting to their commanding officer. His response: "Well, don't worry about it."

A BLAZING ROUT. The Japanese could hardly believe their luck. As they flew over Ford Island, they counted eight battleships—the Pacific fleet's big guns—anchored like sitting ducks.

The Japanese pilots went into a bombing frenzy. Nearly all of the battleships were seriously damaged, but none took a worse beating than the *Arizona*. As the attack began, several bombs slammed directly into her. While Japanese planes strafed the decks, sailors tried to man the *Arizona*'s guns and suffocate deck fires. Battling the blazes, many caught fire themselves.

As the *Arizona*'s crew struggled to battle the flames, another tremendous explosion rocked the ship. A bomb had blown up her powder magazines. The bow of the *Arizona* seemed to rise straight into the air and then crash back down into the water. Suddenly a giant ball of fire rose from the ship, a geyser of flame spurting five stories into the air. The explosion was so fierce it blew men off nearby ships. On the *Arizona*, four-fifths of the crew, a thousand men, died then and there.

When navy crews thought they had taken all that the Japanese could send them, another wave of planes attacked. Airfields and bases were slammed by bombs. Army fighter planes, parked in neat rows, were smashed and burned before they could take off.

In just a few hours, the fleet at Pearl Harbor was gutted. The pride of the U.S. Navy billowed in black smoke. Never in U.S. naval history had there been such a disaster.

PRESIDENT DECLARES WAR. The Japanese ambassador was instructed to deliver an ultimatum to the United States before the attack. But it had been decoded slowly and delivered late. The Japanese had therefore staged a "sneak attack." President Roosevelt called the raid an act of cowardice. The attack had killed more than 2,400 people, sixty-eight of them civilians. The United States was outraged.

On December 8, 1941, President Roosevelt asked Congress to declare war against Japan. Three days later, Germany and Italy declared war on the United States. The nation, once sworn to neutrality, was now committed to war.

PACIFIC WAR 1942–1943

On the same day that they bombed Pearl Harbor, the Japanese attacked Guam and the Philippines. They moved quickly to grab U.S. island bases in the Pacific. Japan's military leaders knew that the United States would soon make good its losses at Pearl and mount a counterattack. They had to press their advantage while the United States was still weak.

BRUTAL CONQUESTS. After the surrender in May of Bataan and Corregidor in the Philippines, the Japanese forced American and Philippine captives on a long march to prison camps. With no food and only table-spoonfuls of water to drink, many died en route. Japanese treatment of U.S. prisoners infuriated Americans. U.S. war posters depicted the Japanese as inhuman monsters.

In the early months of 1942, Japanese forces moved south as well, trouncing Malaya and then Singapore. They forced Singapore's surrender by seizing its water supply and threatening to bomb the population.

Japan invaded Burma, defeating the British forces stationed there. Then it was on to Indonesia, the Dutch East Indies, New Guinea, and Java. The Dutch, who controlled Java, offered some stiff resistance. But Japan's naval forces destroyed most of the tiny fleet opposing them. The Japanese seemed unstoppable.

DOOLITTLE RAID. Though the United States was not yet ready to battle Japan in earnest, the U.S. military command was determined to do something. From American carriers, a squadron of B-25s set off to bomb Tokyo and other Japanese cities on April 18. Lieutenant Colonel James Doolittle led the raid. This daring attack startled the Japanese. Their home islands were no longer safe.

The United States also had some other surprises in store. In the attack on Pearl Harbor, Japan had missed two aircraft carriers that were temporarily at sea. The omission was a serious one. The two carriers, the *Lexington* and the *Enterprise,* would soon stop the Japanese momentum.

BATTLE OF THE CORAL SEA. In May, Japan and the United States fought their first aircraft carrier battle in the Coral Sea. The Japanese were intent on using parts of two fleets to cut off Australia from the rest of the world.

U.S. intelligence, though, was way ahead of them. Using decoded enemy messages, the Pacific Fleet's commander in chief, Admiral Chester Nimitz, already knew about the Japanese plan. And he had one of his own. He assembled two carrier task forces around the *Lexington* and *Yorktown,* backed up by a task force of Australian and U.S. cruisers.

THE SECRET OF THE *JUNEAU*

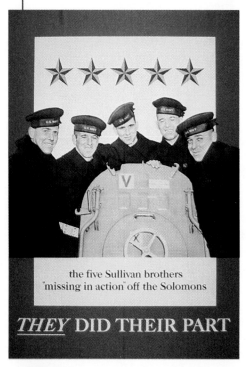

the five Sullivan brothers
'missing in action' off the Solomons

THEY DID THEIR PART

The USS *Juneau* was part of a navy convoy supporting the fight for Guadalcanal. During a sea battle with the Japanese, it was severely damaged along with several other ships.

The vessels were on their way back to port when the *Juneau* was torpedoed. An explosion ripped through the ship, killing most of the 700-man crew. More than a hundred men, though, were thrown free. They ended up in the thick, oil-covered water. Many were badly injured. Three rafts had been tossed off the ship; some of the men boarded these. The seriously injured were hung in nets from the side.

Other ships had seen the explosion, so the men thought for sure they would be rescued. In fact, though, no one reported the incident. The other ships were under instructions to maintain radio silence. The men continued to suffer in the hot sun. Eventually a search plane spotted them, but its officer simply filed the sighting in his daily report.

The survivors of the *Juneau* had no drinking water or food. They had been in the water for three days. Sharks surrounded them, feeding on the men who died each day. Eventually many of the survivors went mad.

One of them was George Sullivan, one of five Sullivan brothers stationed on the ship. After the explosion he searched in vain for his four brothers, calling their names out over and over again. After days of waiting, George Sullivan thought he could swim to shore. He jumped out of the raft and was immediately attacked by sharks.

It took six days before the men from the *Juneau* were rescued. By then only ten were left alive.

The deaths of the five Sullivan brothers were used immediately to promote the war effort, but the true story of the *Juneau* survivors was not made public until 1994.

An F6F crash-lands on the Enterprise. *A weakened U.S. fleet fought to hold back the Japanese tide in the Pacific.*

The battle was a draw. The *Lexington* was sunk and the *Yorktown* damaged. The Japanese lost the carrier *Shoho*, but the Japanese invasion fleet turned back. Remarkably the fleets never sighted each other during the entire battle.

BATTLE AT MIDWAY.

The fight in the Coral Sea kept Japan from landing at Port Moresby and thereby cutting off Australia. The tide was slowly turning against the Japanese. This became very clear in the Asian nation's next bout with the U.S. Pacific Fleet at Midway Island.

Harvard-educated Admiral Isoroku Yamamoto had overseen the raid on Pearl Harbor. Now he planned an attack on Midway Island, an important U.S. naval outpost. He assembled the most powerful Japanese fleet ever mustered: aircraft carriers, destroyers, battleships, submarines. With it he hoped to cover Japanese troops invading Midway. More importantly, he wanted to destroy the remaining U.S. Pacific Fleet, to finish the job he had started at Pearl Harbor.

Intelligence from MAGIC, however, came to the rescue, revealing Yamamoto's plan. The information allowed Nimitz to lay a trap for the Japanese. He ordered U.S. carriers to ambush the enemy fleet as it moved on Midway. Japanese carrier planes bombed Midway early on June 4, 1942, unaware that American carriers lurked nearby. Scout planes from the *Yorktown*, *Enterprise*, and *Hornet* then spotted Yamamoto's fleet.

At first, his defending Zero fighters blunted every attack from the U.S. carriers—the Zeros shot down 37 of 41 torpedo planes. But the sacrifice of these low-flying torpedo pilots left the Japanese unprotected above. Screaming down at the crucial moment, American dive-bombers sent bomb after bomb into Japanese carrier decks packed with fuel and bomb-laden warplanes. Wreathed in flames, three Japanese carriers went down, followed by a fourth late in the day. Without air cover, Yamamoto had no choice but to retreat. Even though a Japanese sub sank the battle-damaged *Yorktown*, the Midway defeat cut the offensive heart out of Yamamoto's fleet.

BATTLE FOR GUADALCANAL.

The Japanese held the tiny "rain-sodden, malaria-ridden" island of Guadalcanal, close to Australia. The United States was determined to take it back. Guadalcanal would open the American campaign to force the Japanese back from their gains in the Pacific. The fight for it would be fierce, the first of many dirt-clawing, island-scorching actions to come. Both sides bled heavily in the land and sea battle. In the end, though, the victory belonged to the Americans.

Success continued for the U.S. Pacific Fleet in 1943. In early March, the navy attacked a Japanese convoy in the Bismarck Sea near Guadalcanal. Taking few losses, it sank eight transports—every one in the fleet. Thousands of Japanese troops drowned in the salt water.

WAR ON CIVILIANS

In the spring of 1942, Allied forces began attacking the German population from the air. The Royal Air Force (RAF) had been running bombing raids on Germany since 1940. The raids, though, had been carried out by a few small bombers and had little success hitting their targets, usually factories.

BOMBING OF CIVILIANS.
Now the battle plan changed. Instead of aiming for specific factories, RAF bombers would go after built-up areas, especially workers' neighborhoods (see sidebar). At the end of May, in a spectacular and punishing attack, 1,000 RAF planes raided the city of Cologne.

Other cities would follow. In July 1942, the United States also flew its first daylight raids against "Fortress Europe."

JEWS TARGETED.
Within Europe's fortress, Hitler continued his outrageous treatment of the Jewish people. After the invasion of Poland, Jews who were not immediately killed were herded into ghettos in the larger cities. The Germans used the ghetto residents as slave laborers. They were given little food or medicine. Where one family had lived, several were crowded together. People, especially the old or weak, became sick. Without medicine or proper care, they usually died.

The immediate fate of Russian Jews was even worse. When Hitler invaded the Soviet Union, death squads forced Jewish villagers to dig large trenches. When they were finished, German soldiers machine-gunned them into the opened graves. These executions were so grisly that the Nazis had difficulty finding soldiers to carry out the killings.

EXTERMINATION CAMPS.
Still, Europe's Jews were not dying fast enough for Hitler. He and his staff members worked out plans for a "Final Solution." At the Wannsee Conference on January 20, 1942, senior Nazi officials laid out plans to sweep all Jews from Europe. Those who were able to do hard manual labor would build roads and do other work until they were dead or no longer needed. The rest would be exterminated.

Mass executions began at Auschwitz concentration camp in Poland. Soon work began on other camps: Sobibor, Treblinka, Chelmno, Belzec, and others (see map). These camps were equipped with gas chambers that could kill thousands of Jews every day.

Non-Jewish Germans were warned against feeling sorry for the Jews. Hitler's propaganda minister, Joseph Goebbels, wrote: "Feelings of sympathy or pity are entirely inappropriate." The Jews, he insisted, were only getting what they deserved.

Hitler's program for extermination was carefully controlled; there was little opportunity for anyone to protest. To make matters worse, anti-Semitic feelings in many countries in Europe caused some people to aid the Nazis in their brutal treatment of the Jews.

FIRESTORMS

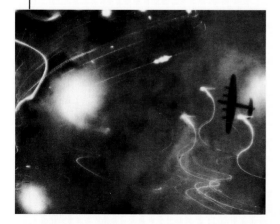

In the spring of 1942, British Air Marshal Arthur Harris took over the Allied Bomber Command. Instead of aiming for specified military or industrial targets in Germany, the Allies began mass bombing raids. These raids used hundreds of bombers to smash Germany's most populated cities. Nearly 600,000 German civilians died in these attacks. More than 3 million homes were destroyed. Nearly every major city in Germany was heavily damaged.

The rain of incendiary bombs and explosives was so fierce that, in a few cases, firestorms occurred. In closely built-up areas, multiple fires created a storm with superheated hurricane winds. Temperatures at the center of the storm reached 800 degrees centigrade. Even people in bomb shelters were poisoned by smoke, suffocated, or burned to death.

The first firestorm occurred in Hamburg in late July 1943. About 40,000 people died. One bomber pilot described the scene as "an active volcano… Our actual bombing was like putting another shovelful of coal into the furnace."

A German teenage girl, running from the flames in Hamburg, described her neighborhood as the firestorm struck:

"We… couldn't go across the street because the asphalt had melted. There were people on the roadway, some already dead, some still lying alive but stuck in the asphalt. They must have rushed onto the roadway without thinking. Their feet had got stuck and then they had put out their hands to try to get out again. They were on their hands and knees screaming."

German soldiers liquidate the Warsaw ghetto in Poland. The Nazis were systematically murdering European Jews.

Some Jews were able to resist the Nazis, though their fight was usually short-lived. Before they could be rounded up, a few escaped into the forests of Poland and the Soviet Union. From there, some formed partisan groups that worked against the Germans during the war.

> *"One of our greatest mistakes in the First World War was to spare the lives of enemy civilians. We shall... destroy at least one third of the population of all adjacent territories."*
>
> — *German Field Marshall Gerd von Rundstedt*

Large-scale attempts to resist always failed. In April and May 1943, the residents of the large Jewish ghetto in Warsaw, Poland, rose up against their Nazi oppressors. The revolt was brutally crushed.

LIDICE MASSACRE. The Jews were Hitler's principal civilian target, but the Nazis took brutal revenge on many others who tried to stand in their way. In 1942, a Nazi Gestapo leader was assassinated by the Czechoslovakians. In retaliation, the Germans destroyed the Czech village of Lidice. All the men over sixteen

years of age were murdered. The rest of the 1,200 people were sent to concentration camps.

MAJOR NAZI CAMPS (1943-1944)

Greater Germany and occupied territories	Neutrals
German Allies or dependent states	Extermination camps
Allies	Other camps

0   500 Mi.

WAR IN NORTH AFRICA

At the end of 1942, the Allies were not yet ready to try an invasion of Nazi-held France. But the Soviet Union could not fight the Germans alone; they needed another front to draw some of Hitler's heat. The Allies decided to strike at Hitler from the south. They would first battle the Germans for North Africa, then invade Italy via the Mediterranean.

FIGHT FOR THE DESERT. Italian troops had moved into Egypt in September 1940, going for the Suez Canal. The British counterattacked, eventually forcing the surrender of Mussolini's troops in February 1941.

Hitler, however, was not willing to let the British defeat his Axis allies. He sent in the crack armored Afrika Korps under General Erwin Rommel. The Germans went on the offensive in February 1941, pushing through Libya. Even though Rommel was outnumbered, the German general was able to shove the British right back into Egypt. On June 21, 1942, the British garrison of Tobruk fell with 33,000 men. The British were humiliated.

BATTLE OF EL ALAMEIN. In late October, the Allied forces were under new command. The British were determined to take back their ground in Egypt. Allied forces led by British General Bernard Montgomery got ready for an offensive.

Montgomery, who believed in having overwhelming superiority in a battle, had it in spades. The Allied army boasted 195,000 men and a thousand tanks. Its crushing offensive finally broke the Axis back at El Alamein. German and Italian casualties were more than 90,000. El Alamein was the first decisive victory on land for the British.

U.S. TROOPS ASHORE. In the second week of November 1942, more than 100,000 Allied troops, mainly Americans, made their way onto the Mediterranean shores of Morocco and Algeria. They hoped to cut off Rommel's line of retreat.

The landings were politically tricky for the Allies. Under the terms of the French-German armistice, these North African French colonies were now in the hands of the Vichy French government. This puppet government was pledged to defend Morocco and Algeria against any attacks. Still there was some hope that the French would not oppose the landings. U.S. soldiers, in fact, faced only slight resistance coming ashore.

During the landings, however, Hitler ordered the seizure of the still powerful French fleet. A total of about 80 warships were at anchor in Toulon, France, when the order came. Before the Germans could get to them, however, the French crews scuttled nearly every ship.

THE U.S. WAR MACHINE

One of the things that really depressed German General Rommel in North Africa was how many spare parts the Americans had. Those spare parts, munitions, and supplies were coming from the biggest factory on the face of the earth—the United States of America. While U.S. soldiers were battling Axis forces overseas, Americans at home were working in the national arsenal. Unemployment vanished; factories stayed open for two or three shifts. Women who had never worked away from home before became the heart and hands of the U.S. labor force.

The staggering output was relief to America's Allies, a terror to its enemies.

During the war, the United States produced, among other things:

- **300,000 aircraft**
- **88,000 landing craft**
- **215 submarines**
- **147 aircraft carriers**
- **952 warships**
- **86,333 tanks**
- **531,000,000 tons of bombs**
- **12,573,000 rifles/carbines**

U.S. production not only supplied American forces, but aided its Allies—Britain and the U.S.S.R. The Axis powers suffered many hardships because of the U.S. entry into the war. But no pill proved as bitter to swallow as the United States' endless supplies.

Rosie the Riveter flexes her muscle. U.S. women took over much of the job of producing arms and supplies for the troops. The war could not have been won without their astonishing effort.

While the British continued to move west, the American troops, commanded by General Dwight D. Eisenhower, would move east. If the plan worked, the Allies could trap the Axis armies in one of the greatest pincer moves in military history.

Most U.S. soldiers landing in North Africa had never seen combat. They weren't up to fighting battle-hardened German troops. Nor was their equipment. Americans were unpleasantly surprised at Chouigui when their M3 cannon shells bounced right off German tanks. Heavy air attacks from the German *Luftwaffe* made it impossible to keep advancing.

By January, Rommel was in Tunisia, having been flogged across North Africa by Montgomery. For now, Rommel believed the Americans could be handled. He promised to give them "an inferiority complex of no mean order."

KASSERINE PASS. Rommel soon got his chance to humiliate American soldiers. In February 1943, U.S. troops were chased across the middle of Tunisia, having lost two battalions at Sidi Bou Zid.

The Americans holed up in a range of mountains known as the West Dorsal. Along the ridge was the

> *"Gentlemen, you have fought like lions and been led by donkeys."*
>
> —General Rommel to captured British officers after Tobruk

Kasserine Pass, an important gateway to Algeria. It was also the gate to the town of Tebessa, an important supply and communication base.

During the day on February 19, the Americans managed to repel a tank attack along the Kasserine from the Afrika Panzer Korps. But later that night, German infantry worked their way up the hills and caught the Americans by surprise. By the following day, Axis forces had broken through the American lines.

RETREAT FROM VICTORY. The Americans, confused and shocked at first, learned their lesson quickly. They would not easily be overrun again. The U.S. Army also had munitions and materiel to spare. German supplies were down to practically nothing. Rommel himself was sick with jaundice and heat. He decided to call it quits.

The battle at Kasserine Pass would be Field Marshal Rommel's last victory in Africa. From that point on, he had lost faith that the campaign in North Africa was winnable. The Afrika Korps would, in fact, surrender in May. By that time, Rommel was long gone: Hitler had called him back to Germany to help defend the French coast.

CASABLANCA CONFERENCE. While Allied and Axis soldiers were battling it out in Tunisia, Roosevelt and Churchill were meeting in Morocco. The Allied leaders were trying to decide where to strike next. Roosevelt wanted to make a decisive blow against Hitler in France. Churchill, who had watched the humiliating evacuation of Dunkirk, wasn't so sure. He thought it might be smarter to "nibble" at Hitler. A decisive blow could be struck later when the time was right.

Eventually the Allies compromised. After victory was achieved in North Africa, Allied forces would attack and occupy the island of Sicily. The Germans were weakest in the Mediterranean. If the Allies attacked here, they could carry the war up into Greece and Turkey. The Germans would then be caught between a rock and a hard place—between them and the Russians.

THE INVASION OF ITALY

After the Allies captured the remaining Axis troops in North Africa in May 1943, they turned their attention to the European continent. The British argued for an invasion of Sicily and Italy, into what Churchill called the "soft underbelly" of Europe. Surprising Hitler and Mussolini, the Allies struck at Sicily, coming ashore in early July 1943.

SICILY. The tired Italian defenders didn't offer much resistance—some even helped unload the Allies' landing craft. But the German divisions fought hard, keeping open an escape route to Italy across the Straits of Messina. From there most of the German troops managed to retreat from Sicily between August 12–17. The Italian Army had lost its will to fight. On July 25 the Italian government had already arrested Mussolini, and by early September the country announced it was joining the Allied cause.

This infuriated Hitler. He rescued Mussolini and poured fresh troops into Italy, demanding that Field Marshal Albert Kesselring hold the peninsula. Hitler had acted just in time. On September 9, the United States and British troops stormed ashore at Salerno, just south of Naples. The landings went easily at first, but the Germans counterattacked, nearly splitting the beachhead in two in a series of bloody assaults. Only massive air strikes and naval artillery were able to stop the German attacks. By early October, the British Eighth and American Fifth armies had conquered all of Italy south of the city of Naples.

THE MEAT GRINDER. Italy was anything but a "soft underbelly" to the Allied troops that fought there. Mountains almost 10,000 feet high ran up and down the peninsula's spine, and rocky spurs stretched toward the Adriatic and Mediterranean coasts. Swift rivers ran from the heights down to the seas, forming a series of obstacles to the invading Allies. Nature wasn't the only enemy. North-south highways ran on the narrow coastal plains, where German guns on the ridges and hilltops could bring tanks and trucks under heavy fire. Hitler's troops held a strong position—the Gustav Line—stretching 120 miles across Italy. The only way to advance was into the jaws of German defenses.

The opposing lines were locked in a miserable battle all through the winter of 1943–44. Winter floods made the rivers impassable. Expert German soldiers pinned down the American, British, Polish, Moroccan, Canadian, and New Zealand divisions struggling northward. Trying to cross the Rapido River in late January 1944, a Texas division ran into a wall of gunfire. The Germans killed 1,000 of the 6,000 Texan infantrymen who tried to cross.

Even when successful, Allied attacks could make only a few miles before being stopped by mud, cold, and a fresh German defensive line. The fighting in Italy was horribly familiar to those officers who'd seen the brutal, muddy trench warfare of World War I.

GEORGE S. PATTON

George S. Patton, even in 1940, was nobody's idea of "politically correct." Commanding troops in the brutal and protracted fight in North Africa and Sicily, Patton was twice reprimanded for verbally abusing and even slapping soldiers suffering from combat exhaustion. "Old Blood and Guts," as he was often called, got into even more trouble when he delivered a charged speech before U.S. troop landings at Messina. The speech, which emphasized the importance of killing German soldiers, was blamed for the massacre of German and Italian prisoners by U.S. troops at Biscari in July and August 1943. Patton's toughness and aggression came close to ending his career.

But General Eisenhower, then Supreme Commander in the Mediterranean, would not let go of Patton. The general with the highly polished boots and pearl-handled pistols was simply too valuable, and Eisenhower knew it—even though Patton's real brilliance had not yet shown. Instead Patton was sent to Britain to take charge of the U.S. Third Army.

As Allied troops were breaking out of Normandy in August, Patton's forces, moving out from Brest (see map on pages 106–107) put a division across the Seine southeast of Paris. His soldiers might have been the first liberation troops to enter the French capital, but that privilege was given to the French-led forces of Charles de Gaulle.

By November, Patton's forces had reached the west wall of the German border. Then disaster struck the Allies further north. The Germans launched the Ardennes offensive. U.S. troops were soon encircled at Bastogne, holding off, it seemed, the entire German Army.

Patton was sent to their rescue. He pushed his exhausted troops northward at incredible speed, chomping at the southern edge of the German line, and relieving the siege at Bastogne. The Third Army's push north has been called one of the most remarkable movements in military history. It wrapped and ribboned Patton's military reputation, showing his aggression in all its lifesaving glory.

U.S. troops are welcomed by Italian children. The fight for Italy would continue until the end of the war in Europe.

THE TRAP AT ANZIO. The Allies tried to break the stalemate with a seaborne landing at Anzio, behind the German lines. Coming ashore with complete surprise on January 22, the Americans soon had a beachhead just thirty miles south of Rome.

But Kesselring recovered quickly, brought up fresh troops, and kept the Americans penned in. Hitler decided to show the Allies what would happen if they tried to invade France and ordered the *Wehrmacht* to crush the beachhead. Anzio became a bloody trap for the Americans. Pinned down under the deadly German guns, U.S. troops would not break out until May 1944.

MONTE CASSINO. In February 1944, the Allies tried to smash past the German Gustav Line on the west coast. General Mark Clark's Fifth Army couldn't move under the artillery fire directed from the 1,400-year-old Benedictine monastery at Cassino. The Germans didn't use the monastery itself, but the rocky hilltops and ridges were just as strong as the ancient fortress on Monte Cassino.

Unable to advance and convinced the abbey was being used as a spotting post by the Germans, the Allies, in frustration, decided to destroy the monastery. On February 16, 135 B-17s bombed the ancient walls into ruins. The elite German defenders—a parachute division—immediately burrowed into the rubble, making the position even more formidable. By mid-March, the third in a series of bloody Allied assaults ended in failure. Cassino's hillsides were a moon-cratered wasteland. Only in May would Polish Allied troops seize the hilltop in a final, savage assault.

ROME FALLS. Bogged down in the bitter winter fighting, the Allies searched for some crack in the German armor. They used air attacks on railways and bridges to deny supplies to the German troops. Fresh Allied soldiers, expert in mountain warfare, replaced those sent back to England for the invasion of France.

In May, catching the defenders off guard, the Allies finally broke out from around Cassino. At last Allied tanks rolled toward Rome. Had they turned eastward and cut off the Germans' retreat, the Italian campaign might have ended much earlier.

Instead U.S. General Mark Clark, intent on being the liberator of Rome, pressed toward the Eternal City, which was liberated on June 5, 1944. Kesselring's German Army slipped away.

Not until the spring of 1945, after months of bitter fighting, would the Allies break out into the plains of northern Italy. In fact, when the war ended in May 1945, the Germans still held on in the Alps.

The campaign in Italy, instead of opening up Germany's back door, diverted Allied troops from a faster buildup to the invasion of France. Italy's liberation cost the Allies a staggering price—paid in lost opportunity and in lives.

THE NORMANDY INVASION

From the moment the United States declared war on Germany, a cross-channel invasion of France was at the heart of the plan to defeat Hitler. On the morning of June 6, 1944, that landing—Operation OVERLORD—became a reality.

INVASION PREPARATION. An enormous effort led up to the invasion. The United States would furnish sixty divisions for the assault; the British and Canadians another twenty.

President Roosevelt had appointed General Dwight D. Eisenhower Supreme commander of the invasion forces. Roosevelt liked "Ike" and considered him a good soldier and general. More importantly he believed Eisenhower had the political sense to forge cooperation among the other Allied leaders. Eisenhower proved up to the task. When he met with the other invasion commanders he insisted that it mattered less what they agreed to do, than that they all agreed to do it.

STANDING HIS GROUND. Eisenhower, though, would no pussyfoot around issues he believed essential. His firs concern, in preparing for the invasion, was cutting com munication lines into France. To do that he would need to use Allied bombers. Most were now busy hitting tar gets in Germany.

The other Allied air commanders objected to switch ing the bombing to France, but Eisenhower wa adamant. He threatened to resign if the bombers were not made available. The rail lines, as well as bridges, had to be cut to keep the Germans from quickly sending in reinforcements once the Allies had landed.

The bombing raids began in January 1944. After con sulting weather and tide reports, the invasion was set fo the fifth day of June.

DECEIVING THE GERMANS. The Germans were expecting an invasion across the English Channel, but they didn' know when or where. The Allies decided to take advan tage of German uncertainty. They created a huge fake military buildup and a fictitious army group under General George Patton.

The operation, code-named FORTITUDE, wa designed to make the Germans think the invasion would come across the narrowest part of the Channel—a Calais. Workers built fake barracks and depots. The Allies used ULTRA intelligence (see page 116) to make sure the Germans were swallowing the bait.

The real invasion would arrive at Normandy, farthe

DWIGHT D. EISENHOWER

The pensive, sometimes even stricken face of Dwight Eisenhower became for many the icon of the United States' struggle in World War II. One of seven sons born into a poor Mennonite family, Eisenhower detoured from his religion's pacifism to become a West Point cadet. Some thirty years later he would be Supreme Allied Commander leading the invasion against Hitler's Fortress Europe.

Within a week of the Japanese attack on Pearl Harbor, Eisenhower was called to Washington. In mid-1942 he was sent to London. There he began to oversee plans for what would become the D-Day invasion. Overseeing several Allied generals, some of whose egos rivaled his Texas home state in size, Eisenhower somehow managed to create a working harmony.

While continuing plans for D-Day, Eisenhower led the North African campaign. North Africa was a political and military trial by fire for Ike. When U.S. troops landed at Algiers they were fired on by Vichy French troops, and the French fleet, which might have fallen into German hands, had to be destroyed. Tunisia was near-disaster for green U.S. troops fighting top-of-the-line Germans under Erwin Rommel.

Ike, however, had a capacity to fix what was broken. He learned from the initial horrors of North Africa and from American mistakes in the hard fight in Italy. "(U)nity, coordination and coopera-tion are the keys," he wrote while he forged what would become the greatest invasion in the history of the world.

Though Eisenhower planned D-Day with some confidence, others were wary of a potential disaster. Eisenhower's air commander, for example, had predicted that U.S. airborne divisions (who would be dropped during the night before the invasion) would suffer 70 percent casualty rates. Eisenhower believed the airborne troops were essential to protect the invasion. Still, he was conscious of the terrible risk these soldiers were taking. The night before the invasion, as the airborne troops were getting ready to fly over the channel, Eisenhower stood among them. He walked through their lines, asked their names, and where they were from. He clamped them on the shoulders and wished them luck. As each plane departed in the dark, the four-star-general stood on the runway, his hand raised in salute.

Eisenhower wishes luck to paratroopers ready to emplane for Normandy, where they would be dropped behind enemy lines.

south on the French coast. Amphibious (land and sea) forces from three nations would storm five beaches, code-named UTAH (American), OMAHA (American), JUNO (Canadian), SWORD (British), and GOLD (British). Three airborne divisions would be dropped in to protect the flanks of the invasion force.

Naval gunfire would "soften up" the German defenses before the landing started. Allied planes, now in control of the air around the coastline, would protect the beaches from a German counterattack by air.

GERMANS PREPARE.
General Erwin Rommel, who had given the Allies so much trouble in North Africa, was now in charge of defending the French coast. He had two armies under his control. One was positioned at the Pas de Calais, where the Germans expected the invasion. The other was stationed farther southwest, in Normandy and Brittany.

The Germans knew that the invasion was on the horizon, and they expected it would come soon, but they thought it would come at Calais. Bad weather over the channel just before the invasion helped to keep them in the dark. They were quite sure the Allies would not risk a landing during the coming storm.

Rommel was so certain nothing was happening, he went home to Germany for his wife's birthday. It was probably the mistake of his life.

STORM FRONT.
Heavy squalls over the channel had threatened to cancel the June invasion altogether. Severe winds and rain would make the invasion crossing nearly

impossible. Tanks and divisions could not land on the beach in five-foot waves.

Eisenhower was beside himself with worry. If he delayed, all the carefully made plans for the invasion might collapse. If he okayed it, the storm might turn the landing into a suicide. In the end he delayed for a day, okaying the invasion to begin June 6, with a break in the weather.

ALL IN READINESS.
On June 5, the preparations for D-Day, the Normandy landing, were completed. The great invasion would be on a scale larger than any before it. Aircraft, ships, men, and supplies—in quantities never seen before or since—prepared to depart from the south of England.

A line of trucks leaving from Dover formed such a gridlock that an ice-cream truck, stuck in the middle of the convoy, got sent to France with the invading forces.

Among many of the commanders on the eve of the invasion, there was a feeling of deep dread. Many of the British officers had experienced the humiliating evacuation of Dunkirk. They could not help but fear a repeat disaster.

Eisenhower himself was vexed with worry. In his pocket was a speech he had written should the invasion collapse. "Our landings...have failed.... The troops, the Air and Navy did all that bravery and devotion to duty could do. If any blame or fault attaches to the attempt, it is mine alone."

D-DAY

During the night of June 5–6, 1944, thousands of ships filled with invasion troops left from ports in England. Most of the Americans were unblooded soldiers—they had never seen battle before. Now they would be facing crack German divisions behind iron defenses.

THE LANDING. The seas, churned and swelled by the squalls, made many seasick along the way. A few talked. Most smoked cigarettes, nursed their sick stomachs, or slept. Some spent time praying. Almost all wondered if they would still be alive in a few hours.

As the thousands of ships approached the beaches, the U.S. fleet's big guns began to slam the Normandy cliffs with shell fire. The more damage done to the Germans from a distance, the easier it would be for the men wading ashore.

But it would be no seaside picnic. Rommel had spent months stiffening the coastal defenses, burying millions of mines all along the coast. Obstacles laced the shallow water to keep boats, or anything else, from landing.

AIRBORNE UNITS. At dawn Allied troops struggled onto the landing beaches; some British and American soldiers were already roaming deeper inside Normandy. Three divisions, a total of 23,400 paratroopers—including the 82nd and 101st American airborne units—had been dropped into the Normandy fields during the night.

Like the soldiers on the beaches, their welcome onto French soil was hardly hospitable. Dropped off-target in a fog, some actually fell into the ocean. Others, still inside the plane, were hit with antiaircraft fire before they got a chance to jump. Some were dropped too low for their parachutes to open and smashed "like ripe pumpkins." Others fell into the flooded ditches of the Normandy fields and tangled in their parachutes.

Allied troops also came in by glider. These "flying coffins" sometimes proved the worst method of any for getting into France on D-Day. Whole crews were killed when the planes crashed into hedgerows or "Rommel's asparagus" (poles planted in open spaces by the Germans to keep the gliders from landing).

The airborne units were supposed to be dropped much closer together than they actually were, and many were lost on the ground. In a nightmarish scenario, GIs had to find each other without alerting the Germans lurking all around them. To signal friendlies, troops used a small clicker that made a noise like a cricket. Through the night they gathered into groups and went about their missions, taking strategic bridges and crossroads and crushing German positions. They took staggering casualties, but their efforts protected the landing beaches from a German counterattack.

DEATH AT OMAHA. Allied soldiers met resistance at all the invasion beaches, but the worst fight came at Omaha. The Americans who landed there had the misfortune to arrive during a German training exercise.

The seas were still high from the storm, and many

A NORMANDY WOMAN REMEMBERS

Marie-Louise Osmont was a widow living on her farm in Normandy when World War II broke out. Osmont's home was occupied first by the Germans and later by the British. She fought to keep her life and home in some state of order during the occupations. She also managed to keep a detailed diary, which was published in 1995.

Osmont's descriptions of the events just after the invasion are especially fascinating. On June 7, she was wounded as a dogfight went on above her. The passage below makes clear the chaos and terror of those hours:

"Very early in the morning, German airplane [is] shot down in the field of rapeseed. The aviators (young men) tried to jump with parachutes, but in vain. The bodies are badly damaged, burned, hands still clenched on their parachutes.

"Around six o'clock in the morning, dead quiet. We emerge into the coolness of this new day and I go delightedly to stretch out on my bed for a bit. I'm driven from it about eight o'clock by intense cannon fire. Above our heads, sudden and horrifying, an airplane battle. I hug the walls of the outbuildings; I'm terrified. I want to get to the trench, to escape these machine-gun bullets that smack everywhere. I run; when I get to the turn that leads to the farmyard I throw myself flat on the ground, bewildered, glued to the slope. Suddenly everything's erupting, everything's falling around me, I feel a painful blow to the small of my back. I see balls of fire a few meters in front of me. I raise my head instinctively and catch sight of an airplane falling in flames."

Seasick and scared, American troops wade toward Omaha Beach. Casualties in the first waves passed ninety percent.

landing craft foundered, drowning the men inside them. Tanks, specially designed to "swim" onto the beaches, toppled in the surf and sank to the bottom. Burning oil floated on waves, as soldiers desperately tried to wade ashore in a storm of fire.

> *"Almighty God, our sons, pride of our nation, this day have set upon a mighty endeavor... to set free a suffering humanity."*
>
> —*President Roosevelt's prayer on D-Day*

Of the first wave of troops at Omaha, 75 percent were cut down before they made it off the beach. Sheer terror sent a few panic-stricken and screaming back to the boats.

There was no place to run, though—German fire fell all around them. Wave after wave of desperate men somehow struggled toward the beaches. Eventually U.S. Army Rangers and other intrepid soldiers clawed their way up the cliffs to silence the German defenders.

By midmorning, the beach was strewn with dead and dying men. Water-fouled guns, wrecked tanks, blankets, and blood were everywhere. Five thousand men had died, but the worst was over. By midnight the area around Omaha and the other beaches was secured.

Hitler, having issued strict orders that no one wake him, slept through the great invasion.

TO THE EAST. The führer had promised that the Allies would get "the thrashing of their lives" if they tried to invade France. His prediction, at least for the Americans, proved correct. They did get the thrashing of their lives at Omaha Beach.

But it did not stop them. Hitler had banked upon destroying the invasion force on the beaches. But his strategy failed. The Allies used their control of the air to secure those blood-bought acres of ground. In a few days the troops were off the sand and into the pastures of Normandy.

In less than two months, 1.5 million men would land in France. In a very short time the Americans would recover from their losses on the beaches. They would be ready to thrash back, aiming their armor east, toward Hitler and Germany's heart.

TO PARIS AND THE RHINE

It had taken less than a day to get a foothold on the Normandy beaches. It would take another six weeks to secure them. The Allied commanders knew they had to move off the landing area as soon as possible. Hitler had insisted that any invasion had to be stopped on the beaches. The Allies knew they dare not linger.

WHILE HITLER SLEPT. The Allies didn't quite grasp how disorganized the Germans were. Not only had Hitler slept through the invasion, most in the German high command believed the Normandy attack was a ruse. The real attack, they were still certain, would come at Calais farther north.

An entire German Army, which could have been used to strike the Allies, was instead left waiting for Patton's fake invasion army to arrive. Crack Panzer (tank) divisions should have been rushed to the front, too. But they were being held in reserve for the "real" attack.

It took a day before the Germans began to realize the truth. By then, it was too late. Confused orders and the presence of Allied paratroopers everywhere added to German confusion.

MULBERRY LOST. Things weren't running exactly as planned for the Allies, either.

Normandy did not have a natural harbor, so the Allies brought their own. Two artificial harbors, called Mulberries, were put in place to allow replacement troops and supplies to come ashore. Unfortunately, nature had a grudge against the Mulberries. Just days after the first troops landed, a full-force gale struck the coastline, destroying one Mulberry and damaging the other.

TAKING THE PENINSULA. After the breakout from the beaches, the job for the Americans was to cut off the Cotentin peninsula to the west. The British Second Army moved to take the city of Caen.

Neither job proved easy. The Germans clung desperately to each hedgerow on the Cotentin. The Americans pushed forward, though, and without replacements, German resistance gradually thinned out.

By taking the Cotentin, the Americans now had control of Cherbourg. Cherbourg was a genuine port, so replacement troops and supplies could come ashore there. The fragile Mulberry was no longer essential.

THE "LIBERATION" OF CAEN. On their way to Caen, the British met a collection of German armored divisions who stood painfully in the way of their progress. The British had to batter their way into the city using 700 tanks. The fight on the ground as well as bombs from the sky turned the ancient town to a pile of rubble.

JUSTICE FOR COLLABORATORS

When Hitler defeated the French in 1940, he allowed the formation of a new French government under Marshal Henri Philippe Pétain. Pétain had been something of a hero in World War I, and the French people, for the most part, supported the new regime. With the Vichy government in place, the Germans agreed to leave a large part of France unoccupied, and, to a certain extent, free. For the defeated French, Vichy seemed almost a bargain.

As the war progressed, though, the Vichy government began to sit uneasily with many French people. Vichy police helped the Germans capture French Jews and other French citizens suspected of subversion. The line between French policing and Nazi terror began to blur. Support for the Vichy regime, including Marshal Pétain, began to dry up.

Still, large numbers of French people worked for—and with—the Vichy government up until the time of Allied liberation. As the Germans were chased out of France, however, hard times fell upon those who had collaborated.

About 10,000 Frenchmen who helped the Nazis were killed outright by their fellow citizens. Other collaborators were tried in courts. Of the 167,000 tried, 27,000 received jail sentences. Half were acquitted. Among those tried and executed was the Vichy Prime Minister Pierre Laval. Laval had personally overseen the rounding up of French Jews, carrying out the Nazis' brutal orders. Also sentenced to die was the Vichy leader, Marshal Pétain, though his sentence was later commuted to life in prison.

Even small crimes were punished. Women who had had relations with German soldiers had their heads shaved and were publicly humiliated.

We French workers warn you... defeat means slavery, starvation, death

U.S. soldiers use howitzers to shell retreating German troops in France. East and west the Germans were being pushed back.

ASSASSINATION ATTEMPT. Many of Hitler's officers had long believed his direction of the war bordered on insanity. As both the Eastern and Western Fronts collapsed, some of these officers plotted to assassinate him. On July 20, as the fighting at Caen reached a crisis, Hitler met with his command officers at his headquarters in Rastenburg in East Prussia. One staff member, Colonel Claus von Stauffenberg, had a bomb in his briefcase.

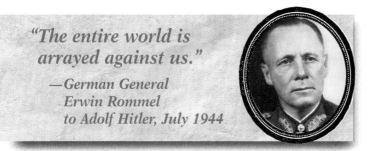

"The entire world is arrayed against us."

—*German General Erwin Rommel to Adolf Hitler, July 1944*

During the meeting Stauffenberg excused himself, leaving the briefcase behind. Minutes after he left, the bomb exploded. Stauffenberg believed the bomb had killed Hitler and was prepared, along with other officers, to launch a new government.

What Stauffenberg didn't know was that Hitler had survived. Someone had shifted the briefcase to the far side of a heavy oak table. The table had protected Hitler from the blast. The coup failed, and Hitler's retaliation was, as expected, severe. Many officers were executed, some hanged with piano wire while cameras recorded the scene for the führer's later entertainment. Others, anticipating their fate, took poison instead. Among these was the man who had led the campaign in North Africa and had supervised the defense of the French coast: General Erwin Rommel. He was forced to commit suicide.

THE END OF THE TUNNEL. On August 25, Paris was liberated by U.S. and French troops. Parisians celebrated the victory with the thrilled Americans. But the war was far from over. Even as the Allies celebrated, German holdouts sniped at them.

The Allies were closing in on the Germans, but the battle for Europe was far from over. In September, British forces led by General Montgomery tried to cross the lower Rhine at Arnhem in Holland. Montgomery was aided by airborne troops dropped in advance. But German resistance was strong, and the British effort failed. Still, the combined Allied armies were advancing in a giant arc. The tide was flowing against the Germans, and they could do nothing to halt it.

THE ARDENNES/ BATTLE OF THE BULGE

During the second half of 1944, the Allied armies had chased the Germans across the European countryside, routing them from France and Belgium. Pushed hastily from their bases in Western Europe, the Germans had no time to turn and fight.

CLOSING IN. Now, as the year closed, the Allies brought their troops up along almost the whole length of the German frontier. But as the Allies closed in on the Rhine and Germany, a desperate Hitler conceived one final surprise: a German counterattack through the Ardennes forest. The move would set American troops and their commanders reeling.

Hitler's grand idea was to divide the Allied armies threatening his border and punch through them to Antwerp, Belgium (see map on page 137). The Belgian city was a major supply port for the Allies. By taking it, Hitler reckoned he could cut off Allied resources and prevent them from continuing their move into Germany.

The Allied armies had been able to push their way across Europe because they controlled the air. Hitler knew his offensive had little chance unless he could somehow keep Allied planes out of the skies. To do that, he decided to launch his offensive during bad weather.

THREE FISTS. Hitler needed power and speed to drive a wedge into the Allied lines. He combined four SS Panzer (armored) divisions into one powerful Sixth Panzer Army. This German fist would push out from the northern Ardennes aiming toward Antwerp. At the same time, another new Panzer Army, the Fifth, would attack in the center of the Allied lines. The German Seventh Army would also move forward in the south (see map).The combined German forces included thirty divisions and what was left of the *Luftwaffe*, about 1,000 planes.

Hitler kept the plans for the offensive a deep secret. When his staff eventually did find out, they believed the plan was too ambitious. But the führer believed this was Germany's last chance.

Allied intelligence, which had brought the Americans and British so far, now abandoned them. The Germans' extreme secrecy, radio silence, and heavy cloud cover all helped to fog Hitler's deadly threat. Nearly all of the commanders believed the Germans were incapable of launching such an offensive.

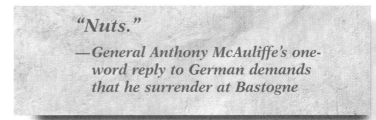

> *"Nuts."*
>
> —*General Anthony McAuliffe's one-word reply to German demands that he surrender at Bastogne*

DAWN ATTACK. The Germans began their big move early in the morning on December 16. German infantry used searchlights reflected from overhead clouds to guide them through the winter darkness. The American lines were weakly manned by green or exhausted divisions. Many were quickly surprised and overrun.

German airborne troops, speaking English and dressed in GI uniforms, were dropped in before the German advance. Their presence behind the American lines added to the GIs intense confusion and fright.

Having achieved a complete surprise, German armored units quickly blew through the Allied lines. They had gone sixty miles before Allied infantry units were able to stop them. As Hitler hoped, foul weather kept Allied bombers on the ground. The German-American slugfest was fought almost entirely on the ground. U.S. soldiers, having struggled across Europe to Germany's border, were now being beaten back with the heavy ax of Hitler's Panzers.

BATTLE OF THE BULGE. Everything that the Allies had

A German soldier signals his unit to advance during the Ardennes battle. Behind him is a wrecked U.S. half-track.

accomplished since the Normandy invasion was in jeopardy. New information from ULTRA now alerted Eisenhower to the Germans' plan to push for the Meuse River (see map). From there Hitler's armies would be in striking distance of Antwerp.

The Americans were managing to stop the German thrust along the northern section of their lines. The worst winter in years, though, was making the defense more than difficult. Even surrender wasn't an option. German SS units had already murdered large numbers of American prisoners.

Along the southern line, the situation was even worse. The Germans had pushed a deep salient, or bulge, into the Ardennes. The Americans had two footholds within the area. One was a line around Saint Vith reinforced by the 82nd Airborne Division. The other was the small town of Bastogne, where the 101st Airborne was holed up with some tank units. Bastogne was now surrounded, but the American defenders refused to give up.

Bastogne was a key road junction, and the Germans needed it for their push toward Antwerp. But the gritty defenders would not budge. Their resistance sucked in thousands of German soldiers. In whole or in part, nine German divisions would lay siege to Bastogne.

PATTON KEEPS HIS PROMISE.
On December 19, General George S. Patton had sworn he would relieve Bastogne in forty-eight hours. No one believed he could do it. Nevertheless, Patton pushed his weary Third Army northward 100 miles. Within days, Patton's troops had broken through the German ring around Bastogne.

The German Panzer troops, the pride of Hitler's army, had no wish to give up their choke hold on Bastogne. They lashed back in a fury against the Third Army again and again. But Patton was nothing if not stubborn. He had marched all this way in the bitter cold. He would give up nothing.

NO MERCY.
Eisenhower knew that the Americans had to hold the line against the Germans here. Everything was at stake; everything could be lost. The American troops, some of whom had never fought at all, were ordered to stand firm on the bitterly contested ground.

Frozen, exhausted, scared to death and beyond, U.S. troops were allowed no mercy in the Ardennes fight. The wounded and shell-shocked, if they could stand and walk, were sent back to the lines. Some were too sick to fight and froze to death in the snow. Casualties exceeded 80,000.

The relief of Bastogne was successful, though it took two more weeks to squeeze out the German bulge. In the meantime, the sky cleared and Allied planes were able to help push the Germans back. The Ardennes fight was the longest and most difficult one the American troops had seen or would see in Europe.

In the end the Battle of the Bulge was won, but at a price too terrible for any to ever forget the cost.

Hitler's last great thrust pushed American troops to the brink—and sometimes beyond it.

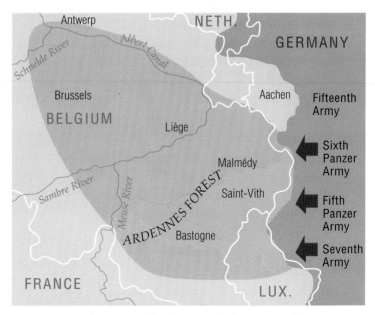

As German forces pushed toward the port of Antwerp, U.S. airborne troops at Bastogne refused to surrender. Patton's Third Army eventually relieved them.

GERMANY FALLS

Throughout 1942–43, the Germans and Soviets had fought epic battles on Soviet soil. More lives were lost on this eastern front than anywhere else during the war.

TURNING THE TIDE. At the **Battle of Stalingrad** in late 1942 through early 1943, Soviet defenders stalled what had been a powerful summer offensive by the Germans. In mid-November, the stall turned into a massive counterattack, as the Soviets trapped nearly 300,000 *Wehrmacht* troops. The raging German tide was finally turned.

In July of 1943, the final German offensive on the eastern front collapsed. At the Battle of Kursk, the largest tank battle of the war, the Soviets used their air superiority to completely thrash the Germans.

Although both sides lost massive amounts of men and materiel, the Germans could no longer replace their losses. The Russians, now being aided by the United States, could. Soviet forces drove the Germans west, into Poland.

By January 1945, massive Russian armies had pushed into Germany itself. By the end of the month, General Georgi Zhukov's forces had reached the Oder River. There he met the forces of Konstantin Rokossovksi. Together, the combined armies turned north, trapping 500,000 German soldiers against the Baltic Sea. The German troops—and more than one million civilian refugees—had to be evacuated by boats.

ALLIES MOVE WEST. As the Russians were marching west, the Allied armies continued to drive relentlessly east, pushing the Germans back to the Rhine. The German Army was caught between two huge and powerful war machines, both moving fast and both aiming a deathblow at Germany's heart.

As destruction ran riot on the ground, Allied bombers rained it from the air. American and British raids finished off the last of Germany's industrial targets and smashed German cities, including Dresden.

Of all the Allied bombing raids on Germany, the one on Dresden created the most controversy. Dresden was a stunningly beautiful, historic city with little military or industrial importance. Its only significance as a target was that it was a communications hub, or center, for northern Germany. It had few, if any, bomb shelters.

In February 1945, as refugees from the east flooded into the city, nine Mosquitoes and 796 British

A PILOT'S LETTER

As Allied armies moved east, Allied planes moved ahead of them, smashing German military targets and cities. Facing intense antiaircraft fire, pilots flying these missions had little hope of making it through the war. Quentin Aanenson, a P-47 fighter pilot with the U.S. Ninth Air Force, wrote this letter—but never sent it—to his fiancée.

"Dear Jackie,

"I have purposely not told you much about my world over here, because I thought it might upset you.… I still doubt if you will be able to comprehend it. I don't think anyone can who has not been through it.

"I live in a world of death. I have watched my friends die in a variety of violent ways. Sometimes it's just an engine failure on take-off resulting in a violent explosive crash.… Other times it's the deadly flak that tears into a plane. If the pilot is lucky, the flak kills him. But usually he isn't and he burns to death as

the plane spins.… I've watched close friends be killed in their parachutes by the German gunners, or worse yet, have their 'chute catch fire so they just fall helplessly to their death.

"If we aren't being killed, we are killing. The worst was one mission in late August.… I spotted some German troop trucks loaded with German soldiers… My wingman's guns were jammed, but mine were live and the switches on. They [the German soldiers] never had a chance.… I made three passes, firing until I burned out my gun barrels. [We] counted over 40 separate bodies. I don't know how many more were in the ditches that we couldn't see. The emotional impact on me was terrible.… I couldn't grip the control stick. I had to land by laying my arm on top of the stick and shifting my left hand back and forth between the throttle and the stick. I have recurring nightmares about that mission.

"Yes, there are a lot of things I haven't told you. I haven't mentioned a mission on

September 6th [when] I was hit by an 88mm shell right behind the cockpit and it almost tore my plane in two. I could look behind me and see sky all around. How the plane held together I don't know. When I landed, all the plane behind my back armor plate broke off. The control cables dragged the back half of the plane down the runway behind me. When the guys looked at the wreckage, they couldn't figure out how I got back or how I lived through the landing. Neither could I.

"So far I have done my duty in this war. I have never aborted a mission or failed to dive on a target no matter how intense the flak. I have lived for my dreams for the future, but like everything else around me, my dreams are dying, too. In spite of everything I may live through this war and return to Baton Rouge. But I am not the same person you said goodbye to on May 3rd. No one could go through this and not change. We are all casualties…"

U.S. soldiers move through a smoke-filled street in Germany. The Allies were closing in on Berlin.

Lancaster bombers attacked in two waves. The planes dropped more than 2,500 tons of bombs on the city. The resulting firestorm killed perhaps 50,000 people. The next day U.S. B-17 bombers struck the city, smashing what little remained of Dresden's center. Approximately 100,000 people lay dead from the raids, many crushed under tons of rubble. Hundreds of thousands were injured in a city with little or no hope of taking care of them.

CROSSING THE RHINE. The Germans had hoped to stop the Allies as they crossed the Rhine River into Germany. They didn't move quickly enough, though, to destroy the Ludendorff Bridge over the Rhine at Remagen. American forces stormed across the bridge on March 7, the first bridgehead over the Rhine.

Other British and American troops followed. The German Army's resistance was faltering, its supplies drying up. During the middle of April, 300,000 German troops surrendered in the Ruhr Valley.

DEFENDING THE HOMELAND. The Germans, however, were still fighting hard on the Eastern Front. The German Army had devastated Russia in its eastern offensives. The Russian Army, the Germans believed, would now have little mercy on them.

As the Red Army pushed toward Berlin, German soldiers fought to spare their homes and families from what they expected would be unspeakable horrors. As German troops scratched to hold every acre, hundreds of thousands of German refugees behind them staggered toward the West.

The Red Army reached Berlin on April 22, 1945. But it took another ten days of vicious fighting before the city surrendered. Hitler ordered every person to stand to the last in the defense of the city. Young boys were taught to use antitank weapons. Eight out of ten of them would die in the fighting. Anyone refusing to fight was publicly executed.

The Russians, however, would not be stopped by a few civilians. They well remembered the millions of Russians that had died in ditches or starved to death at the hands of the Nazis. They poured their terrible vengeance down on Berlin. Corpses littered the streets. The smoke from burning tanks and trucks choked the air. Block after city block was reduced to bloody rubble. Berlin became Hitler's last and most frightful nightmare.

On April 30, as the Red Army fought block to block in Berlin's last battle, Hitler and his new wife, Eva Braun committed suicide. Their bodies were brought to a clearing outside the bunker where they had lived for the last six months. SS guards doused them with gasoline and set them burning.

The Third Reich—and Hitler himself—were reduced to ashes. After another week of hand-to-hand fighting, Berlin surrendered to the Red Army.

PACIFIC 1944

As the Allies were closing in on Germany, U.S. seaborne forces were waging an island-to-island campaign across the Pacific. At the same time, the American fleet was doing all it could to destroy Japan's navy.

STRUGGLE FOR SAIPAN. With the Allies making an all-out push to take Germany, the United States carried most of the burden of the war in the Pacific. But the effort was vital. Left alone, Japan might easily make the Pacific into an impenetrable fortress. Japanese defenders had already begun fighting to the death, preferring to commit suicide rather than surrender.

The 1944 push began in February as U.S. forces landed at the Kwajalein and Eniwetok Atolls. Two Japanese garrisons—with a combined force of 10,000—were defeated. These hard, but confined, fights were just a prelude. More wrenching battles were to follow as U.S. forces pushed closer to Japan itself.

In June, Americans landed on Saipan (see map on page 119). Saipan was one of the Mariana Islands, defended by about 30,000 Japanese soldiers. Before the invasion, a massive bombardment had cut into the island's defenses. Saipan's air bases had been pounded hard, so few Japanese planes were left to provide air support.

The bombardment, however, didn't really hamper the huge Japanese fighting force on the ground. Saipan was mountainous and covered with dense jungle. This made rooting out the thousands of dug-in soldiers a prolonged nightmare. In a bloody three week campaign, U.S. Marines, with an extra Army division, pushed the Japanese back across the island. In a last, desperate charge, thousands of Japanese flung themselves against the Americans, only to be cut down.

Civilians living on Saipan were told American forces would brutalize them if they were captured. Along with the remaining Japanese soldiers, hundreds of them jumped from cliffs to their deaths before American soldiers could stop them. The capture of Saipan was an essential victory for the Americans. Japan was now within range of U.S. B-29 bombers.

The fall of Saipan was felt at the highest levels of the Japanese government. In its aftermath, Japanese prime minister General Hideki Tojo fell from power.

BATTLE OF THE PHILIPPINE SEA. As U.S. Marines trudged through the jungles of Saipan, nearby a fight was raging in the Philippine Sea. Admiral Jisaburo Ozawa's naval forces were facing the U.S. 5th Fleet.

Ozawa had a total of nine carriers, three of which were large, but his pilots were inexperienced. On June 19–20, American flyers shot them down by the hundreds in what became unofficially known as the Great Marianas Turkey Shoot. By the end of June 20, Japan had lost 450 aircraft and pilots.

Several Japanese battleships and three aircraft carriers, two of them large attack carriers, fell victim to American submarines during the battle. One of the large carriers, the *Shokaku*, was a prize for the Americans. The *Shokaku* had participated in the raid at Pearl Harbor.

CHESTER W. NIMITZ

"**Y**ou've wanted this all your life," Admiral Chester W. Nimitz's wife reminded her anguished husband when he took command of the Pacific Fleet just after Pearl Harbor. "But sweetheart," Nimitz protested, "all the ships are at the bottom." Though badly outnumbered in a vast ocean, the new commander not only managed to contain the Japanese but led a rebuilt U.S. Navy to total victory.

Nimitz was just fifty-seven when he was promoted over twenty-eight senior admirals to pick up the shattered reins of the Pacific Fleet. At first, he could do little but stage hit-and-run raids on Japanese outposts, but these strikes boosted American morale and avoided a lopsided battle with the stronger Japanese. Using decoded enemy radio messages, Nimitz moved swiftly to block a Japanese invasion force in the Coral Sea. A month later, in June 1942, the admiral threw his last three aircraft carriers and their escorts against Admiral Yamamoto's 185-ship Midway strike force.

Yamamoto thought he could crush the small U.S. fleet. But Nimitz laid an ambush. His carrier commander at Midway, Raymond Spruance, said of the admiral: "Nimitz combined so many fine qualities that you could not put your finger on any one of them and say 'Here is the key to the man.' The one big thing about him was he was always ready to fight…" Catching the Japanese by surprise, the outnumbered U.S. fleet sank four big carriers and put the Japanese on the defensive for the rest of the war.

The white-haired Nimitz bore the strains of command calmly. He never raised his voice in a crisis, and in his brilliance and confident manner he resembled another great American commander, Robert E. Lee. Nimitz devised the island hopping strategy for bypassing the strong Japanese defenses in the central Pacific. His forces seized only key islands needed for the next advance, leaving powerful Japanese garrisons cut off from supplies, helpless to interfere with American moves. Promoted to five-star or "fleet" admiral in 1944, the Pacific Fleet's commander in chief watched the Japanese surrender their forces on the deck of the U.S. battleship *Missouri* in September 1945.

U.S. soldiers plant a flag on Iwo Jima. The brutal battle for the Pacific islands was unlike anything seen in Europe.

TO THE PHILIPPINES. From April into July, the Allies continued to battle Japanese forces in New Guinea. Gradually, the Japanese were pushed from towns and bases across the islands. But they would continue to fight in the New Guinea jungles until the end of the war.

As the summer came to a close, U.S. forces took Guam and Tinian in the Mariana Islands. Again the Japanese defenders refused all calls to surrender. Ten thousand of them fought to the death in the struggle for Guam alone.

The Philippine Islands remained a great prize for the Allies. General MacArthur had promised to return to liberate the Philippines when they were captured by the Japanese in 1942. Japan was determined to stage a bitter fight to keep the Philippines under its control.

IWO JIMA. The Allies were gradually leapfrogging across the Pacific, but the Japanese were not giving up. Every foothold, every beach, every island would have to be paid for in blood.

This would prove unbearably true in the fight for Iwo Jima. This tiny volcanic island had three airstrips. These were vitally needed to provide extra air bases for American bombers hitting targets in Japan.

The Americans knew Iwo Jima would be hard to take. They spent two months before the invasion softening up the defenses with near-continuous air strikes. But the bombs sent the island's defenders into ever-deeper bunkers. When U.S. Marines landed on February 19, 1945, the Japanese pounded them with machine guns and mortars as they crawled across the beaches.

The fight to take the five-mile-long island eventually sucked in 800 warships and 330,000 men. An operation that was expected to take two weeks took more than a month. In one day of action alone, five marines merited the Congressional Medal of Honor. The Japanese, for their part, fought back with "astonishing bravery."

The pitiless warfare on Iwo Jima would make the battle famous and the marines who fought it heroes. Their heroics, though, would cost many their lives. Before the fighting on Iwo was over, 5,931 Americans were dead, another 17,372 were wounded. Japanese loses, however, included more than 23,000 dead; only 1,000 were captured alive.

Japan's desperation to keep its hold in the Pacific had become near-madness. But madness alone would not prevent Americans from invading Japan, at least not for long.

LEYTE GULF; OKINAWA

As American ships, planes, and troops leapfrogged toward Japan, the emperor's military leaders sought to hold onto gains made early in the war.

FIGHT FOR THE PHILIPPINES.

If the United States took back the Philippines, Japan's lifeline to oil in the East Indies would be choked off. By seizing island bases close to Japan, U.S. bombers could also bring devastation to industrial sites in Japan's home islands. From late 1944 into mid 1945, determined Japanese soldiers fought the most savage battles of the Pacific war, trying desperately to hold off the Americans.

General Douglas MacArthur had promised the Filipino people in 1942 that he would return, and on October 20, 1944, American troops landed on Leyte Island, keeping MacArthur's pledge. As the army poured ashore, the Japanese activated a plan to destroy the American fleet near Leyte. Three separate Japanese fleets converged on the Philippines, hoping to crush the ships supporting the American landings. U.S. submarines and carrier aircraft slowed, but did not stop, the Japanese center force on October 24, sinking the super-battleship *Musashi*. But the northern force of Japanese aircraft carriers lured Admiral William Halsey's powerful U.S. carriers and battleships away from the Leyte beachhead. The Japanese plan was working.

SURPRISE AT LEYTE.

Before dawn on the morning of October 25, the Japanese southern force steamed into a trap in Surigao Strait, south of Leyte. Six U.S. battleships, five of them raised from the mud of Pearl Harbor, rained down armor-piercing shells from their big guns. The outnumbered Japanese lost two battleships, a heavy cruiser, and three destroyers.

This smashing victory was nearly reversed when the Japanese center force regrouped overnight and burst into a group of small American carriers and destroyers north of Leyte Gulf. These ships were the only force between the Japanese and the precious landing zones. A half dozen light carriers and seven small destroyers were facing four Japanese battleships, six heavy cruisers, and more destroyers than the Americans could count. By 7 A.M.

JAPANESE INTERNMENT

In the aftermath of Pearl Harbor, Japanese-Americans in western states faced extreme prejudice. Even though many were U.S. citizens, people suffering from anti-Japanese hysteria saw them only as enemies. This bitterness was fanned by reports of the viciousness of Japan's treatment of POWs. Though President Roosevelt was personally opposed

to relocation, under intense pressure he signed Executive Order 9066 authorizing internment.

During the early months of 1942, more than 100,000 Japanese-Americans—more than half of them U.S. citizens—were relocated. They were forced to leave their homes and jobs and live under harsh conditions in internment camps.

The ten camps in which Japanese-Americans were confined were in remote rural areas where the climate was often severe. Seven people died of heat stroke within days of their arrival at one Arizona camp. At Camp Minidoka in Idaho, temperatures dropped to 25 below zero in winter. Sanitation was poor, and there was little privacy. Internees were paid but had to perform hard labor. Guards had orders to shoot on sight anyone who tried to escape.

Military and public officials tried to justify the internment. They claimed that Japanese-Americans represented a threat to security. They might become spies or collaborators. No evidence was ever found to support this point of view.

The United States never interned Americans of German and Italian descent, even though the U.S. was also at war with Germany and Italy. For the most part, it ignored a small but outspoken Nazi movement in the United States.

As the war went on, Japanese-Americans turned out to be some of the proudest and most loyal Americans. Japanese-American soldiers—some of whom fought while their families were interned—formed the most decorated unit of the war.

In December 1944, having safely won reelection, Roosevelt finally ordered the camps closed. The freed Japanese-Americans had spent an average of 900 days in confinement. They had lost an estimated $400 million in property alone. For many, however, the real injury was loss of pride. Many had been model citizens in their communities and valued their U.S. citizenship. To be accused of being disloyal was a bitter humiliation.

In 1948, Congress approved the distribution of $37 million to internees, in an effort to compensate them for their lost property and civil rights. In 1988 the government issued an official apology and paid survivors $20,000 each as further compensation.

The USS Bunker Hill *billows with smoke after being hit by two kamikaze planes. The suicide attacks took many lives but did not alter the course of the war.*

the monster battleship *Yamato*, the biggest warship afloat, was shooting at the slow, stubby U.S. carriers.

But the plucky American destroyers laid smoke-screens and launched torpedoes at the Japanese battlewagons. Hiding in rain showers, the carriers dodged the huge shells while throwing every fighter-bomber they had into the air. Then, just when the Japanese were beginning to triumph, sinking the carrier *Gambier Bay* and three destroyers, Admiral Takeo Kurita decided to retreat. He'd lost two heavy cruisers and feared even more air attacks from the American fleet.

Admiral Thomas Sprague's force had lost two carriers (one to a kamikaze), three destroyers, and 1,130 men. But, in one of the bravest fights in naval history, it had held off a powerful Japanese fleet, protecting the landing beaches from a slaughter.

OKINAWA. With the Philippines recaptured, the Americans next moved to secure islands close to Japan. These could be used as bases for the planned invasion of the enemy homeland. Okinawa was only 350 miles from Japan and offered good harbors and airfields. But with the home islands at stake, the Japanese were certain to fight to hold onto Okinawa with everything they had.

The Okinawa landings were the biggest amphibious assault of World War II. By the end of April 1, 1945, 50,000 troops were ashore. Amazingly, the Japanese had hardly fired a shot in their defense.

At Iwo Jima in February, the defenders had met the landing craft with an avalanche of fire right on the beaches. General Mitsuni Ushijima pulled his 117,000 soldiers on Okinawa into a series of intricate defensive

lines and waited for the Americans to come to him. His plan was to bleed the invaders so badly that the U.S. soldiers wouldn't dare try to invade Japan itself.

Offshore, the U.S. Navy protecting the landings came under terrifying kamikaze assaults. Hundreds of Japanese planes daily savaged the fleet. While American fighters and antiaircraft guns shot them down by the dozens, a few crashed on the decks of U.S. carriers, destroyers, transports, and battleships.

Flaming gasoline from the planes burned and disfigured hundreds, while the bombs the kamikazes carried could break the back of a destroyer in one blow.

Over the next three months, the kamikazes sank nearly a hundred U.S. ships and killed more than 5,000 American sailors. Their bravery in fighting off these suicide attacks was a story matched nowhere else in the course of the war.

The kamikaze assaults did nothing to help the Japanese on Okinawa. General Simon Buckner's troops pushed doggedly south against Ushijima's dug-in bunkers and pillboxes, gaining ground yard by bloody yard. As the Americans closed in, deadly Japanese artillery and machine-gun fire killed more than 7,000 soldiers. General Buckner was killed by Japanese guns late in the battle.

In June, U.S. troops seized the rubble of Shuri Castle, the last stronghold. General Ushijima committed suicide as American soldiers closed in.

Okinawa was the most savage, unrelenting land battle of the Pacific war; all but a few thousand of the 110,000 Japanese defenders fought to the death.

HIROSHIMA; NAGASAKI

The bitter fighting on Iwo Jima and Okinawa had a powerful effect on those planning the eventual U.S. invasion of Japan. If a tiny postage-stamp island could devour more than 20,000 men, what would a full-scale invasion of Japan cost?

THE COST OF AN INVASION. Japan could still muster about 10,000 planes, perhaps half of them kamikazes. Two million soldiers could be expected to defend the home islands. For those estimating American casualties in an invasion of Japan, the numbers were no longer in the thousands but in the millions.

BOMBING RAIDS. The United States still hoped that heavy bombing raids might persuade Japan to surrender. But as spring approached, B-29 raids had had only limited success against Japan's industrial base. Daylight targets were generally covered by clouds. Radar, still in its infancy, was unreliable. The United States was losing plenty of planes, too, both to enemy fire and to accidents.

General Curtis LeMay decided to change the U.S. bombing strategy. Instead of going for specific industrial targets by day, LeMay developed a plan to bomb civilian areas around industrial sites. American planes would rain incendiary bombs on heavily built-up areas. These firebombs could easily create firestorms (see sidebar on page 124) in packed residential districts.

On the night of March 9, 1945, Tokyo was the target. LeMay put 334 bomb-laden B-29s into the air. For three hours, the bombers swarmed over Tokyo, releasing their terrible cargo. Tokyo was soon blazing. Sixteen square miles of the city—with 100,000 inhabitants in each square mile—became an inferno. Water in the city's small canals literally boiled. Between 80,000 and 100,000 people died. With hundreds of thousands of buildings in cinders, more than a million people were left without homes.

The civilian bombing campaign was now part of the American strategy in the war against Japan. But though the general of the U.S. Army Air Force claimed that the incendiary attacks were a bargain, massive bombing raids weren't exactly cheap.

This dilemma could be solved by a single weapon that could reap as much destruction as hundreds of bomb-laden planes. That very weapon was now ready.

ATOMIC SUCCESS. Since 1942, U.S. scientists had been laboring on a secret atomic bomb. Instead of TNT, the bomb would use the explosive power of nuclear fission to achieve mass destruction. Early on, the bomb was developed for possible use against Germany. Now the U.S. military and the president hoped that the powerful new weapon would shock the Japanese into surrender.

THE ATOM BOMB

In 1932, a British scientist, James Chadwick, discovered an atomic particle, the neutron. This particle could penetrate the nucleus of an atom and cause it to separate. The divided atom, in some cases, would throw out other neutrons to split other atoms: A chain reaction would occur. In each chained event, as each nucleus broke down, more energy, and therefore more destructive power, would be released.

Scientists found that these chain reactions occurred only in radioactive materials. In the late 1930s, German scientists achieved good success as they bombarded uranium (a radioactive element) with neutrons. Their success, however, caused anxiety among many physicists in other countries, including the United States.

One of them was Albert Einstein. Einstein eventually wrote a letter to then-President Franklin Roosevelt, warning him of the incredible destructive power of a weapon based on a nuclear chain reaction. It was not, however, until 1942 that Americans began work on their atomic weapon. Under the Manhattan Project, more than 600,000 people participated in building a weapon of astonishing killing power.

Many of those who participated were torn about creating such a weapon. Robert Oppenheimer, who headed the Manhattan Project, watched with trepidation as the first atomic bomb was exploded:

"We knew the world would not be the same. A few people laughed. A few people cried. Most people were silent. I remembered the line from the Hindu scripture—the Bhagavad Gita. [The god] Vishnu…says, 'Now I am become Death, the destroyer of worlds.'"

An atomic bomb explodes over Nagasaki. Japan soon surrendered.

In July 1945, scientists began the final phase of the Manhattan Project (see sidebar) at an old ranch house in southern New Mexico. On July 16, the first atomic bomb was successfully tested in the nearby desert.

President Truman immediately approved plans to drop the bomb on targets in Japan. After much discussion, Hiroshima was selected as the first target. Hiroshima was chosen because it had not been hit by previous large-scale B-29 raids. U.S. military officials believed the Japanese would be more impressed by an attack on a city that was still intact.

Kyoto was another possible site, but the historic city was rejected because it was considered too beautiful to be destroyed.

HIROSHIMA DESTROYED. At 8:15 A.M. on August 6, 1945, an American B-29 bomber piloted by Colonel Paul Tibbets ferried the bomb to Hiroshima. There it was dropped on target, exploding about 2,000 feet above the ground. The heat at the point of detonation was hotter than the surface of the sun. The explosion created a monstrous shock wave.

> *"It was as if the sun exploded."*
> —A Hiroshima resident

A fireball immediately formed, which emitted atomic radiation and searing heat. People close to ground zero were vaporized. Thirteen square miles of landscape was reduced to ashes. Nearly 63 percent of all the buildings in the city were destroyed. Immediately or very shortly afterward, 70,000 to 80,000 people died. One survivor later wrote:

" *…there were so many injured people that there was almost no room to walk. This was only a mile from where the bomb fell. People's clothes had been blown off and their bodies burned by the heat rays. They looked as if they had strips of rags hanging from them. They had water blisters which had already burst, and their skins hung in tatters… Some had lost their eyes. Some had their backs torn open so you could see their backbones inside. They were all asking for water.*"

NAGASAKI DESTROYED. Japan did not immediately surrender after the attack. So on August 9, another bomb-laden B-29 departed for the Japanese city of Kokura. However, that city was spared because of heavy cloud cover. The bomb was instead dropped on Nagasaki.

Though the destruction of Nagasaki was not as extensive as Hiroshima, the bombing had another tragic consequence. About 2,500 of the people in Nagasaki were forced laborers from Korea. These people had been taken to Japan against their will. The bomb killed about half of them, along with more than 100 American prisoners of war.

SOVIETS DECLARE WAR. On the same day that Nagasaki was destroyed, the Soviet Union declared war on Japan. During the next four days, the Soviets destroyed the Japanese Army in China and took over most of occupied Manchuria. The Red Army was moving across the Yalu River into Korea when Japan finally surrendered to the Allies on August 15.

World War II was finally over.

AFTERMATH

In the aftermath of World War II, the Allied powers sought to carve out areas of influence both in Europe and the Pacific. The Soviet Union had been particularly savaged by the Germans during the war and had no intention of letting itself be trampled again.

THE CURTAIN COMES DOWN. Led by the aggressive and crafty dictator Joseph Stalin, the U.S.S.R. determined to gain political control of the Eastern European countries that surrounded it. It sought to build, as Winston Churchill put it, an "Iron Curtain" around its neighbors.

For the United States and other countries that had led a "crusade for democracy," the lowering of the Iron Curtain following the war was a crushing blow.

BERLIN BLOCKADE. The Cold War, a standoff between the Communist world and the Western democracies, began—and would end—in the city of Berlin. Many of the Cold War's subsequent crises would be played out in this city during the coming decades.

In 1945, Berlin became a divided city. At the end of World War II in Europe, the Allies had carved up Germany and its capital into sectors. Each of the Allied powers occupied one sector. After a period of time Germans, including Berliners, voted for the type of postwar government they wished to have.

Stalin had absolutely no intention of abiding by election results that went against the Communists. He wanted control of all of East Germany, and since the city of Berlin was within East Germany, he wanted all of Berlin, too. He wanted the Allies out of the city. To get them out, Stalin established a blockade. As of June 22, 1948, no food or supplies could enter Berlin over land from the West.

The United States was not about to let West Berlin slip away to the Communists. It organized an airlift to support the besieged Berliners. A fleet of C-47 and C-54 cargo planes carried tons of fuel and food into Berlin. The Soviets did not immediately relent. They maintained the blockade for nearly a year, calling an end to it only in May 1949. The wrangling over Berlin did not end there, however. The city's division would be the source of yet another crisis in the early 1960s.

REDS AMONG US. In the late 1940s, several events called attention to the activities of Communists in the United States. In 1949, British agents revealed that Klaus Fuchs, a physicist who had worked on the atomic bomb, was a spy.

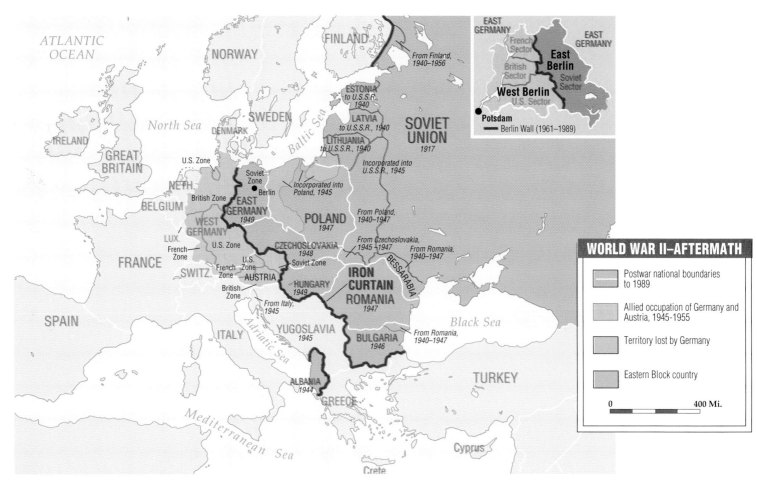

WORLD WAR II—AFTERMATH

- Postwar national boundaries to 1989
- Allied occupation of Germany and Austria, 1945-1955
- Territory lost by Germany
- Eastern Block country

0   400 Mi.

A sailor kisses a nurse on Times Square. The end of the war brought overwhelming relief to those whose lives hung in the balance.

The revelations about Fuchs followed hard upon the sensational trial of an American diplomat, Alger Hiss. Hiss was also accused of being a Communist spy. The evidence presented against him was weak and it was unclear at the time whether Hiss had done any real spying or not.

These events—and the generalized fear of communism—triggered a spree of investigations conducted by the House Un-American Activities Committee (HUAC). In addition to the House committee, a Republican senator, Joseph McCarthy of Wisconsin, began to hold hearings after claiming that communists had infiltrated all walks of American life. The committee interrogated hundreds of Americans from every walk of life. Film directors, government employees, and army officers were investigated. Many hearings were based on no more than shreds of evidence. People were compelled to name friends who they knew had associations with the Communist Party. Many of those interrogated ended up with their reputations tainted, their careers in shambles. A few committed suicide.

As the hearings wore on, the sheer nastiness of the procedures—particularly Senator McCarthy's meanness—caused a few people to speak out against this blatant violation of the spirit of the Constitution. Republican Margaret Chase Smith scolded her fellow Senators in 1950:

"Freedom of speech is not what it used to be in America."

— *U.S. Senator Margaret Chase Smith, June 1, 1950*

"I think it is high time that we remembered that we have sworn to uphold and defend the Constitution. I think it is high time that we remembered that the Constitution, as amended, speaks not only of the freedom of speech but also of trial by jury instead of trial by accusation...."

"Those of us who shout the loudest about Americanism in making character assassinations are all too frequently those who, by our own words and acts, ignore some of the basic principles of Americanism: the right to criticize; the right to hold unpopular beliefs; the right to protest; the right of independent thought...."

A THREATENING WORLD. Immediately following World War II, the United States had banked on the atomic bomb as its ultimate defense. With it, the nation and its president felt they could stave off any threat from any country. But the American ace in the hole became decidedly less impressive in the summer of 1949. In August of that year, U.S. Air Force sensors picked up strange elements in the Soviet atmosphere. The Russians had exploded their own bomb. The Cold War was now a lot hotter.

If the troubles with the Soviet Union weren't enough, the United States was now facing another potential threat. The Chinese had been waging a civil war since the 1920s (see sidebar on page 118). In the conflict, the United States had backed Chiang Kai-shek, whose Nationalist forces opposed the Communists led by Mao Tse-tung. In 1948, however, communist forces had won a series of major victories that had, for all practical purposes, ended the war. The following year, Chiang Kai-shek was forced to flee to Formosa (Taiwan), a nearby island. The United States had one less friend and one more powerful enemy in Asia.

In East and Southeast Asia, too, communist movements were on the rise. A movement for independence in colonial Vietnam turned into a full-scale war in 1946, pitting France against communist Vietminh forces led by Ho Chi Minh.

Trouble was brewing in Korea, too—trouble that would soon be front-page news in America.

THE KOREAN WAR

In the early 1950s, the Cold War that had frosted relations between the United States and the Soviet Union sparked a very hot conflict in Asia. The war in Korea would be the first contest between the Communist and non-Communist world. Korea would also be the United States' first limited war. Instead of fighting to all-out victory, the United States would limit its aims and compromise. This new concept of warfare prompted serious questions—questions that would haunt U.S. policy makers for decades.

PRELUDE TO WAR
In the middle of World War II the Allied powers—the United States, Britain, and China—had made a promise. Once Japan was defeated, Korea would become "free and independent." This was restated at the postwar Potsdam conference in July 1945. The promise was also agreed to by the Soviet Union when it declared war against Japan during that same summer.

KOREA SPLIT. After Japan unconditionally surrendered to the Allied forces, General Douglas MacArthur outlined the procedures for the surrender of Japanese forces in Korea. (Japan had annexed Korea as a colony in 1910.)

MacArthur's plan, General Order One, created an artificial line at the 38th parallel in Korea. The line roughly split the country in half. Japanese forces above the line were to surrender to the Soviet Union. Those below the line would surrender to the Americans.

The United States considered the 38th parallel separation temporary, but the Soviets had a different idea. Russia had traditionally claimed the northern part of Korea as a vital southern buffer zone. Almost immediately after accepting Japan's surrender, the Soviet Union stopped all movement across the line. The United States saw the Soviet action as a hostile move, contrary to the agreement reached at Potsdam. The United States turned to the United Nations for help. The U.N. shared the U.S. belief that Korea should be united. It sent a delegation to Korea to help monitor free elections.

When the delegates arrived in Korea in 1948, they were refused entry to the North. As a result, free elections were held only in the South. Syngman Rhee was elected president of the Republic of Korea—south of the 38th parallel. Rhee was a long-standing Korean nationalist who had been educated in the United States.

SOVIETS STYLE THE NORTH. In North Korea, the U.S.S.R. wanted to create a government based on its own communist model. When Rhee was elected in the South, Soviet-backed Kim Il Sung became the new leader of the Democratic People's Republic of Korea in the North.

The Soviets were also training and supplying troops in the North. The United States, in turn, was doing the same for the South Korean Army.

The United States was in the process of developing a postwar foreign policy. The main goal was not to defeat but to "contain" communism wherever possible. The Soviets' attempt to dominate North Korea posed the first challenge to this policy of containment.

PARALLEL BREACHED. By 1950, there were rumors that North Korea was planning to invade the South.

These rumors were realized when Communist forces from the North crossed the 38th parallel in a surprise attack. North Korea declared war on the South. With its 135,000 troops, it quickly overpowered the weaker army of the Republic.

The United States was stunned by the swift invasion. President Truman had already been accused of losing China to the Communists. Now, it seemed, Korea would suffer the same fate.

Truman made a stopgap decision. He instructed General MacArthur to supply the South Koreans with ammunition and equipment but made no mention of sending in American ground troops.

1950

North Korean forces invade South Korea in a surprise attack *(June 25)*.

The United States with the U.N. intervenes. Seoul falls to North Korean forces (NKPA). United States blockades Korean coast, begins bombing campaign *(June)*.

Inchon falls to NKPA. First U.S. ground troops land in Korea *(July)*.

Major Allied invasion at Inchon. U.S. forces liberate Seoul *(Sept. 27)*.

Chinese Communist Forces (CCF) begin secretly to move large units into North Korea. South Korean and U.S. forces capture North Korean capital of Pyongyang *(Oct.)*.

United States suffers severe losses to CCF at battle of the Chosin Reservoir *(Nov. 27–Dec. 1)*.

Pyongyang falls to NKPA. South Korean cities Wonsan, Inchon, and Hungnam evacuated. U.N. passes resolution seeking a cease-fire *(Dec.)*.

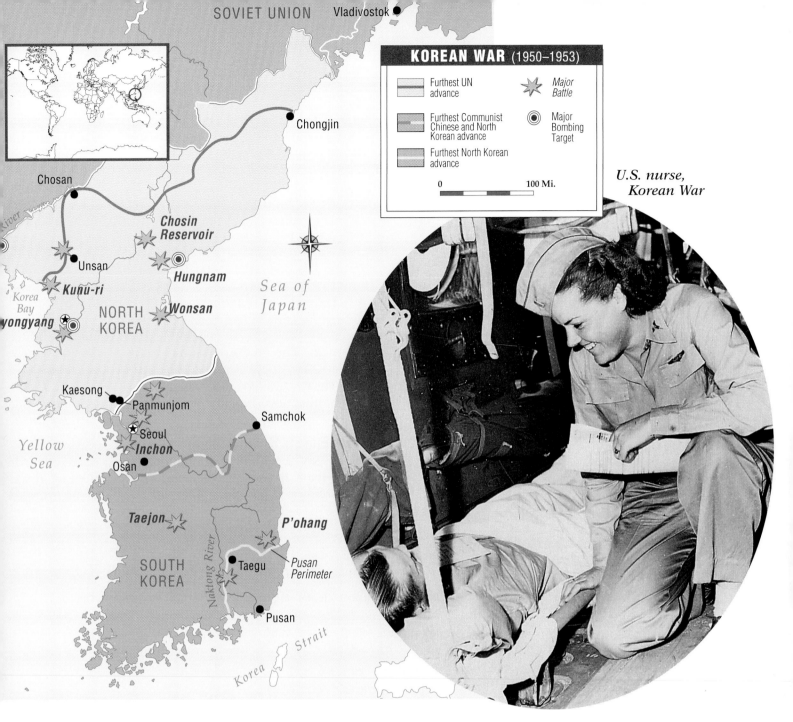

KOREAN WAR (1950–1953)

Legend	
Furthest UN advance	✦ Major Battle
Furthest Communist Chinese and North Korean advance	◉ Major Bombing Target
Furthest North Korean advance	

0   100 Mi.

U.S. nurse, Korean War

SOVIET UNION

Vladivostok

Chongjin

Chosan

Chosin Reservoir

Unsan

Hungnam

Kunu-ri

Korea Bay

Wonsan

NORTH KOREA

Sea of Japan

Pyongyang

Kaesong

Panmunjom

Samchok

Yellow Sea

Seoul

Inchon

Osan

Taejon

P'ohang

SOUTH KOREA

Naktong River

Taegu

Pusan Perimeter

Pusan

Korea Strait

U.N. RESOLUTION. Just after the invasion, the United Nations called the Security Council into a special session. It declared the attack a "breach of peace" and demanded that the North withdraw to the 38th parallel. It also asked all U.N. members to give "every assistance to the United Nations in the execution of this resolution…"

Normally the U.S.S.R. would have been expected to veto such a resolution. But the Soviet representative was boycotting all Council meetings. He was protesting the Council's refusal to acknowledge the new Communist government in China.

1951

Seoul and Inchon abandoned. U.S. Army counterattacks CCF in Operation THUNDERBOLT *(Jan.)*.

Seoul recaptured *(March)*.

President Truman relieves General MacArthur. Allied forces reach line "Kansas." CCF launch spring offensive *(April)*.

U.S. Air Force makes a major strike on the Yalu River. U.S. Army drives enemy forces out of South Korea *(May)*.

CCF and NKPA agree to armistice talks *(July 10)*.

Battle of Bloody Ridge *(Aug. 31–Sept. 3)* and Heartbreak Ridge *(Sept. 13–Oct. 15)*

1952

Pyongyang is bombed in largest air raid of the war *(Aug.)*.

Armistice talks are disbanded indefinitely *(Oct.)*.

1953

Armistice talks resume *(April)*.

Korean armistice signed *(July)*.

U.N. ACTION

Just four days after Communist forces invaded South Korea, its capital, Seoul, fell. Truman, using the U.N. resolution for justification, began a naval blockade of the Korean coast. He also authorized a bombing campaign in the North.

POLICE ACTION. The measures, though, were too little, too late. The South was unable to halt the advances of the North Korean People's Army (NKPA).

General MacArthur, soon to take command of U.N. forces, recommended that the United States put some American ground troops into the fight. On June 30, President Truman agreed. Still, Truman wanted to downplay the idea that the United States was at war. He called the conflict a "police action." The United States, he maintained, was simply responding to the Korean crisis as part of the U.N. effort.

A LESSON IN INTELLIGENCE. The Central Intelligence Agency (CIA) was an infant organization when the Korean War began. Agency reports from Korea, however, were considered very valuable. Important information like enemy troop strengths were relayed to the president. By early 1952, the CIA claimed to have nearly 1,500 agents working in North Korea.

But all was not as it seemed. The problem was revealed by John L. Hart, when he was appointed head of the CIA station at Seoul. His first shock came when he discovered that no Americans in the station spoke Korean.

The contacts in North Korea were known as "principal agents." Hart had serious suspicions about them. He ordered an investigation and gave the PAs polygraph (lie detector) tests. The results were disappointing to say the least.

Hart discovered that most of the information collected by the station had been false. In fact, most of it had been concocted by the enemy just to mislead U.S. intelligence. The agents hadn't been working for the Americans; they'd been helping out the Communists.

The CIA was so embarrassed it tried to hide the failure from other government agencies. In fact, it's unlikely that even President Truman was told about the CIA fiasco.

THE EIGHTH STANDS ALONE. The great American forces from World War II had long since been dismantled. In 1950 the U.S. Army consisted of just 591,000 men. It was the weakest it had been since the 1930s. Given the state

---

A REPORTER'S UP-CLOSE VIEW OF THE WAR

Marguerite Higgins had covered the Second World War in Europe when she was just out of college. When the conflict in Korea broke out, she returned to the front lines. In the summer of 1950, Higgins was holed up in an abandoned schoolhouse with the 27th U.S. Infantry when the North Korean Army attacked:

"Half a dozen regimental staff officers, myself, and Martin [another correspondent] were fin-ishing a comparatively de luxe breakfast in the schoolhouse (powdered eggs and hot coffee) when suddenly bullets exploded from all directions. They crackled through the windows, splintered through the flimsy walls. A machine-gun burst slammed the coffeepot off the table. A grenade exploded on the wooden grill on which I had been sleeping, and another grenade sent fragments flying off the roof…

"One of the officers suddenly said, 'I'm getting out of here,' and dove out the window into the courtyard in the direction away from the hill. We all leaped after him and found a stone wall which at least protected us from the rain of fire from the high ground …

"A ruckus of yelling was raised in the opposite corner of the courtyard. I poked my head around in time to see an officer taking careful aim at one of our own machine gunners. He winged him. It was a good shot and an unfortunate necessity. The machine gunner had gone berserk in the terror of the surprise attack and had started raking vehicles and troops with machine gun fire ….

"I started to say something to Martin as he crouched by the telephone methodically recording the battle in his notebook. My teeth were chattering uncontrollably, I discovered, and in shame I broke off after the first disgraceful squeak of words."

Known for her fire and stubbornness, Higgins survived the surprise attack on the schoolhouse. She reported her experiences in a book, *War in Korea: The Report of a Woman Combat Correspondent*, published in 1951. Higgins eventually received a Pulitzer Prize for her coverage of the Korean War. In the 1960s, she brought her pen into battle again, this time in Vietnam.

After losing a buddy in action, a grief-stricken soldier is comforted by another GI. U.S. troops were unprepared for the ferocity of the fighting in Korea.

of the army, General MacArthur felt the only way to respond was to commit troops piecemeal—a little at a time. This would not stop the NKPA, but it would definitely slow it down. In the meantime, U.S. forces could prepare a full-scale attack.

The U.S. Eighth Army, under General Walton H. Walker's command, was the first to arrive in Korea. The American military was racing the clock. To buy time, Walker's men stood alone against the NKPA. The situation continued to be desperate. When one battalion commander arrived, Walter told him, "I'm sending you up the river to die."

FIGHT AT TAEJON. The first large-scale battle of the war for the Americans took place in July at Taejon. The Eighth Army had begun what it thought was another delaying action—stalling the North Korean advance. However, on July 19, the NKPA attacked the American force. A full-scale battle rocked the town.

The North Koreans put up a roadblock, cutting off Taejon and trapping the American soldiers. By the following day the NKPA had pushed its way into the city, forcing U.S. soldiers to back off. But the action did buy the U.S. Army a little more time. Soon the Eighth Army was reinforced as other American troops joined the fight.

By August 1950 the Eighth Army had withdrawn to the Naktong River (see map on page 149). The river formed part of what would soon become known as the Pusan Perimeter. (The area encompassed the city of Pusan, Korea's largest port.)

> *"If the best minds in the world had set out to find us the worst possible location in the world to fight ... the unanimous choice would have been Korea."*
>
> —U.S. Secretary of State
> Dean Acheson

The U.S. Army Command believed the only way to stop the North Koreans from capturing the entire South was to defend the perimeter. The army could then build up strength for a counterattack. General Walker told his men they had to hold the line around Pusan, and they did. The NKPA attacked over and over throughout the summer. But by September they had lost their advantage, as more U.S. troops came to aid the besieged Eighth Army.

THE TIDE TURNS

In the beginning of September 1950, things began to look up for the American troops in Korea. Reinforcements had arrived, and the troops were gaining momentum and morale. While the fighting continued in the Pusan Perimeter, U.S. forces were taking the offensive for the first time since the fighting began.

INCHON. General MacArthur had been planning a way to reverse the enemy's offensive even while his army was getting beaten up at Taejon. He came up with one of the boldest military operations in history.

The plan called for a large amphibious landing on the west coast of South Korea at the port of Inchon. Once the American forces were ashore, the plan was to push the enemy back and recapture the capital of Seoul.

At the same time, the Eighth Army would break out of the Pusan Perimeter and head toward Seoul. The theory was that the NKPA would be trapped and crushed under the weight of two advancing armies.

Washington opposed MacArthur's plan. Naval specialists thought the landing in Inchon harbor would be impossible. They pointed to the severe tidal range, maybe the most extreme in the world. During high tide, the water rose thirty to forty feet. At low tide the sea sank to a muddy marsh.

MacArthur, in spite of the complaints, pushed his plan through. He assembled a force of nearly 70,000 men to take part in the landing. The invasion was scheduled for September 15, 1950.

HITTING THE BEACHES. The first wave of the invasion began in the morning. Supported by the air force and the navy, the troops stormed the beach of Wolmi-do and secured it within an hour. The second wave of troops waited for the next high tide that came at evening. By midnight American troops had captured the port. The invasion had cost fewer than 200 casualties.

While the invasion troops were pushing on to Seoul, the bottled-up Eighth Army started making progress against the NKPA around the Pusan Perimeter. The success of the American landing panicked the North Korean Army, and it retreated to the 38th parallel.

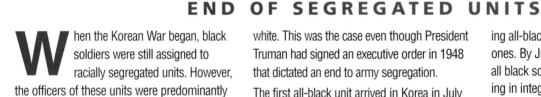

END OF SEGREGATED UNITS

When the Korean War began, black soldiers were still assigned to racially segregated units. However, the officers of these units were predominantly white. This was the case even though President Truman had signed an executive order in 1948 that dictated an end to army segregation.

The first all-black unit arrived in Korea in July 1950 amid one of the darkest periods of the war. It launched the first successful counterattack of the war. The victory was the first major victory the U.S. Army had scored since the war began.

By the end of the summer more all-black units were arriving in Korea. But the army's segregation policy began causing problems. While thousands of more qualified black soldiers were ready and waiting, white units were desperate for replacements.

Eventually military necessity overpowered racism. By early 1951, black soldiers were getting assigned to all-white units. By the end of the year, General Ridgway—now in command of U.S. forces—acknowledged the need to integrate the army. From that point on, remaining all-black units were combined with white ones. By July 1953, more than 90 percent of all black soldiers serving in the war were fighting in integrated units.

The Air Force had moved to desegregate long before the Army. Even before the Korean War began, its units were almost totally integrated. The Marine Corps had also integrated its units to gear up for the landing at Inchon. The U.S. Navy was the last to alter traditional separation. It didn't integrate its force until a decade after the Korean War ended.

More than 3,000 black soldiers were killed in combat in Korea. Those who returned found that the country had not caught up with its military. Segregation was still the norm in Southern states. Returning black veterans were still barred from attending many public universities or even sitting down at local restaurants. State laws, particularly in the South, made it nearly impossible for many to vote.

Marines use scaling ladders to storm ashore at Inchon. MacArthur's invasion gamble would pay off brilliantly.

Seoul was recaptured on September 27. The success of the Inchon landing was so complete many thought the war was over. The North Koreans had been expelled from the South, and Syngman Rhee was reinstated as head of the Republic of Korea. The United States and the United Nations had achieved the goals they had set when the war began.

GREAT EXPECTATIONS. The Communists were contained behind the 38th parallel. That was a victory in itself. However, the Americans were so encouraged, they now thought they could push their victory further. They might be able to unite the country under Rhee and expel communism from Korea altogether.

In order to unite Korea, U.S. forces would have to cross the 38th parallel. They would have to destroy the remaining 30,000 NKPA troops who had refused to surrender. Many in Washington advised against this policy. They felt that neither the Soviet Union nor China would stand still for this kind of intervention. China had already said that it would "not stand aside should the imperialists wantonly invade the territory of their neighbor."

Both the Soviet Union and China considered North Korea to be an essential buffer state. But Syngman Rhee was not content to have the Communists control half of Korea. He maintained that no matter what the United

States decided to do, his Republic of Korea forces would cross the 38th parallel and attack the NKPA.

Rhee made good on his promise. When South Korean troops crossed into the North on October 1, 1950, President Truman was cornered. He reluctantly authorized U.N. forces (90 percent of whom were U.S. soldiers) to follow suit.

WAKE ISLAND. On October 15, President Truman and General MacArthur met to discuss what they thought would be the final phase of U.S. involvement in Korea. The conference took place on Wake Island in the middle of the Pacific Ocean.

Truman called the meeting because he was concerned about the possibility of China intervening in the war. But MacArthur felt he understood the Chinese perspective. He was certain China would back off from the conflict in Korea. He assured Truman that the war would be over by Thanksgiving. Both men were confident when they left Wake Island.

Neither Truman nor MacArthur would have been nearly as confident if they could have seen what was going on in North Korea. The Chinese had already started a military buildup there. At the time of the meeting, nearly 300,000 Chinese troops were poised and ready to take on the charging U.N. forces.

THE CHINESE ATTACK

In late October, MacArthur moved his troops northward toward the Yalu River. Intelligence reports about the Chinese, however, had begun to reach Washington. They were giving President Truman shivers. He started to have doubts about MacArthur's advance into the North.

CHINA STRIKES. MacArthur knew Washington was nervous. So he sidestepped Washington entirely, no longer clearing his movements with the Pentagon. He ordered his troops to "drive forward toward the North with all speed…" This was a direct violation of his instructions. Truman had insisted that only Republic of Korea forces were to be used in provinces close to the Chinese border.

On October 25, the Chinese launched their first-phase offensive. Chinese forces attacked Republic of Korea (ROK) forces north of Unsan. The South Koreans were beaten so badly by the Chinese forces they were unable to help the Americans at all. As a result the Eighth Army was left exposed and vulnerable to a Chinese attack.

Even though the ROK forces had been completely smashed by Chinese troops, MacArthur still believed the Chinese were a small enough force to be defeated. But MacArthur's intelligence officers failed to detect the movements of nearly 200,000 Chinese troops into the area. By November, Washington could see clearly that the Chinese were invading on a huge scale.

OVERRUN AT UNSAN. On November 1, the Chinese attacked the Americans for the first time. U.S. troops were occupying the town of Unsan when they were startled by the sound of bugles and whistles. The small scare tactic was followed by a stunning punch—the Chinese Army advanced in waves. The Eighth Army fought back, but the situation was beyond desperate. The moment troops thought they had slowed the attack, another wave of Chinese would converge upon them.

Literally thousands of Chinese soldiers overran American positions. Hundreds of Americans were killed, and the rest were forced to retreat. At the end of two days of fighting, more than 600 Americans had died.

THE YALU RIVER BRIDGES. MacArthur refused to accept that anything could stand in the way of his conquering all of North Korea. He felt that U.S. forces could stop the further movement of the Chinese at the Yalu River (see map on page 149) The general ordered the destruction of the northern ends of the Yalu bridges. Once again, he did it without first clearing his decision with Washington.

The Pentagon was already set against the plan. If the bombs landed on the Manchurian side of the bridges, the Chinese would likely step up their fight against U.N. forces. The Pentagon postponed the bombing before MacArthur's orders were carried out.

MacArthur was incensed that his orders had been overridden. Not bombing the bridges, he said, would

MOBILE ARMY SURGICAL HOSPITALS

During World War II, survival rates of wounded soldiers had been poor. Wounded soldiers often had to face long hours of transport before they reached an operating room. Half the time they didn't make it there alive.

By the time the Korean War began, the army had worked out a way to provide quicker treatment of casualties. The result was a small hospital that could work just behind the lines of fighting. These units provided quick and efficient care for wounded soldiers. And that care was only minutes away from the heavy fighting. Once a wounded soldier arrived at the MASH, his chances of surviving were excellent: from 97 to 98 percent.

The M in MASH was for mobile. The hospital staff could pick up and move out at a moment's notice. This meant no long-term recovery was available for patients. Once treated and stabilized, the wounded were evacuated to hospitals farther away from the fighting. The speed at which patients had to be treated led to some important improvements in emergency care.

MASH units were popularized by the feature film *M*A*S*H* and by the television series of the same name. The antiwar attitudes expressed boldly in both the film and the series were more a part of the Vietnam War than Korea. But many of the medical problems and plots were right on target.

U.S. Marines move forward with close air support. The Chinese offensive turned the war around.

have "a disastrous effect" on U.S. troops. He also insisted that the matter be brought to the president's attention.

Truman, under pressure to secure the position of U.S. forces, authorized the bombing. But he insisted that the act might result in a Chinese escalation. The Soviets, too, he believed, might interpret bombing the bridges as an attack upon Manchuria.

In fact, the bombing campaign enraged the Chinese and changed the course of the war. One top official in Washington noted: "We sat around like paralyzed rabbits while MacArthur carried out this nightmare."

OFFENSIVE. As of November 17, MacArthur informed Washington that he was going to make a final drive to the Yalu. The Pentagon warned him to stop at the high ground overlooking the river and to go no further.

MacArthur, though, was confident that his bombing campaign had curtailed the Chinese advance. By November 24, the drive was underway. China's forces were on the move the very next day.

The Chinese had control of the high ground; they trapped the Americans in the valley. From a wing formation, they spread open their lines and surrounded the American troops. To prevent a rear escape, a smaller Chinese unit closed off the last exit.

CHOSIN RESERVOIR. The Americans were in big trouble. Nonetheless, on November 27, the second part of MacArthur's planned offensive went into effect. A force of 10,000 Marines and a U.S. Army Infantry Division began their advance along the only road that led north. It passed through the Chosin (Changjin) Reservoir in northeastern Korea. The reservoir stood in a valley surrounded by steep cliffs.

Though the Americans and MacArthur didn't know it, a trap was waiting for them. The Chinese had 120,000 troops hiding in the mountains waiting to attack.

The Chinese had waited weeks to ambush the Americans. They moved out from the mountains and took up positions on the hills overlooking the reservoir. The first night, as U.S. troops struggled to warm themselves in the bitter cold, 30,000 Chinese soldiers attacked. The attack at Chosin would go down as one of the most brutal ambushes in history. The Chinese used machine guns to pound U.S. soldiers as they tried to get through the valley. On the eastern shore of the reservoir, the Army's 31st Infantry Regiment, including 700 ROK soldiers, was pinned down by heavy Chinese fire.

Other units in the Chosin area were unable or unwilling to come to the regiment's rescue. The besieged troops were advised to make their way to the village of Hundong where a tank regiment could help them. By this point, however, more than 500 soldiers were wounded and the temperature had dropped to perhaps 35 degrees below zero. They were in no condition to go anywhere. Still the regiment tried to move out with the wounded on trucks. As they advanced, though, Chinese mortars rained down on them. Napalm followed it, mistakenly dropped by U.S. aircraft. When they reached Hundong, they found the tank regiment had abandoned them. The regiment's wounded froze to death. Close to 3,000 men, nearly the entire force, were lost.

The remaining divisions continued to travel the gauntlet from the reservoir to the port of Hungnam. It wasn't until the middle of December that the last of the units—or what remained of them—were evacuated.

CHANGE OF COMMAND

December 1950 was a tough month for the U.N. forces in Korea. The NKPA recaptured the North Korean capital of Pyongyang, and the Americans were virtually shoved out of the North. The Truman administration had to rethink its goal of unifying Korea. The North could not be overrun. The new objective was to hold and secure the South.

STATE OF EMERGENCY. President Truman began to worry that the Soviets might use the struggle in Korea as a pretext for starting a global war. In fact, Washington intelligence was watching for signs of Communist activity in hotspots around the world, especially Berlin, Germany.

Truman's anxiety about the situation became extreme. On December 16, he declared a national emergency. The Chinese, said Truman, have shown "that they are willing to push the world to the brink of a general war to get what they want." Because of the emergency, Truman said it was essential that the United States increase its armed forces as quickly as possible.

NEW COMMANDER. Meanwhile, in Korea, the Eighth Army was retreating behind the 38th parallel. Soon after, General Walker was killed in a car crash. Washington ordered Lieutenant General Matthew Ridgway to replace him. He took command of all U.S., U.N., and Republic of Korea forces engaged in the war, though he was still under MacArthur's command.

Unlike MacArthur, Ridgway favored Truman's policies in Korea. He was confident, too, that he could effect important changes there. Morale had sunk to a new low after Chosin. The army was underfed and badly equipped. Ridgway set about improving conditions for the troops. He also felt it was time for the Americans to start fighting the way the Chinese fought, in the hills and off the road.

On the eve of the New Year, the Chinese launched another attack. They boasted that they would now rid Korea of all U.S. and United Nations forces. The Eighth Army was forced to back up again, this time into an area around Seoul.

That wasn't the end of the retreat. By January 4 the troops had pulled out of Seoul and the port of Inchon. At this point the Communist offensive seemed to be losing steam. The Eighth Army finally dug in forty miles south of Seoul, ending a 275-mile retreat.

DOUGLAS MACARTHUR

The son of a Civil War hero who fought at Missionary Ridge, Douglas MacArthur was probably one of the greatest military minds the United States has ever produced. The Arkansas native graduated first in his class at West Point. In World War I, he received seven Silver Stars for bravery in combat. In WWII, MacArthur again proved his brilliance, particularly in the use of air power. He achieved his objectives in the Pacific and had the lowest casualty rate of any major U.S. commander during the war.

Taking command of United States and Republic of Korea forces in Korea in 1950, MacArthur stopped fast-advancing North Korean troops from conquering all of Korea. His invasion at Inchon is considered one of the all-time brilliant moves in U.S. military history.

MacArthur was undaunted until faced with invading forces from Communist China. The general divided his army and lost just about all the territory U.S. forces had gained. Afterward he wanted to attack the Chinese, to bring the war to their border, and Truman would not let him.

What finally undid MacArthur—and what ultimately caused Truman to fire him— was the five-star general's six-star ego. MacArthur believed he knew how to conduct the war better than Truman did. The general thought he could deal effectively with the Chinese Communists; Truman thought not; he reckoned a serious challenge to the Chinese could land the U.S. knee-deep in World War III.

The world will never know what might have happened if MacArthur had been able to wage war against the Chinese as he wished. But MacArthur's error was larger than just offending the president. He was violating a tenet of the U.S. Constitution. That Constitution mandates that the U.S. military is in the hands of the president—a civilian. No matter how popular MacArthur himself was, he was still bound to obey Truman. In disobeying the direct orders of the president, MacArthur was violating his oath as a soldier.

When MacArthur faced Congress after his firing, an irate senator reminded the general of a statement MacArthur had made in 1932. The then U.S. Army chief had said that the head of state alone should determine a war's objectives and the means of attaining them. It was a statement MacArthur had somehow forgotten.

A seemingly endless line of refugees slogs through the snow. The fighting in Korea made millions homeless.

Ridgway's philosophy hinged on coordination, cooperation, and communications. He set out to train his men and improve intelligence gathering. By the end of January, the Eighth Army was in top shape, ready to fight and ready to win.

Operation Thunderbolt became the U.S./U.N. forces' first offensive in two months. Troops set out on a drive north toward the Han River near Seoul. Within ten days the allied forces had once again secured Inchon. They were on their way to Seoul.

OPERATION KILLER.
The Communists were tired out now. Far from their supply bases, they had used up most of their food and ammunition. Ridgway planned to attack just as the Chinese were at their weakest.

Operation Killer's main purpose was to destroy as many Communist soldiers as possible in the drive for Seoul. Given the situation, Ridgway was planning "a war of maneuver, slashing at the enemy when he withdraws and fighting delaying actions when he attacks."

Ridgway 's success bothered MacArthur. He was not in favor of limited war. He felt that true victory would only come if Korea was unified under Rhee once and for all. Some believed that MacArthur was simply being vain. They thought that his objections might have more to do with his legendary pride than his military strategy.

On March 7, before the launch of the new offensive, MacArthur flew to Korea. He declared that a stalemate was all but certain.

The troops' newly restored morale took a beating. "Die for Tie" became the soldiers' new slogan as they began to realize they would be risking their lives in a war they could not win. In spite of this, Allied forces recaptured Seoul by March.

> "We owe it to the men in the field—and to the God to whom we have to answer for these men's lives—to stop talking and act."
>
> — *General Matthew Ridgway, to the Joint Chiefs of Staff*

SEARCH FOR PEACE.
Truman was eager to end the war, which was becoming increasingly unpopular at home. He planned to announce that he would seek a cease-fire as the first step in a settlement. Before he had the chance, however, MacArthur spoke instead.

In effect, MacArthur issued an ultimatum. He told China to withdraw completely from Korea or face an awesome attack from U.S./U.N. forces. He called the Chinese forces a defeated army, saying that they had "exaggerated" their military power. The general's statement was made without clearing it first with the president.

Truman was furious. He relieved MacArthur of his duties on April 11, 1951, and replaced him with General Ridgway.

RESOLUTION

By mid-April 1951, the Korean War had reached a stalemate. United States and United Nations forces continued to trade offensives with the Communist Chinese. By the end of May, the enemy was driven from all of its positions in South Korea. The Allied forces found themselves back at the position they held the previous autumn.

TALKS BEGIN. The Truman administration felt that it would be a good time, once again, to consider ending the war. The Communists had suffered nearly 200,000 casualties by the end of May. The American public was losing patience for a war that had already injured or killed 75,000 of its children.

On June 30, General Ridgway announced that the United Nations was ready to discuss an armistice agreement. On July 1, Kim Il Sung and the commander of the Chinese forces agreed to the talks. They began on July 10.

In August, a group of armed Chinese soldiers violated the neutrality of the conference zone and threatened the U.N. delegation. The talks were called off. The Chinese promised there would be no more incidents. The talks resumed a few days later.

Later that month, though, the Communists turned around and accused U.N. forces of violating the conference zone. Ridgway claimed the charges were fake and refused to apologize. The Communists walked out on the talks. The negotiations would not resume until October. In the meantime the war raged on.

THE BLOODY PUNCHBOWL. The most intense fighting of the Korean War took place while the talks were suspended. At the end of August, Ridgway ordered a new offensive. He believed that this new attack would force the Communists back to the table.

U.S. Marines were sent in to take control of a series of hills surrounding a valley known as the Punchbowl. Their main objectives were Bloody Ridge and Heartbreak Ridge (see sidebar). The hills were named after the battles were over, and the descriptions were apt. It took a long month of brutal fighting for the Marines to seize Bloody Ridge. The battle for Heartbreak Ridge lasted until the middle of October. Six thousand Americans were carried away dead from the two hills.

TALKS RESUME. During the break in the negotiations, Communist casualties totaled more than 200,000. By October 7, they were ready for another round of peace talks. Negotiations began again on October 25.

Though both sides talked for more than two months, the negotiations were going nowhere. Finally the issue of prisoners of war came up. The U.N.'s official position was that it would repatriate POWs who wished to return home. All those who said they did not want to return home would be given political asylum. The Communists

TWO LITTLE HILLS IN KOREA

In the summer of 1951, the U.S. Army held almost all of the hilltops around an area in Korea known as the Basin. There were, however, two ridges held by the enemy. They would eventually be known as Heartbreak Ridge and Bloody Ridge. Jean Larteguy, a French correspondent, wrote about the battle for those ridges in his book, *The Face of War*:

"In that month of October 1951, two entire American divisions were thrown into the assault on Heartbreak Ridge and were massacred. Fifteen hundred American corpses remained on its slopes. The Chinese and the North Koreans were solidly entrenched, and they put their artillery to its best use. It was impossible to cut it off. Individual artillery pieces were brought out from under cover— from a cave or overhang—one at a time. Each fired two or three rounds and then withdrew, while another took its turn. They were never grouped in a battery—were always isolated. Their losses were thus slight....

"I saw the parts of the American units that had survived coming back down all the little twisting trails from Heartbreak Ridge. The GIs carried long bamboo poles on their shoulders and bore the bodies of their friends like hunting trophies. Many, many soldiers had gone mad. Stupefied by their experiences, some would suddenly begin to howl, or to leap about in a frenzy, until it became necessary to stun them in order to quiet them."

Larteguy was wounded himself on Heartbreak Ridge. He was evacuated by helicopter after being hit by a grenade. Larteguy's report is filled with exhaustion and despair. It is much more pessimistic than earlier work on the war. (Compare *A Reporter's Up-Close View of the War* on page 150.)

Panmunjom, Korea—site of peace negotiations. For the soldiers in the field, the talks seemed to go on forever.

demanded that all prisoners be returned. They were furious at the U.N.'s proposal.

There were also disagreements regarding the number of Americans held. The North Koreans claimed they had only 3,000 American prisoners, while the United States was missing some 11,000 men.

DESPERATE MEASURES. By May 1952, the POW issue had created a complete stalemate. But the United States was still anxious to end the war. In June, Truman again decided that the way to break the stalemate was through military force.

On June 23, more than 250 allied planes attacked the power plants along the Yalu River. The Communists still wouldn't budge. Again, in July, U.S. and U.N. troops turned up the heat. More than 1,200 fighter bombers dropped 1,400 tons of bombs and 23,000 gallons of napalm (jellied gasoline) on Pyongyang. The Communists still showed no signs of moving.

The Allied forces warned the Communists that the raids would continue if they did not give in. The Communists held fast, and the bombs rained down throughout the summer. Finally, on August 29, in the biggest attack of the war, 1,403 planes targeted Pyongyang. The raid had no effect, and talks were suspended again on October 8.

NEW LEADERSHIP. Dwight D. Eisenhower was elected

President of the United States on November 4, 1952. The president-elect set out for Korea in December. Eisenhower had led U.S. forces to victory in World War II. Now he was deciding what to do with the conflict he inherited from Truman. After looking at the situation, Eisenhower said that it wouldn't be easy to actually win the war without risking a larger conflict. Basically he faced the same thorny issues that Truman had. The stalemate continued.

On March 5, 1953, however, Soviet Premier Joseph Stalin died. Stalin's iron will had charted the course for Communists around the world. With his death, there was suddenly a vacuum in world Communist leadership. The Communists were now ready to talk. They agreed to the U.N.'s demands.

The next month, discussions began on the exchange of sick and wounded prisoners. It was decided that all POWs would be turned over to a neutral-nation commission after the armistice. Those who wished to return to their homes would be allowed to do so. After that, each government could try to change the minds of those who did not want to go home.

Fighting in Korea continued throughout June and into July. Finally, it was agreed that the fighting would end twelve hours after the armistice was signed. Each side was to withdraw two kilometers from its positions. The vacated area would become the demilitarized zone. On July 27, 1953, the armistice was finally signed.

AFTERMATH

Korea was the United States' first limited international war. The U.S. had to settle for something less than complete victory. Although it was frustrating, limited warfare often seemed the best choice in a nuclear world. Throughout the Cold War, both the United States and the Soviet Union were tempted and provoked by the possible use of nuclear weapons. In the end, both sides refrained.

SEND IN THE SPIES. Restrained from direct military action, the United States increasingly turned to covert, or undercover, acts to stop the spread of communism around the globe.

In 1945, the Central Intelligence Agency (CIA) had taken over from the Office of Strategic Services, the agency that had overseen much of World War II spying. Soon, the CIA oversaw the toppling of two governments.

In July 1953, U.S. agents in Iran helped oust left-leaning Mohammed Mossadegh and replace him with the pro-U.S. Shah in that oil-rich Middle Eastern land.

The following year CIA-trained exiles and mercenaries forced Guatemalan leader Jacobo Arbenz Guzmán from power. Arbenz had provoked the United States when he "nationalized" property of a huge U.S.-owned fruit company in the small Central American country. Arbenz wanted to end workers' grinding poverty. Although his replacement was more sympathetic to U.S. interests, Guatemala was plunged into chaos that lasted for decades.

AT THE BRINK. The threat of using nuclear weapons was a part of U.S. defense strategy. Secretary of State John Foster Dulles insisted that the nation "depend primarily [upon its] great capacity to retaliate, instantly." Dulles also espoused the idea of brinkmanship—going right up to the brink of war in the interest of avoiding it. "You must take chances for peace," he said, "just as you must take chances in war."

Since the United States still held a great advantage in numbers of nuclear weapons in the early 1950s, some thought Dulles had a point; others weren't so sure. Frightened Americans built and stocked bomb shelters in the hope of surviving a nuclear attack.

In 1954, U.S. scientists designed the Intercontinental Ballistic Missile (ICBM), which could carry a nuclear weapon from U.S. bases to the Soviet Union in just twenty minutes. Within three years, the Soviets had developed their own weapon-carrying ICBMs. Now both countries had powerful hydrogen bombs and a fast and efficient means to deliver them. A nuclear strike—and retaliation for it—could occur in less than an hour. It would kill hundreds of millions, if not billions, of people.

MIXED SOVIET SIGNALS. In 1956, Soviet Premier Nikita Khrushchev exposed the brutal crimes committed by his predecessor, Joseph Stalin. Stalin had ruled through terror and intimidation, executing millions. Others were confined to deadly work camps. Stalin even rounded up children of "suspect" parents and put them in institutions.

By admitting these atrocities, Khrushchev eased tensions with the West. People within Communist countries, however, became disillusioned by the revelations.

REVOLUTION IN HUNGARY. On October 23, 1956, a revolt against the Communists began in the eastern European city of Budapest, Hungary. A reform government was allowed to take over, and Soviet troops withdrew.

However, the new leader, Imre Nagy, made more changes than the Soviets anticipated. He announced that Hungary would withdraw from the alliance of Communist-controlled countries in Europe called the Warsaw Pact. In less than a month, the Soviets stormed back in. Nagy was captured and executed. Between 100,000 and 200,000 people fled.

> "We will bury you."
> —Soviet Premier Nikita Khrushchev

MISSILE GAP. President Dwight D. Eisenhower was under pressure to add more nuclear weapons to the U.S. arsenal. Eisenhower was determined to keep the U.S. defense budget under control and had no wish to buy unnecessary weapons. In fact, there were ten U.S. missiles for every Soviet missile, but the Pentagon could not verify it. One report asserted that the Russians were gaining steadily on the U.S., and soon there would be a "missile gap" that favored the Soviets.

Eisenhower, a former general, thought the missile gap theory was hogwash, but he needed proof to assure the public. He had an idea about how he might get it. In 1956, the Air Force had begun conducting secret, high-altitude flights over Soviet airspace with a new Lockheed spy plane. Code-named U-2, the plane had a camera that could photograph an individual car from fourteen miles up. Unfortunately, the plane could be spotted by radar, and the Soviets knew all about the flights. In 1960, as Eisenhower prepared to meet Khrushchev for their first summit meeting, the U-2 made one last surveillance flight.

An East German soldier bolts over the border between East and West. The Berlin Wall dramatized Cold War tensions.

The Soviets shot it down. Not only did they get the wreckage of an enormously sophisticated plane, the pilot was alive. Air Force Captain Francis Gary Powers was captured as a spy.

First, the United States denied there was a plane. When the wreckage was exhibited, Eisenhower insisted it was a weather plane. Then, to the nation's and president's embarrassment, Powers confessed to spying. The summit was cancelled.

TROUBLE IN CUBA.

Meanwhile, on the Caribbean island of Cuba, another revolution had taken place. A small band of rebels, led by Fidel Castro, launched a guerrilla war against dictator Fulgencio Batista. Between 1956 and 1958, they managed to take control of the entire island. Batista fled, and Castro took over.

To the horror of the United States, Castro began taking over American-owned businesses and oil refineries. Further alienating the United States, just ninety miles to the north, Castro took aid from the Soviet Union. Communist support grew as U.S. support diminished.

In 1961, John F. Kennedy took office as president. His predecessor, Eisenhower, had already begun to work out a plan to overthrow Castro's government. Kennedy's advisers were split over whether he should continue the plan or leave Castro alone. The president eventually approved the invasion but refused to back it with U.S. air power.

On April 17, 1961, Cuban exiles stormed the beaches of Cuba's Bay of Pigs. They were pinned down almost instantly by Castro's forces. Wary of provoking the Soviets into defending Castro, Kennedy abandoned the invasion forces.

The Soviets took Kennedy's caution as proof that he could be intimidated. Over the next two years, the young president would be forced to prove to the Soviets that he would not back down again. Although Kennedy was no advocate of brinkmanship, the United States would be brought to the brink of thermonuclear war.

THE BERLIN WALL.

Since the division of Germany after World War II (see map on page 146), East Germans had been crossing to the West. This migration was so large that it threatened the stability of East Germany. Overnight on August 19, 1961, a barricade was thrown up through the divided city of Berlin. It cut through neighborhoods and even graveyards.

For Kennedy, the wall was a poignant symbol of the difference between the Communist and the free world. Just months after the wall went up, he came to Berlin and made an impassioned speech. "There are many people in the world who really don't understand, or say they don't, what is the great issue between the free world and

the Communist world. Let them come to Berlin… Democracy may not be perfect," he said, "but at least we don't have to build walls to keep our people in."

CUBAN MISSILE CRISIS.

In the autumn of 1962, the worst nuclear crisis of the Cold War occurred. Satellite intelligence showed that the Soviets had installed missiles and heavy bombers in Cuba. President Kennedy announced that the United States would blockade Cuba until they were removed. He made it clear that if the Cubans attacked any nation in the Western Hemisphere, the United States would regard it as a Soviet attack and retaliate.

The Pentagon prepared to invade Cuba, and Soviet forces were put on maximum alert.

Kennedy and Khrushchev exchanged a series of tense letters. Within a short time, the Soviet Union backed down and agreed to dismantle its missile bases. Around the world, people breathed a sigh of relief.

THE VIETNAM WAR

Part of the Cold War fight against Communism, the Vietnam War was, by U.S. standards, a military failure. The conflict in Southeast Asia, though never officially declared a war, tested the United States like no other war had. The longest conflict in U.S. history threatened to tear the country apart. The nation survived Vietnam, but it changed in the process. Having swallowed the loss of 50,000 of its citizens and a chunk of its pride, the United States no longer thought it could solve every problem, everywhere. It had found its limits.

PRELUDE TO WAR

In the mid-1800s, the French, looking for trade routes to China, came to Vietnam. By 1884, France had annexed the entire country and placed it under colonial rule. While France continued its colonial domination, some Vietnamese armed themselves, hoping to get rid of the Europeans. In 1921, Ho Chi Minh created the Vietminh, a nationalistic party seeking independence from France.

When World War II broke out and France fell to the Nazis, Vietnam became a twin colony. The Japanese and French were both telling the Vietnamese what to do. An estimated 2 million Vietnamese died of starvation because of Japanese-French policies during these years.

When Japanese forces surrendered to the Allies in 1945, Ho Chi Minh launched a full-scale revolt. By the end of the summer, the Vietminh took control of the cap-

ital city, Hanoi, forcing the emperor, Bao Dai, to abdicate. On September 2, 1945, Ho declared Vietnam independent and announced the creation of the Democratic Republic of Vietnam.

FRANCE REFUSES RECOGNITION.

Ho's Vietminh hoped to cash in on the Allies' postwar commitment to support the self-determination of all colonized peoples. In reality though, the French were trying to find a way to "reconquer" their former "property" in Indochina.

As a result, France refused to recognize Vietnam's independence, unless it was within the framework of the French Union. When the French arrived in Saigon at the end of September 1945, Vietnamese nationalists revolted. The rebellion kicked off the First Indochina War, with the French battling the Vietminh.

By 1946, the French had reestablished themselves as the rulers of Vietnam. Ho's Communist Party was forced to retreat to guerrilla outposts in the countryside. Intense guerrilla warfare began against the French.

Meanwhile, the French had reinstalled Bao Dai as a puppet emperor of the "free state of Vietnam." They established a new capital in Saigon.

U.S. SUPPORTS FRANCE.

By this point, though, the Vietminh already controlled most of Vietnam's countryside. When China fell to Mao Tse-tung's Communist Party (see sidebar on page 118), France, as well as the United States, worried that the entire Asian region would become communist.

President Truman decided to support Bao Dai and the French. Truman began sending military supplies and money to the French effort. In the end, the United States would end up footing nearly the entire cost of the French war in Vietnam.

By 1953 it was obvious that France was losing the war and looking for a way out. The United States, though, was still fully committed to defending Vietnam against "Communist imperialism." When a French army surrendered at Dien Bien Phu on May 7, 1954, the fighting ended.

In July 1954, a cease-fire agreement was signed in Geneva, Switzerland. A buffer zone would divide Vietnam north from south. The Communists, with Ho Chi Minh as president, would get control of the northern section and the capital of Hanoi. Ngo Dinh Diem would be interim premier in the South. For the French, the trial in Vietnam was finally over. But American troubles were just beginning. Few could imagine what terrible troubles those might prove to be.

1964–1966	1967	1968	1969	1970
Tonkin Gulf Resolution is passed by Congress giving the president power to repel attacks against U.S. troops in Vietnam *(Aug. 7, 1964)*. Sustained aerial bombing of North Vietnam (Operation Rolling Thunder) begins *(Feb. 1965)*.	General Nguyen Van Thieu is elected president of South Vietnam.	Base at Khe Sanh is besieged by North Vietnamese Army forces. The Tet offensive begins *(Jan. 31)*. Vietnamese civilians massacred by U.S. troops at My Lai. Peace negotiations open in Paris *(May 10)*.	Nixon begins gradual withdrawal of troops, which had reached a high of 550,000. Massive antiwar demonstrations in United States	South Vietnamese forces supported by U.S. helicopters attack Communist bases in Cambodia. Antiwar demonstrations continue on U.S. college campuses. At Kent State in Ohio, four students are shot and killed during a protest.

CHINA

Dien Bien Phu

Viet Tri

Hanoi

Haiphong

Harbor mined

Nam Dinh

Zhanjiang

Haikou

Gulf of Tonkin

☆ *Gulf of Tonkin incident*

HAINAN

LAOS

NORTH VIETNAM

Mekong River

Vientiane

THAILAND

Demilitarized Zone

Invasion of Laos

Khe Sanh

Quang Tri

☆ *Hue*

A Shau Valley

Da Nang

South China Sea

Ho Chi Minh Trail

Dak To
Kontum

An Khe

Pleiku

Ia Drang

CAMBODIA

Tonle Sap

Invasion of Cambodia

Phnom Penh

Mekong River

An Loc

SOUTH VIETNAM

Tan Son Nhut

Saigon

Rach Gia

VIETNAM WAR (1964–1975)

Areas of continuous fighting

◎ Major bombing target

☆ *Major battle*

0   75   150 Mi.

*U.S. Marine,
Vietnam War*

1971

Antiwar protesters numbering 500,000 demonstrate in Washington.

President Nixon withdraws another 100,000 troops.

1972

North Vietnamese Regular Army forces invade South Vietnam.

Bombardment of North Vietnam resumes. United States mines North Vietnamese harbors.

1973

Bombing over North Vietnam is suspended. Agreement is reached in Paris to end the war *(Jan. 27)*.

Last American combat troops leave South Vietnam *(March 29)*.

American prisoners are released.

1974–1975

In spite of the truce, fighting continues throughout South Vietnam, Cambodia, and Laos.

North Vietnamese troops enter Saigon, capital of South Vietnam. Remaining Americans and some South Vietnamese are evacuated. South Vietnam's president announces unconditional surrender *(April 30)*.

THE U.S. GETS INVOLVED

After the Geneva agreement was signed in 1954, 900,000 Vietnamese non-Communists in the North fled to the South. Many were fleeing from the severe treatment handed out to Vietnamese "traitors and landlords." Thousands had been killed by the Communist regime.

KEEPING THE STATUS QUO. The Indochina Treaty signed in Geneva specified that elections would be held to determine the fate of both Vietnam and Laos. No foreign troops would be permitted inside either country to influence the outcome. The U.S.-supported Diem regime in South Vietnam had refused to sign the accord. Diem also refused to participate in the Vietnamese elections in 1956. Instead Diem proclaimed the Republic of Vietnam and became its president with U.S. support.

Eisenhower, however, had lived through the Korean conflict (see page 148) and had no desire to fight a war to unify Vietnam. He could tolerate the division of Vietnam, as long as the Communists stayed in the North and left the South alone. For a few years, at least, that is what happened. Both Diem in the South and Ho Chi Minh in the North worked to consolidate power within their own territories.

Under the terms of SEATO (the Southeast Asia Treaty Organization), a U.S-led defense alliance, the United States continued to supply technical, military, and financial aid to the South.

KENNEDY REACTS. By the time President Kennedy took office in 1961, however, the situation was getting worse. Communist forces in Vietnam, and especially neighboring Laos, were becoming more aggressive. In 1961, Communist insurgents, the Vietcong, carried out attacks in the Kontum province of South Vietnam. The U.S. began talking about air strikes against North Vietnam and China.

Kennedy, however, was cautious. He sent another 100 military advisors to Vietnam as well 400 Special Forces soldiers. Additional U.S. military aid helped to bolster the Vietnamese Army. Kennedy also agreed to have U.S. troops stationed in Thailand. Things quieted down for a while, but the situation remained shaky.

A CORRUPT GOVERNMENT. One of the biggest problems for the United States was that Diem's rule was corrupt. Diem had taken control by force, and he had never been elected by the people of Vietnam, North or South.

During the late 1950s, as the Communists used terror to "purify" the North, Diem was wielding his own political bullwhip in the South. He installed village officials throughout the country and used corrupt means to control them. To his enemies he showed no mercy. He was particularly harsh with Communists in the South.

Diem's authoritarian control was not only a moral problem for the United States, it was also a practical problem. His corruption gave further ammunition—and power—to the Vietcong Communists in the South. Many times with encouragement from local peasants, they assassinated Diem's village authorities.

FIERY PROTESTS

More than any other group, a few determined Buddhist monks brought about Ngo Dinh Diem's downfall in Vietnam. The monks were determined to protest Diem's persecution of Buddhists, and they did it in an unforgettable way.

On June 11, 1963, a seventy-three-year-old monk from Hue, Thich Quang Duc, had gasoline poured on himself in the middle of a Saigon street. He lit the gas, then burned to death as Saigon residents looked on.

After Thich Quang Duc's death, other Buddhist leaders delivered a funeral address. They pleaded for assistance from the U.S. military to help them in their plight in South Vietnam.

The protest caused a stir but no immediate changes. In mid-August, four more monks went up in flames. Eventually thirty monks and nuns died by self-immolation.

Diem's powerful sister-in-law, Madame Nhu, said: "Let them [the monks] burn, and we shall clap our hands." But Diem was worried about the protests. He responded by attacking Buddhist temples. Thousands were arrested.

For President Kennedy, the spectacle was too much. U.S. support for Diem evaporated. Vietnam's ruler would soon join the monks in death.

Vietcong prisoners captured by South Vietnamese forces. Though Vietnam was largely a civil war, U.S. policy makers never saw it that way.

Diem responded by locking up the peasants in fort-like hamlets, but this only made him more unpopular. Cries against Diem's authority reached a screaming pitch when Buddhist monks set fire to themselves in public protests (see sidebar).

MILITARY CHALLENGES. The South Vietnamese Army was another problem. It was weak and poorly trained, no real match for the passionate Vietcong. Kennedy received much advice on how to relieve the problem. His military advisor, General Maxwell Taylor, suggested sending in a few thousand soldiers to help. The Joint Chiefs of Staff were more aggressive. They thought about 40,000 to 128,000 troops would "clean up" the situation.

Kennedy sent Vice President Lyndon Johnson on a fact-finding mission to Indochina. Upon his return, Johnson had determined that the United States needed to take a strong position in Vietnam, or Communists would soon take all of Southeast Asia.

Kennedy was unsure about how much of a threat the Communists posed in Indochina. He refused to make a major military commitment there. But he did continue to send troops, and he let it be known in February 1962 that they would fire back if fired upon.

Late in his administration, Kennedy withdrew support from the Diem regime. A group of unhappy Vietnamese generals, urged on by the United States, threw Diem out of office. Diem, along with his brother, was murdered the next day. A military junta, headed by General Nguyen Khanh, took power.

JOHNSON TAKES COMMAND. In November 1963, President Kennedy was shot to death by an assassin in Dallas, Texas. He was replaced by Vice President Johnson. Johnson was wary of further involving the United States in the conflict but saw no real way of getting the country out of its commitment to the Vietnamese. "I don't think it's worth it," Johnson said to an advisor, "and I don't think we can get out."

Early in 1964, Johnson ordered military planes into Laos. In August, the destroyers USS *Maddox* and USS *Turner Joy* reported that they had been attacked by North Vietnamese torpedo boats in the Gulf of Tonkin off the North Vietnamese coast. Later investigations would lead to suspicions that the ships had not been attacked at all. Instead, it seemed possible that navy personnel had been confused by radar blips. No enemy vessels were discovered after the "attack."

The day after the reports, Johnson ordered immediate strikes against naval bases, patrol boats, and oil depots along the North Vietnamese coast. The American raids cost the life of one navy pilot. Another became the first U.S. prisoner of war taken in Vietnam.

TONKIN GULF RESOLUTION. Congress followed up the raid with a resolution allowing the president to "take all necessary measures to repel any armed attack against the forces of the United States." This blanket resolution would give President Johnson and his successors permission to wage war in Indochina for the next eight years. Congress would come to regret it.

By the end of 1964, about 20,000 U.S. soldiers were already in Vietnam.

THE AIR WAR

After passage of the Gulf of Tonkin Resolution, the war in Vietnam quickly heated up. U.S. troops found themselves openly opposed by guerrilla forces throughout the South.

VIETCONG ATTACKS. At the end of November 1964, the Vietcong mortared a South Vietnamese air base at Bien Hoa. Four Americans were killed in the attack, and seventy-two were wounded. Dozens of American aircraft were damaged or destroyed.

The following month a Vietcong bomb exploded outside the Brink Bachelor Officers' Quarters in Saigon. More than fifty Americans and South Vietnamese were injured; two U.S. servicemen died. Two months later, the Vietcong boldly attacked a U.S. Army barracks at Pleiku, killing another eight Americans and wounding more than a hundred.

AID FROM THE NORTH. The United States knew that supplies for the Vietcong were coming mostly down from the North. Materiel and arms were being moved over the Ho Chi Minh Trail (see main map on page 163). In order to stop this stream of supplies, the Pentagon began a bombing campaign early in 1965. It was code-named Operation Rolling Thunder.

With Rolling Thunder, the United States hoped to cut supply and communication lines connecting the North to the South. It would do this by hitting bridges and other targets above the DMZ (the demilitarized zone between the North and South). The Pentagon hoped that the bombing would force Hanoi to stop helping the Vietcong or even negotiate a peace settlement.

President Johnson decided to limit the bombing to particular areas of the North. Most of the supplies making their way down the Ho Chi Minh Trail were coming out of Hanoi and Haiphong. But the Air Force was not allowed to bomb there. The idea of raiding heavily populated areas at this point had been rejected.

NO SUCCESS. Throughout 1965, thousands of sorties were flown against Vietcong lines of supply. Still, U.S. bombs weren't stopping the flow of supplies.

Bomber pilots faced all sorts of problems. The biggest difficulty was the Vietnamese landscape. Much of the Ho Chi Minh Trail ran through heavy forests and jungles. It was difficult, if not impossible, to find a target. In the downpours of monsoon season, from October through March, pilots could rarely fly missions at all.

Now, too, enemy forces were starting to fight back. The number of antiaircraft guns in the North doubled. North Vietnam began to use Russian-made SAMS (surface-to-air missiles) to shoot down U.S. bombers. By the end of 1965, more than fifty Navy and Air Force planes had gone down. Some of the pilots had been captured and imprisoned (see sidebar).

At the end of 1965 (Christmas through the New Year), President Johnson ordered the bombing of North Vietnam stopped. He wanted to see if Hanoi would react positively. But the result was disappointing. The pause allowed the North Vietnamese to repair damaged roads and bridges. In the interval, they were able to increase the flow of supplies to Vietcong in the South.

CAPTURED U.S. PILOTS

Few issues incited American passions more than the treatment of Navy and Air Force pilots held prisoner in Vietnam. The North Vietnamese had little mercy on those who had been bombing their troops, roads, cities, bridges, and factories.

Captured flyers were frequently paraded through the streets of Hanoi, where they could be jeered at and beaten by onlookers. Most spent their time locked up in dark concrete boxes, occasionally even in cages. They had no windows, no light, little food. Almost all were tortured—physically and psychologically broken—by their captors. Virtually every right they were guaranteed under the Geneva Convention was violated. The Convention articles, ratified in 1949, mandated the way sick and wounded combatants should be treated in captivity.

U.S. Navy Captain Howard Rutledge was shot down in his F-8 in 1965. He was imprisoned for seven years in Hanoi. In his memoir, *In the Presence of Mine Enemies*, he talks about his time in solitary confinement:

"Nobody can teach you to survive the brutality of being alone. At first you panic. You want to cry out. You fight back waves of fear. You want to die, to confess, to do anything to get out of that ever-shrinking world. Then, gradually a plan takes shape. Being alone is another kind of war, but slowly I learned that it, too, can be won."

A U.S. Skyraider makes a napalm drop over Vietnam. The air war harassed the traffic into the South but didn't stop it.

JOHNSON REACTS. Just after the monsoons ended, in the spring of 1966, Johnson ordered heavier strikes on the North. This time targets in Hanoi and Haiphong were included. The stepped-up raids finally produced some results—although the number of Vietcong attacks was still high, the forces carrying them out were smaller.

Sorties continued through the following September. Although the raids were supposed to be limited to military targets like fuel depots, power plants, and rail lines, the reality was somewhat different. In October, bombers attacked the city of Phuly, thirty-five miles south of Hanoi. Nearly all the homes and buildings were destroyed.

HANOI RESPONDS. The bombing was having an effect on Hanoi, but it was not the one Washington wanted. As the bombing raids grew heavier, the North Vietnamese dug in. They put extra effort into repairing damaged bridges and rail lines. They hid their supply bases underground.

Worse still, more U.S. planes were tumbling out of the sky. The North Vietnamese continued to fire on American bombers and fighters with deadly SAMS. Now, North Vietnamese pilots, flying Russian-made MiG 21s, had begun fighting for their own airspace.

U.S. Air Force Phantom jets were fast, but the MiGs were easier to maneuver. Air-to-air combat grew more common and more and more deadly. By the end of 1966, 455 American planes had been lost.

In January 1967, President Johnson okayed bombing sites nearer Hanoi. As the targets got closer to the city, chances grew that there would be large numbers of civilian casualties. But moving closer to Hanoi allowed the navy and air force to hit industrial and communication sites. These were at the heart of the supply operation to the South.

Hanoi fought back once again, putting nearly 100 MiGs into the air. On January 2, 1967, Phantoms and MiGs engaged in the largest aerial fight of the entire war. The Phantoms shot down seven MiGs in twelve minutes with no losses. From 1965 through 1968, U.S. Navy and Air Force pilots managed to level most North Vietnamese "military targets" near and in Hanoi. An estimated 52,000 civilians were killed during the period.

IGNORING THE SOURCE. The United States was winning the war in the air, but the real problem lay elsewhere. The bulk of the supplies for the Vietcong were coming through the Haiphong harbor. Here a relentless stream of aid from the Soviet Union and China was pouring in. Bombing it, however, and the ships inside it meant taking an inconceivable risk—war with either China or the Soviet Union or both.

The air force and navy were eager to do it, but Johnson refused. The risk, he thought, was simply too great. Haiphong remained a sanctuary.

GROUND WAR

In the face of constant bombing raids, the North Vietnamese simply dug in. They used manholes to make individual bomb shelters, while children and many civilians were sent to live in the countryside. Extensive tunnels were built and entire villages lived day-to-day beneath the ground.

GROUND TROOPS SENT IN. It was clear to the U.S. military that bomb attacks in the North were not going to be enough to win in Vietnam. From 1965 on, it began sending in ground combat forces. These ground units would work with the South Vietnamese Army to try to control guerrilla activities throughout the South. The ground war in Vietnam, however, was very much an "air" war. Much of the transportation and firepower of the ground forces continued to be supplied by aircraft, especially helicopters (see sidebar).

The Vietcong made a series of attacks against U.S. and South Vietnamese forces during the first half of 1965. They destroyed an entire South Vietnamese regiment at Kontum and attacked in and around the U.S. base at Da Nang. The attacks rattled U.S. forces. Clearly, in order to fight the war, U.S. forces had to get—and maintain—control of certain areas of South Vietnam.

In late summer, in Operation Starlight, American marines went on the offensive, destroying most of the Vietcong's first regiment. At An Khe, in October, U.S. airborne troops fought another large battle, killing 226 Vietcong.

IA DRANG BATTLE. North Vietnamese attacked the Special Forces camp at Plei Me in October. In response, the U.S. sent in airborne troops, dropping them in the Ia Drang Valley near the Cambodian border. Unfortunately, the troops landed astride the camps of three North Vietnamese regiments. The NVA troops recovered quickly from the overhead invasion and attacked fiercely, overrunning several American infantry companies.

The fighting lasted for days and was hand-to-hand at times. The American soldiers were forced to call for artillery and airstrikes just a few yards in front of their own lines. While the three enemy units were eventually crushed, more than 300 Americans died in the battle. The Air Cavalry's C-Company was virtually destroyed.

The campaign in Ia Drang taught U.S. commanders a painful lesson about air assault in the thick jungles of Vietnam: Look before you leap.

The North Vietnamese were learning lessons, too. It was clear to them that they could not win the war by confronting U.S. troops directly. Instead they would continue guerrilla attacks, draw out the war, and defeat the U.S. by attrition. They believed if they bled Americans badly enough, they would convince them, like the French before them, into giving up the war and going home.

THE GUERRILLA WAR. Guerrilla activities continued to be heaviest around the DMZ and along the Ho Chi Minh Trail. The United States bombed the trail almost daily, but it was quicky and efficiently repaired, and the stream of supplies was never completely cut off.

The United States finally decided it had to control the hamlets that supported the supply operation along

THE HELICOPTER WAR

The helicopter was a vital weapon in the ground war in Vietnam. Tanks and armored personnel carriers that the American Army had relied upon in previous conflicts were useless in the jungles and rice paddies of Vietnam. Roads were few, and Vietcong ambushes made them dangerous for troop movements. The helicopter, on the other hand, could move men anywhere, anytime.

An entirely different kind of fighting unit was organized around the helicopter, the U.S. Army Air Cavalry. The "Air Cav" rode into combat in troop carrier helicopters like the Bell UH-1 "Huey."

Other Hueys tagged along, carrying rockets and M-60 machine guns to clear a Landing Zone (LZ) for the troop carriers.

Once on the ground, the infantry could call on extra firepower from fighter-bomber strikes, or artillery barrages from nearby "fire-bases." Air support could reach the LZ in a few minutes. A spotter plane would then guide bombers to the target.

The helicopter war was, however, a dangerous one. Troops were often dropped into areas rife with booby traps and snipers.

The North Vietnamese/Vietcong also soon learned that an immediate assault on just-landed, lightly armed infantry was their best bet. They could hit the helicopter units before reinforcements followed them in.

A wounded soldier finds a lost comrade. In a brutal war, the loyalty forged between soldiers meant more than anything else.

the trail. Helicopter-borne troops were sent in to surprise villages that were suspected of being communist. Communist supporters were identified and arrested. Village houses and croplands were burned, and the residents were forced to move to another location.

The raids were never entirely successful. U.S. troops had difficulty identifying which peasants were communists and which were not. The tension of these raids against an often invisible enemy resulted in U.S. soldiers committing massacres of civilians, like the attack at My Lai (see sidebar on page 170).

Many Vietcong fled American attacks only to return later. This was probably the biggest dilemma for the military—even if American troops successfully cleared an area, chances were it wouldn't stay clear for long. The North Vietnamese and Vietcong remained an elusive enemy, capable of withstanding most of what the U.S. military threw at it and rising to do battle another day.

Meanwhile, the fighting for U.S. ground troops grew more and more brutal. The Vietcong and NVA were experts at mine warfare. Thin wires stretched across a trail would trigger "booby traps," mines concealed in thick jungle undergrowth. The infantryman leading his troops along the trail lived a harrowing existence. A destroyed foot or leg, or even an excruciating death, might be a step away.

URBAN ENEMIES. The jungles and rural villages of Vietnam were not the only areas where the Vietcong were strong. They also maintained a presence in or near large Southern cities. In particular, the VC controlled a large area called the Iron Triangle, only twenty-five miles outside Saigon. Though U.S. troops tried repeatedly to destroy this guerrilla base, they never succeeded. The strength of the Vietcong in this area would be proven during the 1968 Tet offensive.

Other Southern cities like Da Nang and Hue resisted the South Vietnamese government of Prime Minister Nguyen Cao and the American presence. Although these cities were not necessarily communist strongholds, Ky said they were and insisted on clearing them out. His actions provoked bitter protests, especially from Buddhists, who boycotted the 1966 elections. They weren't the only ones who didn't vote. Ky had barred 2.5 million people in Vietcong-controlled areas from the polls.

The United States brought in more and more troops to wage the ground war. Though communist soldiers were dying in large numbers, American casualties kept rising, too. The communists showed no signs of giving up the offense. In March 1966, a Special Forces camp in the A-Shau Valley came under massive attack from the North Vietnamese. In April of the following year the NVA attacked the Marine base at Con Thien.

In 1965, the South Vietnamese Army reported that 90,000 of its men had deserted during the year. The U.S., intent on bringing the war to a close, determined to take on the main burden of the conflict.

Newly-elected South Vietnamese President Nguyen Van Thieu wanted even more. Publicly, he expressed the desire that the United States invade North Vietnam.

KHE SANH; TET

From the Khe Sanh camp near the Laotian border, Green Berets routinely patrolled the trails through the thick forest, keeping track of any Communist forces moving along the Ho Chi Minh Trail.

UNDER ATTACK. In January 1966, however, Communist forces began shelling the camp at Khe Sanh. Marines went in to man and reinforce the base, while the Navy Seabees put in a steel airstrip so cargo planes could land troops and supplies. Still, Khe Sanh remained difficult to defend. Not only was the base surrounded by dense forested hills, but it was often blanketed by thick fog. The base, when full, could hold no more than 6,000 soldiers.

In December 1967, U.S. intelligence detected increased enemy activity in the area. Large numbers of North Vietnamese Army (NVA) soldiers were moving into the hills around the camp. Reports indicated that several divisions, including the dreaded 324B NVA, were surrounding Khe Sanh. This meant that as many as 15,000 North Vietnamese soldiers were in attack range.

Such a large military force could overrun Khe Sanh, especially during the upcoming monsoon season when rains could keep U.S. air support grounded.

The news got worse and worse. By the end of 1967, Khe Sanh was surrounded. The NVA had control of all ground escape routes. The single airstrip was now the lifeblood of Khe Sanh. Cargo planes—under heavy mortar and artillery fire—would land without completely stopping, but continue taxiing to takeoff as they were unloaded. Many aircraft did not make it out.

Soldiers or other personnel attempting to fly out of Khe Sanh huddled in trenches off the sides of the airstrip, then ran desperately to board the moving plane while being fired upon. Said one successful marine, "There is no feeling in the world as good as being airborne out of Khe Sanh."

Planes loaded with food and fuel began making parachute drops onto the base. But heavy materials could not be dropped this way, and mounting casualties couldn't be evacuated. For these, the marines at Khe Sanh had to rely on the precious but deadly airstrip.

LANG VEI FALLS. Soon there were serious fears that NVA troops might attempt to overrun Khe Sanh. These fears grew more real when NVA troops in Russian-made tanks crushed a Green Beret outpost at Lang Vei. In one night, more than half of the 400 personnel in this camp—including American and South Vietnamese troops—were killed. The rest fled through the night back to Khe Sanh.

Many worried that the NVA would use tanks against the Khe Sanh base as they had against French forces at Dien Bien Phu in 1954. President Johnson was so obsessed by the possibility of a repeat disaster, he called in the Joint Chiefs of Staff. He insisted they sign a state-

---

THE MASSACRE AT MY LAI

The conflict in Vietnam was marked by startling acts of brutality—on both sides. In the aftermath of the Tet attack on Hue, nearly a thousand shallow graves were discovered—civilians killed by the Communists.

U.S. troops, who had a historic reputation for restraint, also committed acts of unspeakable cruelty in the war.

On November 16, 1969, it was revealed that U.S. soldiers had murdered approximately 150 unarmed civilians in March 1968. The villagers, mostly women, children, and old men, were killed at My Lai, a hamlet in Vietnam's Quang Ngai province.

Photographs of the massacre were taken by a military photographer, Ron Haeberle. The images of dead children lying in ditches

horrified the nation. Some felt that the pictures should have never been released. Later it was revealed that My Lai was only part of a string of massacres committed in the region at the time. Several army officers who were at My Lai were brought up on charges. The platoon commander, William L. Calley, Jr., was eventually convicted.

Seymour Hersh, an investigative journalist, interviewed witnesses at My Lai. He wrote about the events of the massacre in his book, *My Lai 4*:

"The killings began without warning. Harry Stanley [a soldier in the division] told the C.I.D. that one young member of Calley's platoon took a civilian into custody and then 'pushed the man up to where we were standing and then stabbed the man in the back with his bayonet…. The man fell to the ground

and was gasping for breath.' The GI then 'killed him with another bayonet thrust or by shooting him with a rifle…. There were so many people killed that day it is hard for me to recall exactly how some of the people died.' The young man next 'turned to where some soldiers were holding another forty- or fifty-year-old man in custody.' He 'picked this man up and threw him down a well. Then [he] pulled the pin from a M26 grenade and threw it in after the man.' Moments later Stanley saw 'some old women and some little children— fifteen or twenty of them—in a group around a temple where some incense was burning. They were kneeling and crying and praying, and various soldiers…walked by and executed these women and children by shooting them in the head with their rifles. The soldiers killed all fifteen or twenty of them…"

Wounded U.S. troops are evacuated on a tank. The Tet offensive took the United States by complete surprise.

ment saying that Khe Sanh would be held at any cost. The move was not entirely popular, especially among the men defending the base.

Fire for Fire.
Shelling continued for seventy-seven days, with U.S. casualties passing 400. The United States retaliated. Gunships saturated the hills around Khe Sanh with fire, and aircraft dropped more than 100,000 tons of bombs on the hills around the base. Khe Sanh became the most bombarded area in human history, but the air power kept the NVA from mounting an effective attack.

Eventually, most of the NVA troops moved out of the area, and Khe Sanh was relieved. The longest confrontation of the war turned out to be only a distraction. It kept the United States from focusing attention on what would be the major Communist offensive of the war—Tet.

The Surprise Offensive.
Since the war had started in 1964, the U.S. military had tried to secure the area around Saigon. They believed, to a large extent, that they had been successful. A bold attack during the Vietnamese Tet New Year celebration opened their eyes.

The first Vietcong rocket blasts of the offensive hit the American Embassy in Saigon at 3 A.M. on January 31, 1968. The explosion blew in a section of wall at the embassy. Vietcong soldiers jumped into the gap and sprinted into the building.

Thinking fast on his feet, a Marine guard shut the heavy cherry-wood doors that opened into the building's interior. Miraculously they held against the guerrilla fire. But Vietcong were still inside the building. It would take six hours of hard fighting and five American lives to take the embassy back.

The embassy attack came as a complete surprise to the United States. There had been quick raids by the Vietcong on other government buildings and bases since the war began, but this was serious: the Vietcong were intent on taking what should have been the U.S. stronghold.

By daybreak, the streets around the embassy had turned into a complete battlefield. Crouched in door fronts and belly-down in gutters, Vietcong commandos and U.S. Military Police exchanged gunfire. Finally, the last of the Vietcong fell dead. By noon, the Marines controlled the building, once again raising the U.S. flag.

Multiple Strikes.
The attack on the embassy was part of a storm of Vietcong attacks on South Vietnamese cities. Just outside of Saigon, Tan Sun Nhut Airbase came under fire. Farther north, two dozen U.S. aircraft were destroyed or damaged at Danang. The coastal city of Nha Trang was attacked, and the ancient city of Hue was nearly destroyed in heavy fighting.

Though the Tet offensive failed in its military aims, the United States was shaken. The scope of the attack had astonished the U.S. To an already skeptical United States, Tet proved that victory in this conflict, which had gone on for four years and taken 30,000 U.S. lives, was nowhere in sight.

THE WAR AT HOME

The year 1968 was a terrible one for the United States. In the spring, the civil rights leader Martin Luther King, Jr., was assassinated. Riots followed in cities throughout the nation. One of the calm voices in that storm belonged to Senator Robert Kennedy, the slain president's brother. That June, though, Kennedy himself was shot dead. Forces of discontent were threatening to tear the country apart.

VOICES OF PROTEST. Much of the furor in the United States centered on the war being waged in Vietnam. After the surprise Tet offensive, many in Washington and around the country began to feel that enough was enough. Too many young men and women were killing and dying for a cause whose value few could see clearly.

The storm of protest around Vietnam grew too much for President Johnson. He declared that he would not seek another term as president. Johnson's withdrawal from the race made room for other Democratic candidates. Robert Kennedy became one of them. When he was assassinated, the choice came down to Vice President Hubert Humphrey or Senator Eugene McCarthy. Both candidates favored an end to the war, but McCarthy advocated complete and immediate withdrawal.

The choice of who would run on the Democratic ticket was to be made at the party's August convention in Chicago. The convention threatened to be a stormy event. Chicago's mayor, Mayor Richard Daley, expected antiwar protests to turn violent. He assembled 26,000 police, troops, and National Guardsmen to control Chicago's streets.

Initially there was little violence among the protesters. Eventually, though, Chicago police stormed the crowd with clubs and tear gas. Worse violence followed. On the last night of the convention, protesters were chased and beaten bloody by "rioting" police.

NIXON ELECTED. Hubert Humphrey was chosen to run on the Democratic ticket. But it was the Republican candidate, former Vice President Richard Nixon, who won the election for president. Nixon did not advocate immediate withdrawal from Vietnam, although he pledged himself to finding "peace with honor."

Though Nixon had promised to gradually reduce the number of U.S. troops in Vietnam, he "escalated," or widened, the war in other ways. In spring of 1969, the

---

REPORTING THE WAR

Vietnam was the most covered war in history. Virtually anyone with press credentials—from a wire service or a high-school newspaper—was eligible to cover the war. Transportation was provided free by the military, and, for the most part, correspondents could go wherever the action was.

The reports from Vietnam were plentiful and explicit, and they helped to turn public opinion against the war. Some of the best reporting came from the pen of Michael Herr, who was working as a young correspondent for *Esquire*. In his book, *Dispatches*, he describes some of the terror in Hue during the Tet offensive.

"A little boy of about ten came up to a bunch of Marines from Charlie Company. He was laughing and moving his head from side to side in a funny way. The fierceness in his eyes should have told everyone what it was, but it had never occurred to most of the grunts (Marines) that a Vietnamese child could be driven mad too, and by the time they understood it the boy had begun to go for their eyes and tear at their fatigues, spooking everyone…

"On the worst days, no one expected to get through it alive. A despair set in among members of the battalion that the older ones, the veterans of two other wars, had never seen before. Once or twice, when the men from Graves Registration took the personal effects from the packs and pockets of dead Marines, they found letters from home that had been delivered days before and were still unopened…

"In the station there was the youngest-looking Marine I'd ever seen. He'd been caught in the knee by a large piece of shrapnel, and he had no idea of what they'd do with him now that he was wounded. He lay out on the stretcher while the doctor explained how he would be choppered back to Phu Bai hospital and then put on a plane for Danang and then flown back to the States for what would certainly be the rest of his tour. At first the boy was sure that the doctor was kidding him, then he started to believe it, and then he knew it was true, he was actually getting out, he couldn't stop smiling, and enormous tears ran down into his ears."

A young woman screams in horror over a victim at Kent State. The shootings of students shocked the nation.

North Vietnamese had increased the number of troops moving south—routing them now through supposedly neutral Cambodia. Nixon retaliated by secretly bombing Cambodia. However, the secret soon leaked, and protests mounted.

PEACE INITIATIVES.
American-Vietnamese peace talks had begun in Paris in 1968, but the talks had gone nowhere. Nixon advocated secret talks, and he sent a message to Ho Chi Minh asking for them, but Ho did not respond. In fact, Ho was dying and would live only a few more weeks.

Meanwhile protests at home continued to escalate. In the summer of 1969, Vietnam veterans themselves came to Washington to protest the war. Some abandoned Purple Hearts and other combat medals that they had won on the steps of the Capitol. On November 15, hundreds of thousands of people demonstrated in Washington. The march would be the largest protest of the entire war.

Further ammunition against the war was provided the following day when news sources revealed that U.S. soldiers had massacred Vietnamese civilians at My Lai (see sidebar on page 170).

NIXON MAINTAINS COURSE.
President Nixon did not believe that the protesters represented mainstream Americans. He called the demonstrators "mindless rioters and professional malcontents." He instructed the FBI to check the backgrounds of protest leaders for Communist connections.

Nixon believed that the majority of the country was in agreement with his Vietnam policies. He felt that the United States had to keep its commitment to South Vietnam despite the protests.

> "Be the first ones on the block to have your boy come home in a box."
>
> —lyric from "I-Feel-Like-I'm-Fixin'-To-Die Rag"

BORDER ATTACKS.
Cambodia was still being used by the North Vietnamese to stage attacks on South Vietnam. Nixon decided the only remedy for this was to invade Cambodia. Fifteen thousand troops were assembled to cross the border. They penetrated a full twenty miles into Cambodia, but the majority of the enemy had slipped away.

The Cambodian invasion added more fuel to protests against the war. At Kent State University in Ohio, panicky U.S. National Guardsmen fired live rounds into a crowd of protesters and spectators. Four students were killed, and eleven were wounded. Many Americans were horrified by images of college students lying in pools of blood.

WITHDRAWAL

On December 31, 1970, the U.S. Congress repealed the Gulf of Tonkin Resolution. This resolution had allowed President Johnson to send troops into Vietnam. In effect, Congress was asserting *its* right to determine when and where Americans should be sent to fight.

"VIETNAMIZATION." Meanwhile, President Nixon was continuing the withdrawal of U.S. troops in Vietnam. By the end of 1971, there would be fewer than 175,000 U.S. servicemen stationed there, down from half a million. At the same time, the North Vietnamese continued to strengthen their positions in the South.

The United States now wanted to shift the burden of the war onto the shoulders of the South Vietnamese. During February and March 1971, 16,000 South Vietnamese troops crossed the Laotian border. The operation, meant to disrupt a Communist buildup south of the DMZ, was also designed to prove that the South Vietnamese could fight the Communists on their own.

Though no U.S. ground forces participated, the U.S. Air Force, Army, and Marines provided massive air support. The military results were mixed, and the South Vietnamese suffered serious casualties. About half of their soldiers were killed or wounded.

CAMBODIAN WAR. During 1971, the South Vietnamese would also venture into Cambodia. That country was going through a civil war of its own. In 1975, the brutal Khmer Rouge faction would take power after a siege of the capital, Phnom Penh. The unrest in Cambodia contributed to the overwhelming feeling of U.S. unease about the whole region of Southeast Asia.

Nixon felt the tide of American sentiment against the war. He continued to pursue peace negotiations, even as he pulled more and more troops out of Vietnam. By May 1, 1972, only 69,000 American soldiers were still fighting the war.

On December 18, the North Vietnamese delegation walked out of the Paris peace talks. Nixon immediately resorted to more air raids. In what was known as the "Christmas bombing," the United States once again staged massive air attacks on the North. The heaviest air strikes, 729 sorties in total, were made by B-52s. Because North Vietnam had built up its air defenses,

COSTS OF COMBAT

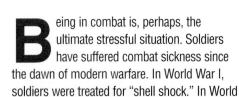

Being in combat is, perhaps, the ultimate stressful situation. Soldiers have suffered combat sickness since the dawn of modern warfare. In World War I, soldiers were treated for "shell shock." In World

War II, it was called battle fatigue. Simply put, soldiers can only endure combat for a limited time before they will break psychologically.

After Vietnam, soldiers and nurses were frequently diagnosed with PTSD (Post Traumatic Stress Disorder). Many had become drug addicted during their tour. Some had recurring nightmares or suffered from guilt for what they had or had not done during the war. In some respects, Vietnam veterans were experiencing many of the same problems as soldiers from previous wars. But in other ways Vietnam vets' problems were different. These soldiers had been trained differently from troops who had fought in most previous wars.

Following World War II, investigations showed that, on average, only 15 percent of combat riflemen fired their weapons in battle. The remaining soldiers did not run away, but they would not kill, even when their own lives were at risk.

For the military, these numbers were shocking. They set about revising basic training so that troops could be relied upon to kill in battle. Situations were set up so soldiers could mock-kill their enemies in close combat.

Troops were verbally encouraged not only to slay their enemy but to relish doing so. The training was effective. During the Korean War, about half of all infantrymen were now firing their weapons.

Still, there were—and are—problems with this kind of training. In order to make most human beings kill, their instincts against killing have to be overcome. Altering human psychology this way can have disastrous effects. Incidents of fragging (soldiers killing their own officers) were unheard of in World War II. In Vietnam more than 200 cases of fragging were reported. U.S. soldiers in Vietnam also committed a series of massacres and tortured enemy soldiers.

Although the war's utter brutality influenced behavior in Vietnam, the way these soldiers were trained may have been a factor. It's clear that some people cannot override their natural aversion to killing without dire consequences to themselves or to society.

A soldier stands beside a Vietnamese mother and child. U.S. presence in Vietnam would soon be a thing of the past.

fifteen of the heavy bombers were shot down, all by Soviet-made SAM missiles. But U.S. planes quickly destroyed these defenses and were soon roaming the North's skies at will.

Nixon also ordered the mining of Haiphong and other North Vietnamese harbors. The mining cut off the flow of seaborne supplies into Vietnam almost overnight.

TREATY NEGOTIATED. Nixon's actions had their intended effect. On January 3, 1973, the North Vietnamese delegation to the Paris peace conference announced it was ready to start talking again. Nixon's aide, Henry Kissinger, and Le Duc Tho, representing North Vietnam, signed the peace agreement on January 27. Remaining U.S. troops were pulled out of Vietnam by March 29, although American planes continued to attack the

Khmer Rouge in Cambodia until mid-August. Americans in North Vietnamese prisons were released starting February 17.

The war in Vietnam for the Americans was over, at least as far as its combat troops were concerned. But though President Nixon declared the United States had achieved peace with honor, that peace would prove more fragile than anyone dreamed. Civil wars in Vietnam and Cambodia would continue. Their results would no longer cost the United States in American blood—but in American pride.

AFTERMATH

The cease-fire agreement signed between the United States and Vietnam in January 1973 did not bring an end to the fighting in Southeast Asia. Though U.S. troops withdrew from the country, the North Vietnamese soon resumed the ground fighting.

SAIGON FALLS. Though still supplied with U.S. weapons, the South Vietnamese Army, by themselves, were no match for the Northern forces. Against failing resistance, the Communists continued to push south. Tens of thousands of refugees fled ahead of them, converging on Saigon.

The capital city provided only brief refuge. On April 30, 1975, Saigon fell to the Communists, and the South Vietnamese government surrendered. The previous day, in a scene of frenzied desperation, seventy helicopters airlifted the last Americans and some lucky Vietnamese from the American Embassy.

REFUGEES. Struck by the plight of the South Vietnamese, Congress voted $405 million to aid them; 140,000 were flown to the United States. Many others were left behind to face "re-education" by the Communists. Some would spend years in camps paying for their collaboration with U.S. forces.

Refugees, numbering near one million, would continue to spill out of Vietnam for the next twenty years. Neighboring countries (with U.S. encouragement) gradually began refusing political asylum to these "boat people," forcing many to return to Vietnam. However, many Vietnamese did make it to a new life in America.

The Berlin Wall came down in 1990. The Soviet Union would soon collapse.

AGENT ORANGE. As soldiers returned from Southeast Asia, many began displaying mysterious symptoms eventually traced to a herbicide (weed killer) known as Agent Orange. Over a period of years it was revealed that thousands of GIs were contaminated by the agent, which caused open sores, bleeding, and skin disintegration. Extreme cases resulted in partial paralysis. More than 65,000 children of Vietnam veterans were born with birth defects, which their parents later attributed to Agent Orange.

The U.S. government refused for many years to admit that the illnesses experienced by returning soldiers were related to Agent Orange. However, in 1984, a group of Vietnam war veterans reached an out-of-court settlement (without a trial) with a group of chemical companies that had produced the herbicide.

INVASION OF AFGHANISTAN. The Soviets had helped supply the North Vietnamese in their battle against the South. Now the U.S.S.R. was about to embark on its own war—in Afghanistan. The Soviets decided to invade their southern neighbor in December 1979. They hoped to replace the Afghan ruler with a Communist puppet.

What was conceived as a brief intervention turned into a major guerrilla war. Afghan warriors, the *mujahideen*, fled to mountain strongholds and could not be dislodged even by powerful Soviet weaponry. Soviet forces had to be reinforced until their numbers swelled to 100,000. The struggle—as unpopular in the U.S.S.R. as Vietnam had been in the U.S.—cost the Soviets 60,000 casualties.

The United States condemned the invasion and early in 1980 placed an embargo on the sale of grain and high technology to the Soviets. At President Jimmy Carter's request, the U.S. Olympic Committee also declined to participate in that summer's Moscow Olympics.

The Soviets finally agreed to withdraw their troops from Afghanistan in 1988–1989, ending an eight-year war.

TROUBLE IN IRAN. The United States was especially concerned by the conflict in Afghanistan because the Soviets were now one step closer to Middle East petroleum reserves. However, more immediate trouble was brewing elsewhere in the Middle East—in Iran.

Since the early 1950s, the United States had supported the government of Reza Pahlevi, the shah of Iran. The alliance, though, had its problems. The U.S. benefited from increasing Iranian oil output (more than 6 million barrels per day in 1974), but the shah's rule in Iran grew more and more dictatorial. He established a security police force to suppress his opponents. Once accused, enemies of the shah could look forward to imprisonment, torture, and sometimes execution.

Using economic and military incentives, the United States tried to coax the shah into a more democratic rule, but those attempts failed. As opposition to the shah increased, Iran grew increasingly unstable. Many thought that a nationalist/Communist regime might topple the shah and gain control.

A veteran grieves at the Vietnam Memorial in Washington D.C. It would take decades for the nation to make sense of the war.

HOSTAGE CRISIS. Instead, an Islamic revolution tore the shah's government apart. Led by the exiled Ayatollah Khomeini, a variety of Iranian religious groups rose up, forcing the shah from power. Returning from his exile in France, Khomeini directed Iran's fury against the United States, which had backed the shah and, in Khomeini's mind, was responsible for corrupting Iran and threatening its independence.

In November 1979, the American Embassy in Teheran was seized by Iranian students. U.S. diplomats, along with their staffs, were taken as hostages.

The following April President Carter ordered a special task force to Iran to free the hostages. The rescue attempt was a disaster. Three of the eight helicopters sent on the mission malfunctioned. When the raid was called off, a helicopter and a transport plane collided and burned trying to return. Eight men were killed in the crash.

The fifty-three American hostages were kept captive for fourteen months. Only when President Carter left office were they finally freed. Anti-U.S. terrorist attacks continued at home and abroad throughout the 1980s and 1990s.

GRENADA INVADED. The United States continued to worry about Communist gains in its own hemisphere throughout the 1980s. In October 1983, President Reagan authorized a U.S. Marine invasion of the tiny Caribbean island of Grenada. The administration justified the raid, saying that American citizens on the island were in danger because of a Marxist-led coup.

Grenada had been torn by internal strife, which the administration claimed was caused by the intervention of both the U.S.S.R. and Cuba. However, it was unlikely that the island posed any threat to U.S. security. Invading troops encountered little opposition. Still, U.S. relations with Britain suffered. Grenada was a member of the British Commonwealth and President Reagan had neglected to inform British Prime Minister Margaret Thatcher that he was planning to invade.

U.S.S.R. CRUMBLES. U.S. fears about Soviet intervention in Grenada, however, were exaggerated. The Soviet Union was on its last legs.

In March 1985, Mikhail Gorbachev was chosen general secretary of the Communist Party. Gorbachev initiated a strong reform program. He expanded political and economic freedoms within the country. His openness, though, brought much criticism from hard-liners within the Communist Party. It also caused unrest in satellite states like Hungary and some of the ethnic republics within the Soviet Union.

An abortive coup against Gorbachev in August 1991 resulted in a general strike. Several republics within the Soviet Union including Russia declared their independence. At the end of the month, the Soviet Parliament voted to suspend the activities of the Communist Party. The Soviet Union officially broke up on December 26, 1991. With it went the last shiver of the Cold War.

THE GULF WAR

In early 1991, half a million U.S. troops fought a short but fierce war with Iraq. They were aided and supported by thirty other countries. For the first time since World War II, the United States collaborated with its longtime enemy, the U.S.S.R.

For U.S. forces, the Gulf War was the first major military action since Vietnam. The conflict would focus attention on the readiness of the U.S. military to take quick and decisive action. It would also test whether the people of the United States were willing, once again, to risk the lives of sons and daughters in a foreign conflict.

PRELUDE TO WAR
In the summer of 1990, Americans were greeted with a news flash from the Persian Gulf: Iraq had invaded its tiny neighbor, Kuwait. News clips showed troop carriers moving through Kuwait City. Iraqi tanks were shelling buildings and blowing up trucks in the Arab capital.

Much of the small Kuwaiti Army was caught by surprise, but some Kuwaitis resisted. They were no match, though, for the Iraqi Army. It was well armed and battle-trained. It was also the fourth largest army in the world.

U.S. intelligence had been keeping track of the thousands of Iraqi troops gathering on Kuwait's border all summer. The buildup caused concern but not alarm. Few thought Iraq's leader, Saddam Hussein, would invade another Arab country.

STRUGGLE OVER OIL PRICES. Hussein had met with the Kuwaiti emir, Sheikh Jabir al-Ahmad al-Jabir, during the summer to discuss oil prices. Kuwait had been produc-

ing more oil than was allowed under Organization of Petroleum Exporting Countries (OPEC) agreements. The extra oil was pushing prices down. Costs per barrel had dropped from $20 in January to less than $14 in June. Iraq was losing a billion dollars worth of revenue for every single dollar drop in oil prices.

It was something the Iraqi government could scarcely afford. Iraq had bled its economy fighting its neighbor Iran from 1980 through 1988. The war had been one of the most brutal conflicts since World War II. Both sides had participated in mass slaughter campaigns with the aid of chemical weapons. Hundreds of thousands of people had died, including many children.

The United States had sided with Iraq during the war. Now, though, it was determined to stay out of the conflict. Just days before the Kuwait invasion, U.S. Ambassador April Glasbie met with Saddam Hussein. She told him that the United States was concerned about the buildup of troops along Kuwait's border. But she tried not to take sides: "We have no opinion on the Arab-Arab conflicts like your border disagreement with Kuwait," she said.

Hussein assured her he would not invade Kuwait. But Glasbie's statement may have led him to think the United States would not interfere if he did. On August 2, Iraqi troops poured over the border. Immediately, both the U.S.S.R. and China voted with the United States to impose U.N. sanctions on Iraq. Ninety percent of Iraq's trade was cut off. With the strict sanctions came a demand that Hussein withdraw his troops immediately from Kuwait.

OIL AND BLOOD. Hussein refused to withdraw. Instead, hundreds of Iraqi troops systematically sacked Kuwait City, stealing and looting throughout the capital. Videotapes showed Iraqis executing civilians in the streets. Refugees told startling stories of Iraqis raping, looting, and torturing Kuwaitis.

The occupation of Kuwait also posed serious economic problems. Hussein now controlled a full 20 percent of the world's oil reserves. He would now be in a position to dominate OPEC and determine oil costs.

Satellite cameras showed that Iraqi troops were moving south across Kuwait toward Saudi Arabia. If they occupied the ports there, Iraq would control 40 percent of the world's oil.

President Bush was committed to protecting Saudi Arabia. But he was also determined that he would take action to get the Iraqis out of Kuwait. "This (invasion) will not stand," he said.

With the cooperation of the Saudis, the United States launched Operation Desert Shield on August 7, 1990.

TURKEY ■ Incirlik

CYPRUS

MEDITERRANEAN SEA

LEBANON

SYRIA

Kurdistan

Mosul ▲ ✦ Erbil ▲

IRAQ

Damascus ✦

Haifa ◎
ISRAEL
Tel Aviv ◎
Jerusalem ◎
Amman ✦

Suez Canal

JORDAN

Sinai

EGYPT

Gulf of Aqaba

Aqaba ■

RED SEA

Baghdad ✦ Salman Pak
Tuwaitha ▲

Euphrates R.

Tigris R.

IRAN

Nasiriyah

Basra ✦

KUWAIT
✦ Kuwait City

Khafji ◎

SAUDI ARABIA

Dhahran ◎

BAHRAIN

Persian Gulf

OMAN

Stra Hor

QATAR

Abu Dhabi ✦

■ ◎ Riyadh

UNITED ARAB EMIRATES

U.S. soldier, Gulf War

GULF WAR (1991)

▨	Neutral countries	◎ Scud attack
▨	Iraq	✳ *Allied bombing*
▨	Allied countries	➤ Allied advance
▨	Kuwait	■ Allied base
▲	Iraqi nuclear site	⚓ U.S. Navy
🚂	Iraqi forces	

0   300 Mi.

1990

Iraqi troops cross border into Kuwait *(Aug. 2).*

United States launches Operation Desert Shield to protect Saudi Arabia from possible Iraqi invasion *(Aug. 7).*

United Nations okays use of force if Iraq does not withdraw from Kuwait by January 15, 1991 *(Nov. 7).*

1991

Operation Desert Storm begins. U.S. forces bomb Baghdad *(Jan. 16).*

Iraq targets Israel with Scud missiles *(Jan. 17).*

Iraqi soldiers open pipeline and release oil into Persian Gulf *(Jan. 25).*

Hussein orders his troops to set fire to Kuwaiti oil wells.

U.S. and coalition forces begin ground attack *(Feb. 23).*

Iraqis defeated *(Feb. 27).*

DESERT STORM

By early September, President Bush had decided to eject the Iraqis from Kuwait. To do this he needed the cooperation of the Soviet Union, a longtime ally of Iraq and its biggest arms supplier. Bush met with Soviet President Gorbachev, who agreed not to stand in the way if the United States wanted to use force to liberate Kuwait.

LAST EFFORTS AT DIPLOMACY. On November 29, 1990, the United Nations okayed the use of force if Iraq did not withdraw from Kuwait by January 15. The coalition against Hussein would include 690,000 troops from twenty-eight countries. Not only American and European nations would be represented but Arab nations as well.

Bush had offered to negotiate with Hussein up until the U.N. deadline. On January 9, Secretary of State James Baker met with Tariq Iziz, the Iraqi foreign minister, but the negotiations failed.

The U.S. Congress then debated the issue of going to war against Iraq. The House had approved the action but debate still raged in the Senate. Finally, the Senate approved the use of force by a slim margin. In the early morning hours of January 16, Bush signed orders for Operation Desert Storm.

AIR WAR BEGINS. The Allied coalition had 1,700 aircraft poised to attack Iraqi forces. The first targets would be in Iraq, particularly Baghdad. The Allies hoped to destroy Iraqi communications. If they were successful, they could cut off Iraqi troops from their commanders and supplies.

Eight Apache helicopter gunships were sent in to destroy two Iraqi radar sites. These radar dishes could warn Iraq of an upcoming attack.

In darkness, the United States sent ten Stealth Fighters into Baghdad. The Stealths were shaped and painted in such a way as to be invisible to radar. But the U.S. Air Force, taking no chances, jammed Iraq's radar anyway.

The jamming alerted the Iraqis to the attack. Even though the bombers weren't visible, Hussein ordered anti-aircraft guns and missile batteries to fire "even if it meant closing their eyes and firing at the sky."

IRAQI RETALIATION. The bombing runs destroyed much of Baghdad's communications system and at least one of Hussein's thirty-nine palaces. Coalition bombers then struck at Iraq's weapons factories. More than 200 targets were attacked, including large stocks of biological and chemical weapons. Only a single U.S. pilot was killed.

Hussein had promised to attack Israel if the United States went to war against Iraq. Within twenty-four hours of the first bombing of Baghdad, he unleashed his stockpile of Soviet-made SCUD missiles against the Israelis. Hussein was banking on the idea that he could provoke Israel into retaliating. If Israel attacked Iraq, it could shatter the fragile Arab-Western coalition.

President Bush pleaded with Israel not to retaliate. To fend off the Iraqi attacks, the United States brought in the

---

KUWAIT, INC.

At the time the Iraqis invaded their Arab neighbor, the average U.S. citizen barely knew where Kuwait was, much less why someone would want to invade it. By U.S. standards Kuwait was a tiny country—smaller than New Jersey— with fewer than two million people.

But Kuwait had plenty to boast about. This tiny country had been one of the world's poorest nations until 1946. In that year Kuwaitis began exporting petroleum. This single product transformed Kuwait into one of the wealthiest nations on earth. By 1990, Kuwait had international capital worth one billion dollars. Underneath Kuwaiti deserts lay close to 100 billion barrels of oil. The Kuwaitis could continue pumping at current rates for another century without running dry. The country's wealth and identity as an oil producer earned it the nickname Kuwait, Inc.

Kuwaiti citizens paid no taxes. Oil income provided free housing, medical care, education and retirement. Most people living in

Kuwait, however, were not Kuwaitis, but other Arabs including Palestinians, Indians, Pakistanis, and Iranians. Non-Kuwaitis (the majority of the population) were not allowed to vote.

The nation of Kuwait was carved out by Europeans after World War I. Its deep-water port area and northern border were scissored out of what used to be Mesopotamia (now Iraq). These arbitrary borders were one of the causes of conflict with the Iraqis.

Kuwait was a British colony until 1961. Upon declaring its independence from Britain, Kuwait was threatened with invasion by Iraq. It wasn't the first time Iraq menaced its neighbor Arab, and it wouldn't be the last.

Smoke billows from a burning oil well during a Gulf War tank battle. The ground war overwhelmed Iraqi troops.

newly developed Patriot missiles. Coalition forces continued to bomb targets in Baghdad and Iraq for weeks, inflicting terrible damage. Still Hussein refused to pull out of Kuwait. President Bush began debating whether U.S. forces should begin a ground attack.

CHEMICAL THREAT.

A ground war against Iraq was a scary prospect. Iraq had fought such a war with Iran in the 1980s. Both sides had suffered dire casualties, but the Iranians had gotten the worst of it. The Iraqis had systematically slaughtered tens of thousands of them using chemical weapons. U.S. forces could face those same weapons in a ground attack.

The threat of gas attacks was a potent one. The Iraqis had already terrorized Israel with the fear of chemical-carrying SCUDs. In Israel, the government distributed gas masks to citizens in case the Iraqis used nerve gas.

On January 25, Hussein ordered his troops to open a Kuwaiti pipeline. Petroleum flooded into the Persian Gulf. The oil destroyed beaches and sea life. It also threatened the desalinization plants that provided drinking water to the Saudis.

A U.S. bombing raid managed to stopper the pipeline, but the spilled oil caused billions of dollars in environmental damage.

PREPARATION FOR GROUND ATTACK.

Iraqi tank units were positioned all along the border with Kuwait. If U.S. forces were to move into Iraq, those positions would have to be weakened.

The air force began attacking the tank positions with B-52s, heavy bombers from the U.S. nuclear strike force. But because of high winds and other problems, most of the high-explosive bombs fell on empty desert. Another plane, the high-tech F-111, took over. Using infrared cameras, the planes easily spotted the heated-up tanks in the desert. With laser-guided bombs, the planes smashed tank after tank. The constant and precise bomb attacks scared the soldiers from their positions. Though the Allies weren't aware of it, 200,000 Iraqis deserted from the border area.

Meanwhile the Soviets tried to negotiate a withdrawal. Hussein would agree to pull his troops out of Kuwait. But he still refused to recognize Kuwait as a nation. And he would not pay compensation to the Kuwaitis, which U.N. sanctions had demanded.

President Bush, however, was no longer willing to bargain. Though Bush needed Moscow's support, he was determined not to let Hussein go unpunished.

FIRES IN KUWAIT.

The coalition was in danger of breaking down. President Mitterand of France called George Bush. Mitterand wanted to delay the ground war.

As the two were trying to reach an agreement, Bush received word that Hussein had ordered his troops to set fire to the Kuwaiti oil wells. Hundreds of oil fires began to blaze, filling Kuwait's skies with thick, black smoke.

President Bush issued an ultimatum: If Iraq did not begin an immediate withdrawal from Kuwait, coalition forces led by the United States would force them out. Hussein did not respond.

GROUND WAR

General Norman Schwarzkopf planned to send in U.S. Marines first, attacking straight into Kuwait (see map on page 179). The general hoped that this would force Hussein to send down his elite Republican Guard units from the north to reinforce Kuwait City, the capital.

STORMING THE DESERT. About 400 miles to the west, American and French airborne troops would helicopter behind the enemy and begin to encircle Hussein's army. A day later Arab troops would support the U.S. attack into Kuwait. Finally the heavy U.S. 7th Corps would swing wide around Iraq's heavy border defenses. They would arc up to destroy the Republic Guard.

Schwarzkopf's plan was strong and simple, but it relied on careful timing. It also depended on Hussein sending his Republican Guard south as expected.

To convince the Iraqis that the attack would come from the sea, the U.S. Navy set up a fake assault. The USS *Missouri* used its big guns to shell the beach in Kuwait City. The Iraqi troops moved as expected, toward the coast and away from the actual Marine attack.

On February 24, 1991, the ground attack began. The Marines poured over Kuwait's border and headed for Kuwait City. Though they had to blast a safe path through desert minefields, they met little resistance. In the first few hours, 8,000 Iraqis surrendered.

Huge numbers of Iraqi soldiers—possibly 75 percent—weren't fighting at all. The Marines were easily advancing into Kuwait City. Their quick success, though, meant that the Iraqi Republican Guard units weren't moving south. Schwarzkopf was afraid they would have time to escape back into Iraq. He ordered the 7th Corps to move up its attack. If it acted quickly, it might be able to catch the Republican Guard divisions before they got away

The Iraqis had set up lines of trenches to defend their tank units. The American 1st Infantry Division had to clear a path for the corps tanks. U.S. soldiers wanted to avoid close fighting with the Iraqis on the ground. So they decided to simply bulldoze over the trenches. The defending Iraqis would have seconds to surrender or escape.

The tactic worked. Tanks fitted with ploughs and armored bulldozers pushed across the trenches burying hundreds of Iraqi soldiers. U.S. casualties were minimal.

TANK BATTLE. On the second day of the ground war, February 25, the U.S. Marine stroll into Kuwait City ended abruptly. Moving out of the blazing air fields, Iraqi army units attacked the Marines' right flank. The largest tank battle in U.S. Marine history began.

The Iraqis had the advantage of surprise, but once again, the U.S. took control in the air. Cobra helicopter gunships joined the Marines on the ground, hitting Iraqi tanks and vehicles. The Iraqis tried to retreat, backing into the smoking oil fields. But the Marines pursued them, destroying over 100 Iraqi vehicles.

WAR COVERAGE (MORE OR LESS)

In some ways Americans were getting better information than ever during the Gulf War. And in some ways they were being told—and shown—less than in any previous war.

During Desert Storm television viewers were routinely treated to a pilot's eye view of bombing sites and combat areas. The screen showed targeting cross-hairs and the eruption of laser-guided "smart" bombs. The view gave a good sense of what it is like to fly a bombing mission, but showed little of what was happening on the ground when the bombs exploded. Most of what Americans were permitted to see was remarkably bloodless.

The news media had almost complete access to combat units during the Vietnam War. Many in the military believed that journalists had helped turn Americans against that war. For this, and for security reasons, they decided to restrict news coverage in the Gulf.

Selected reporters traveled in groups to pre-approved sites. Pictures of dead U.S. soldiers were forbidden. Cameramen were chased off when 28 Americans were killed in a scud missile attack in Saudi Arabia.

Reporters did get one spectacular scoop in the Gulf. In Baghdad, during the first U.S. bombing, CNN (Cable News Network) reporters provided an on-the-scene experience of what it was like in Iraq while the bombs were falling.

Said one reporter: "I can't speak from experience. But this must be what hell is like."

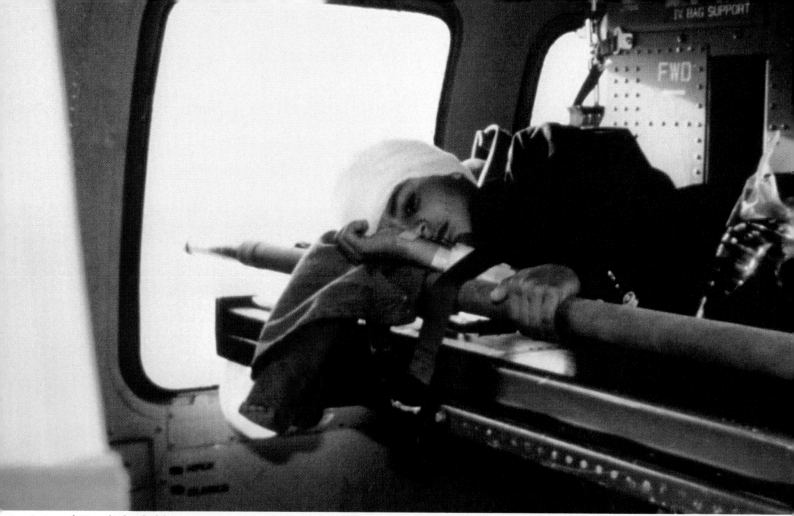

An injured Kurdish child is evacuated by helicopter. Iraq's ethnic minorities continued to suffer after the war ended.

The thick billowing oil smoke and burning tanks scattered across the sand made the battle seem eerie, especially to the flyers. "You almost had to slap yourself into reality," said one pilot.

Hussein was now convinced that Kuwait could not be held. On the night of the 25th, his soldiers pulled out of the city. They headed north back into Iraq.

DEATH HIGHWAY.
The fleeing Iraqi soldiers had been responsible for the sacking of Kuwait. Some had looted the city and tortured Kuwaitis. General Schwarzkopf was determined that they wouldn't walk away unpunished.

An F-15 strike force was sent in to stop the Iraqi convoy. The lined-up vehicles heading toward Iraq's border were easy targets for U.S. forces. The F-15s dropped a string of 500-pound bombs on the trucks, stalling the convoy. Other planes using cluster bombs completed the attack.

The raid produced a massacre. Thousands of Iraqi troops were blasted and burned along the road. The rest ran for their lives into the surrounding desert.

RACE FOR THE REPUBLICAN GUARD.
On the third day of the ground war, the U.S. 7th Corps was racing north. It was trying desperately to catch Hussein's Republican Guard before it escaped into Iraq.

On the afternoon of the February 26, the 7th Corps finally caught up with a Republican Guard Division. The Iraqis turned to attack, and a ferocious tank battle began. The U.S. Abrams tank, however, had a longer firing range than the Russian-built Iraqi tanks. The battle was no contest. While 7th Corps posted no losses, twenty-eight Republican Guard tanks were destroyed.

That evening another Republican Guard division was defeated. Another five of the elite Iraqi divisions were still trying to escape north toward Basra.

An Iraqi rear guard was trying to protect the troops as they retreated. They set up a six-mile defense, with scores of tanks, along a low ridge called Medina. Again the U.S. long-range guns had a deadly advantage. They smashed 300 Iraqi tanks and heavy vehicles. Only one U.S. soldier died in the battle.

Gunships continued hunting for the enemy, attacking the retreating Iraqis wherever they could find them. More than 70,000 Iraqi troops eventually surrendered.

Though the Republican Guard divisions were not completely cut off, President Bush, acting on advice from General Colin Powell, chairman of the Joint Chiefs of Staff, decided to end the killing. The Gulf War, the shortest war in U.S. history, was over, but relations between Iraq and the United States would remain tense.